STOWE IN HER OWN T

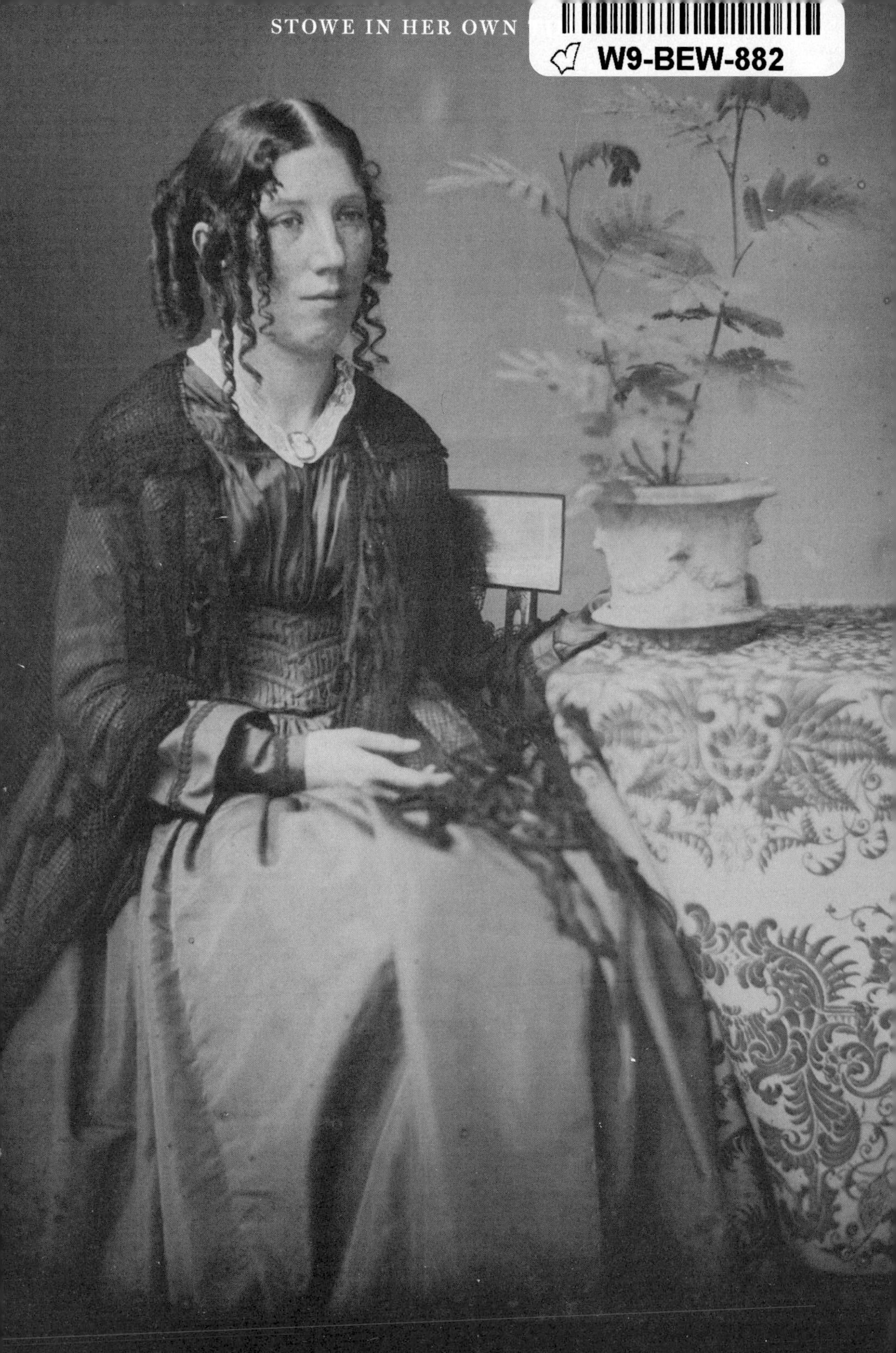

WRITERS IN THEIR OWN TIME  Joel Myerson, *series editor*

# STOWE
## *in Her Own Time*

A BIOGRAPHICAL

CHRONICLE OF HER LIFE,

DRAWN FROM RECOLLECTIONS,

INTERVIEWS, AND

MEMOIRS BY FAMILY,

FRIENDS, AND

ASSOCIATES

EDITED BY

Susan Belasco

University of Iowa Press
Iowa City

University of Iowa Press, Iowa City 52242
Copyright © 2009 by the University of Iowa Press
www.uiowapress.org
Printed in the United States of America

The University of Iowa Press is a member of Green Press Initiative
and is committed to preserving natural resources.

Printed on acid-free paper

Library of Congress Cataloging-in-Publication Data
Stowe in her own time: a biographical chronicle of her life, drawn from
recollections, interviews, and memoirs by family, friends, and
associates / edited by Susan Belasco.
p.    cm.—(Writers in their own time)
Includes index.
ISBN-13: 978-1-58729-782-3 (pbk.)
ISBN-10: 1-58729-782-5 (pbk.)
1. Stowe, Harriet Beecher, 1811–1896.   2. Women and literature—United States—
History—19th century.   3. Authors, American—19th century—Biography.
4. Abolitionists—United States—Biography.   I. Belasco, Susan, 1950–
PS2956.S86 2009
813'.3—dc22      2008043517
[B]

Frontispiece: Harriet Beecher Stowe, ca. 1843–1845. Southworth & Hawes
(Albert Sands Southworth, American, 1811–1894, and Josiah Johnson Hawes,
American, 1808–1901). *Harriet Beecher Stowe,* ca. 1843–1845. ¼ plate daguerreotype,
3 ¾ x 2 ⅞ inches (9.5 x 7.3 cm). The Nelson-Atkins Museum of Art, Kansas City,
Missouri, gift of Hallmark Cards, Inc., 2005.27.13. Photograph by Thomas Palmer.

*For my mother
Peggy Bell Belasco*

# Contents

The Beecher family, ca. 1859, Matthew Brady Studios. Standing, left to right: Thomas Beecher, William Beecher, Edward Beecher, Charles Beecher, Henry Ward Beecher. Seated, left to right: Isabella Beecher Hooker, Catharine Beecher, Lyman Beecher, Mary Beecher Perkins, Harriet Beecher Stowe. Harriet Beecher Stowe Center, Hartford, Connecticut.

# Introduction

In June 1983, over eighty descendants of Lyman Beecher (1775–1863) attended a family reunion at the Harriet Beecher Stowe House in Hartford, Connecticut. This number then represented about one-third of the known descendants of Beecher, patriarch of the famous family to which Harriet Beecher Stowe (1811–1896) belonged. Held just as she was beginning to receive significant scholarly attention and *Uncle Tom's Cabin* was regaining its place in the canon of American literature, the reunion was attended by lawyers, doctors, professors, ministers, engineers, farmers, and business men and women as well as their numerous children from across the United States and Canada. Among the group was a sixteen-year-old Harriet Beecher Stowe III and other descendants named for members of the original Beecher family. A writer for the *Hartford Courant* noted that the Beecher clan had gathered "to update the family photo album," a reference to a photograph of the Beecher family taken about 1859.[1] Indeed, the Beechers held several family reunions during the nineteenth century, and Stowe herself would have loved the twentieth-century event in Hartford.

In the common parlance of our day, Stowe was all about family. Although she formed some close friendships during her later years, especially with Annie Adams Fields, Stowe looked primarily to her family for her intimate relationships. During the course of her life, she was seldom without a family member at her side, and it sometimes seems that when she was not physically with one she was writing to one. Stowe was, for instance, the instigator of the circular letters that family members contributed to and sent on to the next household.[2] She grew up in the midst of her father's large family, worked at her sister Catharine's schools, traveled with her brother Charles and other relatives to Europe, hosted family members for long stays at her several homes, lived down the street from her sister Isabella in her later adulthood, made a home for her adult twin daughters, nursed her husband through a long decline, regularly attended churches where her brother and her son were ministers, and was surrounded by family members at her death on 1 July 1896.

Stowe's family also offered protection and support as she became an increasingly famous person. In its coverage of the 1983 family reunion in Hartford, the *New York Times* observed:

> Mrs. Stowe was one of the first American authors to earn a comfortable living from writing, and the first American woman to achieve fame as an author. Of the more than 30 novels, biographies, poetry, children's books, and nonfiction that she wrote, it was "Uncle Tom's Cabin," translated into 40 languages, that thrust her into the international limelight.[3]

Stowe's international fame was in fact carefully shaped. After an amateurish beginning in which she allowed her husband, Calvin Stowe, to make a disadvantageous deal with the publisher of *Uncle Tom's Cabin*, she shrewdly capitalized on the novel's success and established herself as a major figure in the literary marketplace during the second half of the nineteenth century. As Sarah Robbins has noted, "During her lifetime, family members and friends worked hard to create an image that would appeal to her reading audience."[4] Stowe had a hand in the contemporary biographies and contributed information for many of the articles about her, most of which were designed to present her not just as a woman writer but as a devoted wife and mother with a clear Christian perspective on the world.

*Stowe in Her Own Time* brings together recollections, articles, letters, memoirs, and biographical sketches about Stowe, most of them written by her family and friends, as well as some of her own autobiographical writings. The authors of all of the full-length biographies of Stowe—from Charles Edward Stowe's highly personal *Life of Harriet Beecher Stowe* (1889) to Joan Hedrick's scholarly *Harriet Beecher Stowe: A Life* (1994)— have drawn on at least some of these sources. But the recollections gathered here form another kind of biography, one that is designed to provide several perspectives on Stowe, sometimes in conflict and sometimes in agreement. As in any collection such as this one, there are gaps. I wish, for example, that some prominent figures who knew her well had offered extended commentaries, especially Sarah Orne Jewett, or William Lloyd Garrison, or George Eliot, with whom Stowe enjoyed a friendly correspondence, or her famous brother Henry Ward Beecher. Nonetheless, many others did write about Stowe, and I have been able to select from a rich and

Silhouette of Harriet Beecher Stowe, ca. 1830. Harriet Beecher Stowe
Center, Hartford, Connecticut.

wide array of materials. *Stowe in Her Own Time* is arranged chronologically according to the events of Stowe's life, although many of the recollections were written later and several were written after her death. Readers can trace the ways in which some of the enduring stories about Stowe—her early life as a minister's daughter, the writing of *Uncle Tom's Cabin*, and her meeting with Abraham Lincoln—changed over time. The collection also includes dissenting views of Stowe. Certainly the figure who emerges from this collection is far more complex than the image she helped to construct in her lifetime.

Stowe's life from her birth in 1811 until her marriage to Calvin Stowe in 1836 was in some ways similar to that of many white, middle-class women in the United States. But she was a member of a family with exceptional expectations about education and public life. Born on 14 June 1811, she grew up in Litchfield, Connecticut. Her father, the Congregational minister Lyman Beecher, was determined to reach a wide audience and become an influential public figure. About 1850, her brother Charles Beecher began to help their father prepare his autobiography. In response to her brother's request, Stowe wrote a long letter about her childhood memories. Stowe contributed several other letters which became sections or chapters of the two-volume autobiography of Lyman Beecher, published in 1864. "Memories of My Childhood in Litchfield, 1811–1824"†[5] formed the basis for much of what has since been written about Stowe's childhood, especially the accounts by her son and grandson, Charles Edward Stowe and Lyman Beecher Stowe. Their article, "The Girlhood of Harriet Beecher Stowe,"† first appeared in *McClure's Magazine* and then in their biography, *Harriet Beecher Stowe: The Story of Her Life*, published in 1911, the centennial of Stowe's birth. Stowe's own account of her childhood stresses her early educational experiences, especially in a delightful anecdote about her pride in winning a writing contest. Written just before the publication of *Uncle Tom's Cabin* in 1851 and 1852, this anecdote suggests that Stowe, who was then publishing only occasional sketches and stories, was thinking about her early success as a writer. In their accounts of her childhood, Stowe's son and grandson place a great deal of emphasis on her early religious training. "The Girlhood of Harriet Beecher Stowe" also describes Stowe's early experiences as a teacher and assistant at her sister Catharine's progressive school, the Hartford Female Seminary.

Stowe's budding career as a teacher and a school administrator was disrupted in 1832. That year Lyman Beecher became president of Lane Theological Seminary, and the entire family moved to Cincinnati. Stowe's son Charles devoted a chapter to her experiences there in his *Life of Harriet Beecher Stowe* (1889). "Stowe in Cincinnati, 1832–1836"† draws heavily on Stowe's own letters from the period, and much of the chapter deals with domestic life. Charles Stowe also describes Stowe's early literary efforts and her participation in the Semi-Colon Club, a writing group in which she became friendly with a number of other young people interested in writing including Calvin Stowe and his wife, Eliza Tyler Stowe. This writing group and Stowe's involvement in the growing antislavery movement were crucial to Stowe's later development. Charles Stowe ends his account of his mother's life in Cincinnati with her marriage to Calvin Stowe, whose first wife died in 1834.

Stowe was preoccupied with her growing family and responsibilities as the wife of a professor until 1851, when she began to conceive *Uncle Tom's Cabin*. During these fifteen years, she wrote when she could and published an occasional sketch or article, including "Trials of a Housekeeper" in the popular *Godey's Lady's Book* as well as the introduction for her brother Charles Beecher's *The Incarnation, or, Pictures of the Virgin and Her Son* (1849). She was devastated when her infant son died of cholera in July 1849. It was with some difficulty that Stowe left the comfort of her life with her extended family in Cincinnati to move with Calvin to Brunswick, Maine, where he accepted a teaching position at Bowdoin College in 1850. In a letter to Sarah Buckingham Beecher ("Life in Brunswick, December 1850"†), Stowe describes her new life in Maine with wit and deprecating humor.

A year later, she responded to an inquiry from Sarah Josepha Hale, already famous as the editor of *Godey's Lady's Book*, who asked Stowe for information about herself for a forthcoming book on women writers. In "Harriet Beecher Stowe" (1851)†, the conservative Hale, who carefully avoided the issue of slavery in her magazine, praised Stowe for her domestic stories and articles, little knowing that by the time her book appeared in 1853, Stowe would be in the forefront of the antislavery movement with the publication of *Uncle Tom's Cabin*. The debate over the Fugitive Slave Law (which passed in September 1850) galvanized the Beecher family, and prompted Stowe to write an antislavery sketch, "The Freeman's Dream," which was published in the *National Era*. The editor, Gamaliel Bailey, sent

Postmortem portrait of Samuel Charles Stowe, son of Harriet Beecher Stowe, ca. 1849. The Schlesinger Library, Radcliffe Institute, Harvard University.

her $100.00, asking her for more material. Her sister Isabella wrote Stowe, urging her: "Now Hattie, if I could use a pen as you can, I would write something that would make this whole nation feel what an accursed thing slavery is."[6] Stowe subsequently outlined her plan for a new serialized story in "Letter to Gamaliel Bailey on Writing *Uncle Tom's Cabin*, 1851"†.

The overwhelming success of the novel prompted a great deal of interest in the story of the writing of the novel.[7] Stowe's own account formed the basic narrative, which was used in the family biographies and the recollections of friends. For example, in a toast to American literature at a dinner for the New York press in December 1869, Stowe's friend James Parton (the husband of Stowe's schoolmate Fanny Fern), was reported in the *Hartford Times* as saying:

> I once heard an illustrious American authoress describe the circumstances in which she produced her best novel. Besides her family, too young to help her much, she had a class of eight young ladies, to whom she gave daily instruction. Her only servant was a stout, raw, Irish girl, who could not speak English, but could only do the roughest kind of work about the house. The authoress had to make bread for the family, and even light the fire in the oven. Sometimes after starting the fire, she used to work on her chapter, and sometimes she would get so absorbed in it that the fire would go out, and the bread turn sour; or, if the girl put a finger to it, the green wood would send forth volumes of smoke. Amid this desperate struggle with green wood, green Erin, eight hungry minds, fifteen hungry mouths, "Uncle Tom" was produced.[8]

Stowe also provided additional details, often saying in later years that *Uncle Tom's Cabin* had been a work of divine inspiration and that the Lord Himself wrote it.[9] In an article written for the *Atlantic Monthly* in 1896, the year of Stowe's death, Stowe's neighbor and friend, Charles Dudley Warner, published "The Story of *Uncle Tom's Cabin*,"† which provides the familiar story of the writing of the novel, along with his astute assessment of the ways in which Stowe was influenced by the Fugitive Slave Law in the writing of her novel.

*Uncle Tom's Cabin* made Stowe famous almost overnight. As Henry James recalled, "We lived and moved at that time with great intensity in Mrs. Stowe's novel."[10] Recovering from the birth of a daughter, Elizabeth Cady Stanton wrote a friend: "Just before the baby came I read *Uncle Tom's Cabin*. It is the most affecting book I ever read. I should like to see papa read it. That book will tell against slavery; of that you may be sure."[11] As a celebrity author, Stowe was introduced to other celebrities. In New York City in May 1852, she met the singer Jenny Lind, then touring in the United States, who sent the Stowes complimentary tickets for a concert, writing:

> You must feel and know what deep expression "Uncle Tom's Cabin" has made upon my heart that can feel for the dignity of human existence; so I, with my miserable English would not even try to say a word about the great excellency

of that most beautiful work, but I must thank you for the great joy I have felt over the book.[12]

Life for Stowe in the aftermath of the publication of *Uncle Tom's Cabin* could hardly have been more complicated. On the domestic side, she was busily and reluctantly preparing her family to move again, this time to Andover, Massachusetts, where Calvin Stowe had accepted a position at the Andover Theological Seminary. Completely new to her experience, however, was managing a life in the public sphere and coping with the success of her novel. Henry Wadsworth Longfellow, who entertained the Stowes at his home for dinner in February 1853, later wrote somewhat enviously in his diary: "How she is shaking the world with her Uncle Tom's Cabin! At one step she has reached the top of the stair-case up which the rest of us climb on our knees year after year. Never was there such a literary coup-de-main as this. A million copies of a book within the first year of its publication."[13]

Even as her novel was achieving unprecedented sales, Stowe was obliged to defend its authenticity by writing *A Key to Uncle Tom's Cabin* (1853). In addition, she was preparing for her first visit to England and Europe, as the guest of antislavery societies and, in the absence of international copyright laws, to secure copyrights for her works abroad. Late in 1852, Stowe received a letter from the British antislavery activist Eliza Follen, who asked her to write about herself in advance of her visit to England. Follen distributed Stowe's "Autobiographical Letter to Eliza Follen"† to friends, and it was also published in a number of periodicals. Famously describing herself as "a little bit of a woman—somewhat more than 40—about as thin & dry as a pinch of snuff—never very much to look at in my best days—& looking like a used up article now," Stowe set the stage for her appearances in Great Britain as a self-effacing lady caught up in something larger than herself. Fanny Fern devoted a column to her in the family-oriented newspaper the *Olive Branch*, "Stowe and *Uncle Tom's Cabin*"†, defending "Mrs. Tom Cabin," as she wittily called her, from attacks on her book and her success.

*Uncle Tom's Cabin* was wildly popular in both printed versions and theatrical adaptations. In a 1911 review of *Harriet Beecher Stowe: The Story of Her Life*, an anonymous writer observed:

> *Uncle Tom's Cabin* did more than contribute to the destruction of African slavery. It became a distinct force to help break down the Puritanic hostility against

the reading of novels and the attendance at theaters. In many homes in New England and the Middle West *Uncle Tom's Cabin* was the first novel ever to be admitted, and there are probably tens of thousands of persons still living who saw the inside of a theater for the first time when Uncle Tom and little Eva held the center of the stage.[14]

Stowe herself saw a performance of the play in Boston, in the company of Francis H. Underwood, one of the many editors and publishers with whom Stowe became friends. He wrote an account of seeing the play, "Stowe at a Performance of *Uncle Tom's Cabin*, 1853"†, at the invitation of Florine Thayer McCray, who was gathering material for her *The Life-Work of the Author of "Uncle Tom's Cabin"* (1889). The head of Derby and Miller Publishing Company, which published Stowe's *The Minister's Wooing* (1859), J. C. Derby, wrote a long account of the phenomenon of *Uncle Tom's Cabin* and Stowe's life during the 1850s in his extended memoir, *Fifty Years Among Authors, Books and Publishers* (1884), "Stowe and the Success of *Uncle Tom's Cabin*"†.

Stowe's new celebrity led her to increased involvement in antislavery activities. While white leaders of antislavery groups like William Lloyd Garrison wanted to capitalize on the success of *Uncle Tom's Cabin*, black abolitionists also thought of Stowe as a potential ally. She began to receive a number of appeals for assistance, appeals that the biographies written by members of her family generally ignore. Stowe had been corresponding with Frederick Douglass, whom she had asked for information about slave labor on cotton plantations when she was writing *Uncle Tom's Cabin*, and shortly before she sailed to England she invited him to Andover. Douglass published his recollections of their meeting, "First Meeting with Stowe, 1853"†, in his *Life and Times of Frederick Douglass* (1881). During the visit, Douglass asked Stowe to support an industrial school for former slaves and was bitterly disappointed when Stowe did not. In this case, Douglass's own recollections serve to complicate the friendship presented by the family biographies. Another appeal for help came from Harriet Jacobs, who is not mentioned in any nineteenth-century biography of Stowe. In her "Letters about Stowe, 1852–1853"†, Jacobs recounts a painful episode that reveals Stowe as a woman who could be unfeeling, insensitive, and blind to her own racism. Jacobs, who hoped Stowe might help her publish what eventually became *Incidents in the Life of a Slave Girl* (1861), wrote to abolitionist Amy Post of how Stowe, instead of helping her, wanted to use some of the details of Jacobs's life in her own *A Key to Uncle Tom's Cabin* and, without permission, revealed personal information about her to her employer, Cornelia Willis.

Stowe, who left little written record about these appeals and her methods of handling them, soon embarked on the first of her three trips to England and Europe. She enjoyed an enthusiastic reception wherever she went. Arriving at Liverpool, she was greeted by the Liverpool Antislavery Association. The event was described in "Stowe in Liverpool, 13 April 1853"†, reprinted in the preface to Stowe's *Sunny Memories of Foreign Lands* (1854). Charles Beecher, who accompanied the Stowes and kept a diary during the trip, provides a fond brother's version of the event in Liverpool, "Diary Entry for 14 April 1853"†. At other events in London in May 1853, the Stowes met Sara Pugh, an American Quaker who was serving as an advisor to British antislavery societies. In her diary, "Stowe in London, May 1853"†, Pugh records three events at which the Stowes met the former slaves and abolitionists William Wells Brown and William and Ellen Craft. At a dinner at the Mansion House in London, the Stowes were seated across the table from Charles Dickens and his wife. Dickens offered a gracious toast, saying that he "was in the presence of a stranger who was the author of a noble book with a noble purpose."[15] Dickens later reported that he did not much like Stowe, but the novelist William Makepeace Thackeray, who met Stowe the next month, humorously wrote a friend that when he met Stowe he was

> very agreeably disappointed. In place of the woman I had imagined to myself after the hideous daguerreotype, I found a gentle almost pretty person with a very great sweetness in her eyes and smile. I am sure she must be good and truth-telling from her face and behavior; and when I get a country place and a leisure hour shall buckle to Uncle Tom and really try to read it.[16]

Following the publication of her second antislavery novel, *Dred*, in 1856, Stowe returned to Europe, in part to secure international copyrights for her new book. While there, she attended a performance by Mary Webb, the daughter of an escaped slave for whom Stowe had written a dramatic version of *Uncle Tom's Cabin*, "The Christian Slave."[17] Unlike her treatment of Harriet Jacobs, Stowe helped Webb by arranging music lessons and events to showcase her talents. The *Illustrated London News* reviewed the performance, calling it "an event which would have caused considerable as-

Mary E. Webb reading *Uncle Tom's Cabin*, Stafford House, London. *Illustrated London News*, 2 August 1856, p. 122. Collection of Susan Belasco and Linck Johnson.

tonishment to any gentleman of the Southern States of America who might have happened to be present" and praising Webb for her "considerable and rather peculiar dramatic power."[18] During the trip, Stowe met Harriet Martineau as well as Robert Browning and Elizabeth Barrett Browning at their home in Italy. Barrett Browning and Stowe shared a serious interest in spiritualism, and they began a lively correspondence. Barrett Browning also recorded her candid recollections of Stowe in several letters to friends ("Impressions of Stowe"†).

Back in the United States in 1857, Stowe enjoyed her life in Andover. For the first time, the family finances were in good shape, and she reveled in her home. In "Recollections of Harriet Beecher Stowe at Andover"†, the young Elizabeth Stuart Phelps describes Stowe's life in Andover, paying tribute to the famous writer who encouraged her own literary career. Stowe's happiness at this time was shadowed by the death of her oldest son, Henry Ellis Stowe, a student at Dartmouth College, who drowned while swimming in the Connecticut River. Stowe resolutely continued her work, becoming instrumental in the founding of a new literary journal, the *Atlantic Monthly*, in 1857. Her story "The Mourning Veil" appeared in the first issue and, along with John Greenleaf Whittier and Oliver Wendell Holmes, Stowe was responsible for much of the magazine's early success.[19] Her next novel, *The Minister's Wooing* (1859), was first serialized in the *Atlantic*. Although the novel was a love story with nothing to do with antislavery, it captured the attention of abolitionist Sallie Holley, who, after seeing Stowe at an antislavery meeting, wrote to a friend to ask: "Are you reading her delightful story in the *Atlantic*? I am charmed with it."[20] Despite Stowe's importance to the success of the *Atlantic*, women writers were generally excluded from editorial meetings and the monthly dinners for its editors and contributors. In "Stowe and the *Atlantic Monthly* Dinner, 1859"†, Thomas Wentworth Higginson, a frequent contributor to the magazine, provided a hilarious account of one of the few times in which women were included.

Stowe, who returned from her third and final trip to Europe in June 1860, spent most of the war years in Andover. Now regarded by many women writers as a role model for her influence in the literary marketplace, she was at work on two new novels, *Agnes of Sorrento* (1862) and *The Pearl of Orr's Island* (1862). One of her most important friendships began at the end of her trip in Florence when she met Annie Adams Fields. In an article written

Harriet Beecher Stowe and one of her dogs during the Andover years, ca. 1859 to 1865. Harriet Beecher Stowe Center, Hartford, Connecticut.

for the *Atlantic Monthly*, "Days with Mrs. Stowe,"† Fields describes their first meeting and the nature of their lifelong friendship. In Andover, Stowe saw other literary friends, including Lydia Maria Child and Lucy Larcom. In a letter to a friend ("An Evening with Stowe in 1861"†), Child discusses Stowe's political stance while Lucy Larcom describes meeting Stowe at her home ("Lunch with Stowe, August 1862"†). In early December 1862, Stowe traveled to Washington, D.C., where her son Frederick was a soldier in the Union Army. There, she met with President Abraham Lincoln to encourage him to issue the Emancipation Proclamation. One of the favorite stories of the Stowe family was an account of this meeting, at which Lincoln is alleged to have greeted Stowe by exclaiming, "So you're the little woman who wrote the book that made this great war!" Stowe herself left no written record of the meeting, nor did Lincoln, but the family version of this story has persisted. Charles Edward Stowe and Lyman Beecher Stowe provided the fullest account in a chapter in their 1911 biography, "Stowe and President Abraham Lincoln, 2 December 1862"†.

In 1864, Calvin Stowe retired from Andover, and the Stowes prepared to move to Hartford, Connecticut. They built a grand home, "Oakholm," which Stowe helped design. In the years after the Civil War, Stowe continued her busy publication schedule, beginning with two collections of her *Atlantic* stories in 1865, *House and Home Papers* and *Little Foxes*. Stowe first visited Florida in March 1867, and in the following year, she and Calvin bought a home in Mandarin, where they began spending the winter. In a 1975 article about Stowe's importance to Florida history, travel writer Gene Burnett observed that "the most famous woman in America of that time became also one of the most zealous promoters of the virtues of living in the flower state; and her efforts were no doubt the greatest single contribution to the flourishing growth of Jacksonville as well as other parts of the state in years to follow."[21] Stowe had many visitors there, including William Cullen Bryant, who wrote a friend about the development in east Florida:

> On the more fertile of these spots grow more lofty live-oaks and magnolias, and here the settler makes his openings, and builds his dwelling, and plants his orchard of orange trees. In one of these spots, named Mandarin, Mrs. Stowe has her winter mansion, in the shadow of some enormous live oaks, and here she has planted an orange grove.[22]

When she was not in Florida, Stowe continued her busy social and literary life in Hartford. She continued to meet women writers, including Mary Abigail Dodge (Gail Hamilton), who wrote a brief diary entry about her first meeting with the famous author, "Impressions of Stowe in 1867"†.

Florine Thayer McCray, the author of *The Life-Work of the Author of*

Interior of Oakholm, Stowe's first Hartford home, ca. 1865. Harriet Beecher Stowe Center, Hartford, Connecticut.

*"Uncle Tom's Cabin"* (1889), provides more details about Stowe's life in Florida and especially her writing projects at this time ("Stowe's Life after the Civil War"†). Those projects included a novel, *Oldtown Folks* (1869), and her brief stint as coeditor (with Ik Marvel) of a new journal, *Hearth and Home*, in which Stowe published articles that reveal her increasing interest in women's rights. As famous as she was for her stories, sketches, and novels, Stowe was a prominent example of the ways in which the lack of an

international copyright affected the incomes of writers.[23] In "International Copyright"†, an article written for the *Atlantic Monthly*, James Parton used the story of Stowe's life and publication history as his main example of the inadequacies of current laws. Another of the projects that Stowe pursued at this time was a collaboration with her sister Catharine Beecher. Beecher updated her highly successful and often reprinted *Treatise on Domestic Economy* (1841) by inviting Stowe to contribute several chapters to *The American Woman's Home* (1869). Although the reviews were favorable, Stowe and other members of the Beecher family were beginning to receive a good bit of negative attention in the press, the result of the emerging culture of celebrity which developed after the Civil War. In response, Catharine Beecher wrote an open letter to several periodicals, "Petty Slanders,"† in which she mounted a spirited defense of Stowe's domestic expertise.

Ironically, the letter appeared just one month before the major controversy of Stowe's later career, which was generated by the publication of her article "The True Story of Lady Byron's Life" in the *Atlantic Monthly* (September 1869). As she had written in "Memories of My Childhood in Litchfield, 1811–1824"†, Stowe admired the work of the English Romantic poet Lord Byron (1788–1824) from an early age. The popular and influential Byron led an iconoclastic life filled with love affairs and dangerous exploits. At the time of his death from a fever caught while he was fighting in the Greek War of Independence, he had been long separated from his wife. Stowe became friendly with Byron's embittered widow during her first trip to England. After Lady Byron's death, Stowe decided to write an account of her friend's life, including references to Byron's incestuous relationship with his half-sister.[24] Although the facts of Byron's life were generally known, he was widely revered as a poet in England and as a national hero in Greece. No one had written explicitly about the details of his personal life until Stowe. As her friend and fellow writer Rose Terry Cooke explains in "Stowe and the Lady Byron Controversy, 1869–1870,"† Stowe paid a heavy price for the article, which was controversial in the United States and England. Subscriptions to the *Atlantic* dropped off precipitously and the publication of her book, *Lady Byron Vindicated*, the next year further damaged Stowe's reputation. Women's rights activists such as Elizabeth Cady Stanton came to her defense, but Stowe gradually began to recede from public life.

Calvin Stowe and Harriet Beecher Stowe at Mandarin, Florida, ca. 1880. Harriet Beecher Stowe Center, Hartford, Connecticut.

In 1870, the Stowes sold Oakholm and moved to a smaller and less expensive house in the Nook Farm area of Hartford. Except for their summer trips to Florida, Stowe lived at Nook Farm until her death. For the next decade, she mostly avoided controversial topics and published a series of novels about New York society, *Pink and White Tyranny* (1871), *My Wife and I* (1871), and *We and Our Neighbors* (1875). In order to earn additional money, she toured New England and later traveled to the Midwest, giving a series of popular readings.[25] The *Hartford Courant* reprinted an article from the *Springfield Republican* that described a reading in September 1871: "Viewed as an evening soiree with old friends who have long desired to see a favorite authoress—the favorite authoress, we may say—Mrs. Stowe's reading is a very delightful affair, and will, we trust, be enjoyed by large audiences wherever she goes."[26]

At home, Stowe was friendly with Mark Twain, who described the casual interchange between the families in those years in "Memories of a Neighbor at Nook Farm."† Another friend, George Parsons Lathrop, described an evening he spent with Stowe and Twain, deftly contrasting the differences between the two famous writers in "Stowe at Nook Farm."† The major public event of Stowe's last years was a large party honoring her birthday on 14 July 1882. "The Birthday Garden Party to Harriet Beecher Stowe"† was published as a supplement to the *Atlantic Monthly* and is reprinted here in its entirety. Attended by nearly three hundred people, including a large number of writers, family members, and friends, the celebration included speeches, readings of poems, and other tributes to Stowe. Articles about the event were reprinted widely and many of them included the poems written for the occasion by John Greenleaf Whittier and Oliver Wendell Holmes.

That event was one of Stowe's last public appearances. Stowe spent her time taking walks, enjoying her garden, playing with her grandchildren,

Poem and sketch by Harriet Beecher Stowe for her daughter Hattie, after the death of her cat, Jack Snappy, ca. 1885, from a scrapbook kept by Hattie. Harriet Beecher Stowe Center, Hartford, Connecticut.

and writing occasional poems. Calvin Stowe died in 1886, and Stowe's health began to fail. A number of people visited her and reported on her home life, including one of Twain's friends, Joseph H. Twichell, who wrote "Mrs. Harriet Beecher Stowe in Hartford" (1886)† for the popular "Authors at Home" series in the *Critic*. One of the more unusual visitors was Alexandra Gripenberg, a woman's rights activist from Finland whose "Harriet Beecher Stowe"† was a part of her book of travel essays, *A Half Year in the New World* (1888).

In 1889, the first full-length biographies appeared, Florine Thayer Mc-Cray's *The Life-Work of the Author of "Uncle Tom's Cabin"* and Charles Edward Stowe's *Life of Harriet Beecher Stowe*. McCray, a neighbor in Hartford who had interviewed Stowe and many of her friends, alarmed the family, who were concerned that she might be inaccurate, and the press began to cover the story, calling her an "intruder." The *New York Times* called it "The Stowe Controversy," suggesting that the book, which was published before Charles Stowe's, would "make a stir in the literary world."[27] In fact, both books received a great deal of attention. In a review, the *New York Times* praised the biographies, though it mildly criticized McCray for her "strenuous" appreciation and "unrestrained" eulogy.[28] Perhaps the most moving commentary on the final years of Stowe's life is contained in her correspondence with an old friend, "An Exchange between Stowe and Oliver Wendell Holmes in 1893."†

In the aftermath of Stowe's death at home on 1 July 1896, there were a variety of memorials, presented here as "Eulogies and Remembrances of Stowe at Her Death in 1896."† Articles also appeared in the *American Missionary*, the *Century*, and the *New England Magazine*.[29] Isabella Beecher Hooker published a small pamphlet, *A Brief Sketch of the Life of Harriet Beecher Stowe* (1896)†. Houghton-Mifflin published a sixteen-volume edition of *The Writings of Harriet Beecher Stowe*, which was praised by a reviewer: "None of our writers lived more distinctly in an American atmosphere, or drew more exclusively than Mrs. Stowe on American life for the characters in her books."[30] In the following year, Annie Fields published her *Life and Letters of Harriet Beecher Stowe*. Among the more unusual tributes to Stowe after her death was Paul Laurence Dunbar's "Harriet Beecher Stowe" (1898)†, a poem that hailed Stowe and *Uncle Tom's Cabin* at a time when racial oppression was deepening throughout the United States.

# THE WORKS OF HARRIET BEECHER STOWE.

Uncle Tom's Cabin. A Story of Slavery. Illustrated. 12mo, $2.00. (*See also below.*)

Agnes of Sorrento. 12mo, $1.50.

The Pearl of Orr's Island. 12mo, $1.50.

The Minister's Wooing. 12mo, $1.50.

My Wife and I. New Edition. Illustrated. 12mo, $1.50.

We and Our Neighbors. A Sequel to My Wife and I. New Edition. Illustrated. 12mo, $1.50.

Poganuc People. New Edition. Illustrated. 12mo, $1.50.

The May-Flower, and other Sketches. 12mo, $1.50.

Dred. (Nina Gordon.) New Edition from new plates. 12mo, $1.50.

Oldtown Folks. 12mo, $1.50.

Sam Lawson's Fireside Stories. Illustrated. New Edition, enlarged. 12mo, $1.50.

The above eleven 12mo volumes in box, $16.00.

House and Home Papers. 16mo, $1.50.
Little Foxes. Common Household Faults. 16mo, $1.50.
The Chimney-Corner. 16mo, $1.50.

These three Household books in box, $4.50.

Little Pussy Willow, etc. Illustrated. Small 4to, $1.25.
A Dog's Mission, etc. Illustrated. Small 4to, $1.25.
Queer Little People. Illustrated. Small 4to, $1.25.

These three juvenile books, $3.75.

Religious Poems. Illustrated. 16mo, $1.50.
Palmetto Leaves. Sketches of Florida. Illustrated. 16mo, $1.50.
Uncle Tom's Cabin. *Illustrated Holiday Edition.* With Introduction and Bibliography by GEORGE BULLEN, of the British Museum. With over one hundred Illustrations. 8vo, full gilt, $3.00; half calf, $5.00; morocco, or tree calf, $6.00.

New *Popular Edition* from new plates. With account of the writing of this story by Mrs. Stowe, and frontispiece. 12mo, $1.00.

Flowers and Fruit, selected from Mrs. Stowe's Writings. 16mo, $1.00.

Scenes from Mrs. Stowe's Works. For use in School Entertainments. Selected by EMILY WEAVER. In Riverside Literature Series, extra number, paper, 15 cents, *net.*

HOUGHTON, MIFFLIN AND COMPANY, *Publishers,*

BOSTON AND NEW YORK.

Undated Houghton-Mifflin advertisement for *The Writings of Harriet Beecher Stowe* (1896). Collection of Susan Belasco and Linck Johnson.

*Stowe in Her Own Time* ends with an article from the *New York Times*, one of several articles and stories that appeared in the periodical press in celebration of the one hundredth anniversary of Stowe's birth in 1911. While the tone of this article and most of the others was generally celebratory, Stowe and *Uncle Tom's Cabin* were clearly fading from public memory, despite the efforts of her family. Charles Edward Stowe and Lyman Beecher Stowe's *Harriet Beecher Stowe: The Story of Her Life* appeared in time for the centennial year but was regarded largely as a memorial volume drawn from earlier well-known family papers and earlier biographies. Although one more biography by a family member was published, Lyman Beecher Stowe's *Saints, Sinners, and Beechers* (1934), his dedication was emblematic of attitudes about Stowe: "To My sons, David and Robinson, who quite properly are not interested in ancestors." Forrest Wilson's 1941 biography, *Crusader in Crinoline: The Life of Harriet Beecher Stowe*, did little to revive interest in Stowe.

In fact, through much of the twentieth century, *Uncle Tom's Cabin* was largely unread, living on in negative stereotypes of "Uncle Tom" and racist adaptations of the novel, on the stage, in the movies, and in early television shows. A famous critique first published on the eve of the emerging Civil Rights movement, James Baldwin's "Everybody's Protest Novel" (1949), linked *Uncle Tom's Cabin* with *Little Women* in the sentimental tradition and presented Stowe as a pamphleteer who finally did little to change attitudes in post–Civil War America. Beginning in the 1970s, however, the rise of feminist criticism presented Stowe and her novel in a very different light. Today, interest in Stowe is reflected in a long list of projects: Joan Hedrick's Pulitzer Prize–winning biography; an award-winning electronic archive, *Uncle Tom's Cabin and American Culture*; a flourishing Harriet Beecher Stowe Society; new dramatic adaptations of *Uncle Tom's Cabin*; an annotated edition of *Uncle Tom's Cabin*, prepared by Henry Louis Gates, Jr., one of the foremost African American scholars in the United States; the thriving Stowe Center and Library in Hartford; and dozens of new books and articles on Stowe and her writings which are widely taught in colleges and universities.[31] *Stowe in **Our** Own Time* is clearly an ongoing enterprise.

With the exception of manuscript material which I have transcribed myself, the texts in this volume are from the first printed versions. I have silently corrected obvious typographical or spelling errors in printed texts and altered punctuation marks only for clarity. For example, I have inserted missing single or double quotation marks and closed spaces within contractions. I have also italicized titles of books and periodicals throughout. Entries that are taken from *Life of Harriet Beecher Stowe* (1889) by Charles Edward Stowe, *Life and Letters of Harriet Beecher Stowe* (1897) by Annie Fields, and *Harriet Beecher Stowe: The Story of Her Life* (1911) by Charles Edward Stowe and Lyman Beecher Stowe include long passages from letters that were presented in the original texts as lengthy quotations within quotation marks. For clarity, I have deleted the quotation marks and indented these passages as block quotations. Throughout I have let nineteenth-century spellings stand, and I have modernized all of the texts as little as possible. In this Introduction, a dagger (†) is used to indicate that the referenced text is printed in this volume. I have provided contextual information in an introductory headnote for each selection, and I have written explanatory notes to the texts when necessary. Complete bibliographic information for each entry is given in an unnumbered footnote following the text. The Bibliography at the end of the volume includes all of the texts cited in the Introduction and introductory headnotes as well as other works that readers may want to consult.

I have been helped enormously in the preparation of this volume by a number of people and institutions. My work was supported in part by a grant from the Charles J. Millard Trust Fund, administered by the University of Nebraska Research Council. I am grateful to my colleagues at the University of Nebraska, Lincoln, for their support, especially Joy Ritchie, Kenneth M. Price, Melissa Homestead, and Elizabeth Lorang; and to Charles Johanningsmeier, University of Nebraska, Omaha. Two graduate research assistants at Nebraska provided outstanding help. Kathryn Kruger assisted me in locating and transcribing texts, scanning images, and arranging the chronology, and Daniel Gomes helped me prepare the index. Beth MacKinnon at Colgate University also assisted me in transcribing texts. The staff of the Harriet Beecher Stowe Center, Katherine Kane, Dawn C. Adiletta, and Elizabeth Giard, made archival materials available to me and provided invaluable suggestions for the volume. I am especially grateful to Elizabeth Giard for her lively correspondence and gracious help during my visits to the Stowe Center. (For more information about the Center, please see their website: www.harrietbeecherstowe.org.) Several people at libraries and collections generously provided answers to my questions and helped with texts and illustrations, including: James McQuin and Nancy Horlacher, Dayton Metro Library; Susan Barker, Sophia Smith Collection, Smith College; Diana Carey, Schlesinger Library; Heather Cole, Houghton Library, Harvard University; Matthew Westerby, the Metropolitan Museum of Art; Ralph Marquez, Houghton Mifflin Harcourt Publishing Company; Laurie N. Taylor, Digital Library Center, University of Florida; Sean Casey, Boston Public Library; Mary M. Huth, University of Rochester Library; Cynthia Brennan, American Antiquarian Society; Karen G. Druliner, University of Delaware Press; Cynthia Harbeson, Connecticut Historical Society; Katherine Walters and Carmella L. Orosco, Love Library, University of Nebraska, Lincoln; Simon Lord, Oxford University Press; and Jackson R. Bryer, editor, *Resources for American Literary Study*. Dr. David Wykes, Director, Dr. Williams's Library, London, generously transcribed Stowe's letter to Eliza Follen for my use in this volume. Marcia Matika and Bonnie Linck, Connecticut State Library, kindly helped me piece together missing lines in the microfilm copy of Catharine Beecher's "Petty Slanders." I am thankful to Elizabeth Moyne Homsey for her permission to use her father's translation of the chapter on Stowe in *A Half Year in the New World*, to Jean Fagan Yellin for her assistance with obtaining the illustration of Harriet Jacobs, and to Beverly Peterson for her help with the exchange of letters between Stowe and Oliver Wendell Holmes. I—and all scholars of Harriet Beecher Stowe—owe large debts to Joan Hedrick, author of *Harriet Beecher Stowe: A Life*; Stephen Railton, director of *Uncle Tom's Cabin and American Culture: A Multi-Media Archive* (http://www.iath.virginia.edu/utc/); Sarah Robbins, author of *The Cambridge Introduction to Harriet Beecher Stowe*; Cindy Weinstein, editor, and the contributors to *The Cambridge Companion to Harriet Beecher Stowe*; Denise Kohn, Sarah Meer, and Emily B. Todd, editors, and the contributors to *Transatlantic Stowe: Harriet Beecher Stowe and European Culture*; as well as to the work of Elizabeth Ammons, Jane Tompkins, Mary Kelley, and Eric Sundquist. I thank Joel Myerson for inviting me to edit this volume. I very much appreciated the guidance and good cheer of Holly Carver, Charlotte Wright, and Karen Copp of the University of Iowa Press throughout the process. Jennifer Ushar Dunn, of Mesa Verde Media Services, provided expert copyediting assistance. I have also relied on Steve Scipione and Maura Shea, my friends at Bedford/St. Martins, who have taught me a great deal about preparing anthologies. For over thirty-five years, Pamela Stockton and Reagan Sides have been providing warm friendship and ongoing support.

In a book that is so profoundly about family I am eager to thank my own, especially my mother, Peggy Bell Belasco, to whom this book is lovingly dedicated; as well as Janet, Steve, and Stephen Jenkins; Bill Belasco and Teresa Morales; Roslyn and Vincent Reilly; and Lance Johnson. My stepson, Max Johnson, contributed enthusiastic encouragement and lively diversions. Finally and most importantly, I am grateful to my husband, Linck Johnson, who helped in ways too numerous to count and whose love and laughter make every project possible.

## Notes

1. Christopher J. Bowman, "Beecher Clan Gathers to Update Family Photo Album," *Hartford Courant*, 26 June 1983, p. A4.

2. See Joan Hedrick, *Harriet Beecher Stowe: A Life* (Oxford: Oxford University Press, 1994), pp. 97–98.

3. Eleanor Charles, "Beecher Clan to Catch Up on 124 Years," *New York Times*, 19 June 1983, p. CN25.

4. Sarah Robbins, *The Cambridge Introduction to Harriet Beecher Stowe* (Cambridge: Cambridge University Press, 2007), p. 1.

5. Throughout this introduction, texts included in the volume are indicated by their titles and marked with a †.

6. Quoted in Hedrick, p. 207.

7. For a detailed account of the publishing history of the novel, see Michael Winship, "'The Greatest Book of Its Kind': A Publishing History of 'Uncle Tom's Cabin,'" *Proceedings of the American Antiquarian Society* 109 (2002): 309–322.

8. From a typescript labeled "Mrs. Stowe Wrote 'Uncle Tom's Cabin' Under Trying Circumstances," *Hartford Times*, 3 December 1869. Courtesy Harriet Beecher Stowe Center, Hartford, CT.

9. See Forrest Wilson, *Crusader in Crinoline: The Life of Harriet Beecher Stowe* (Philadelphia: J. B. Lippincott, 1941), p. 270; Charles Edward Stowe, *Life of Harriet Beecher Stowe* (New York: Houghton, Mifflin, 1889), p. 154; Annie Fields, *Life and Letters of Harriet Beecher Stowe* (New York: Houghton, Mifflin, 1897), p. 165; Charles Edward Stowe and Lyman Beecher Stowe, *Harriet Beecher Stowe: The Story of Her Life* (New York: Houghton, Mifflin, 1911), p. 163.

10. Henry James, *A Small Boy and Others* (New York: Charles Scribner's Sons, 1913), pp. 158–159.

11. Letter from Elizabeth Cady Stanton to Elizabeth Smith Miller, 21 November 1852, in *Elizabeth Cady Stanton, as Revealed in Her Letters, Diary and Reminiscences*, vol. 2, ed. Harriot Stanton Blatch and Theodore Stanton (New York: Harper and Brothers, 1922), p. 369.

12. From a typescript labeled "Jenny Lind's letter to Harriet Beecher Stowe May 23, 1852," *Hartford Times*, 6 June 1914. Courtesy Harriet Beecher Stowe Center, Hartford, CT.

13. "February 24th [1853]," *Life of Henry Wadsworth Longfellow*, vol. 2, ed. Samuel Longfellow (New York: Houghton, Mifflin, 1891), p. 249.

14. "The Novel That Overruled the Supreme Court," *Current Literature* 51 (1911): 209–210.

15. "Banquet at the Mansion House, 2 May 1853," *The Speeches of Charles Dickens*, ed. K. J. Fielding (Hempstead: Harvester-Wheatsheaf; Atlantic Highlands, NJ: Humanities Press International, 1988), p. 165.

16. "Thackeray and Mrs. Stowe, London, Friday, 3 June 1863," copy of an undated article from an unknown newspaper, courtesy Harriet Beecher Stowe Center, Hartford, CT.

17. See Eric Gardner, "Stowe Takes the Stage: Harriet Beecher Stowe's 'The Christian Slave,'" *Legacy: A Journal of American Women Writers* 15 (1998): 78–84.

18. "Dramatic Readings by a Coloured Native of Philadelphia," *The Illustrated London News*, 2 August 1856, pp. 121–122.

19. Ellery Sedgwick, *The Atlantic Monthly: 1857–1909* (Amherst: University of Massachusetts Press, 1994), p. 50.

20. Letter from Sallie Holley to Susan Farley Porter, 28 February 1859, *A Life for Liberty: Anti-Slavery and Other Letters of Sallie Holley*, ed. John White (New York: G. P. Putnam's Sons, 1899), p. 168.

21. Gene Burnett, "A Big Push from a Tiny Package," *Florida Trend*, September 1975, p. 81. Courtesy Harriet Beecher Stowe Center, Hartford, CT.

22. William Cullen Bryant to Jerusha Dewey, 9 February 1873, *The Letters of William Cullen Bryant*, vol. 7, ed. William Cullen Bryant II and Thomas G. Voss (New York: Fordham University Press, 1992), p. 106.

23. For a detailed discussion of Stowe and copyright laws, see Melissa J. Homestead, *American Women Authors and Literary Property, 1822–1869* (Cambridge: Cambridge University Press, 2005), pp. 105–149.

24. See Michelle Hawley, "Harriet Beecher Stowe and Lord Byron: A Case of Celebrity Justice in the Victorian Public Sphere," *Journal of Victorian Culture* 10 (2005): 229–256.

25. See Fredrick Trautmann, "Harriet Beecher Stowe's Public Readings in New England," *The New England Quarterly* 47 (1974): 279–289; and E. Bruce Kirkham, "Harriet Beecher Stowe's Western Tour," *The Old Northwest* 1 (1975): 35–49.

26. "Mrs. Stowe's Reading," *Hartford Courant*, 24 September 1871; from a typescript, courtesy Harriet Beecher Stowe Center, Hartford, CT.

27. "The Stowe Controversy," *New York Times*, 13 October 1889, p. 12.

28. "Harriet Beecher Stowe," *New York Times*, 22 December 1889, p. 19.

29. "Harriet Beecher Stowe," *American Missionary* 50 (1896): 244–245; Richard Burton, "The Author of 'Uncle Tom's Cabin,'" *Century* 52 (1896): 698–715; and George Willis Cooke, "Harriet Beecher Stowe," *The New England Magazine* 15 (1896): 3–18.

30. Review of *The Writings of Harriet Beecher Stowe, Independent*, 18 February 1897, p. 18.

31. See, for example, Elizabeth Ammons and Susan Belasco, *Approaches to Teaching Uncle Tom's Cabin* (New York: MLA, 2000); Henry Louis Gates, Jr., *The Annotated Uncle Tom's Cabin* (New York: W. W. Norton, 2007); Denise Kohn, Sarah Meer, and Emily B. Todd, eds., *Transatlantic Stowe: Harriet Beecher Stowe and European Culture* (Iowa City: University of Iowa Press, 2006); and Cindy Weinstein, ed., *The Cambridge Companion to Harriet Beecher Stowe* (Cambridge: Cambridge University Press, 2004).

# Chronology

| 1775 | 12 October | Lyman Beecher born |
| 1811 | 14 June | Harriet Elizabeth Beecher is born in Litchfield, Connecticut, to Lyman Beecher and Roxana Foote Beecher |
| 1816 | | Roxana Foote Beecher dies of tuberculosis at the age of 41 |
| 1817 | | Lyman Beecher marries Harriet Porter |
| 1819 | | Enters Litchfield Female Academy |
| 1824 | | Attends the Hartford Female Seminary established in 1823 by her oldest sister, Catharine E. Beecher |
| 1827 | | Teaches at the Hartford Female Seminary |
| 1832 | | Lyman Beecher named president of the Lane Theological Seminary; Beecher family moves to Cincinnati |
| | | Teaches at Western Female Institute, founded by Catharine Beecher |
| 1833 | | Publishes first book, *Primary Geography for Children, on an Improved Plan with Eleven Maps and Numerous Engravings* |
| | | Begins publishing stories and sketches in the *Western Monthly Magazine*, published in Cincinnati |
| 1834 | April | Wins a prize for "A New England Sketch," *Western Monthly Magazine* |

| | | |
|---|---|---|
| 1835 | | Publishes sketch, "Uncle Enoch," *New-York Evangelist* |
| 1836 | 6 January | Marries Calvin Stowe in Cincinnati |
| | September | Gives birth to twin girls, Harriet (Hatty) and Eliza |
| 1838 | January | Gives birth to a son, Henry Ellis |
| 1839 | | Publishes "Trials of a Housekeeper," *Godey's Lady's Book* |
| 1840 | May | Gives birth to second son, Frederick William |
| 1842 | | Publishes "A Parable," *New-York Evangelist* |
| 1843 | | Publishes *The Mayflower or Sketches of Scenes and Characters among the Descendants of the Pilgrims* |
| 1843 | July | Gives birth to a daughter, Georgiana May |
| 1845 | | Publishes "Immediate Emancipation: A Sketch," *New-York Evangelist* |
| 1848 | January | Gives birth to a son, Samuel Charles (Charley) |
| 1849 | | Writes introduction for Charles Beecher's *The Incarnation, or, Pictures of the Virgin and Her Son* |
| | July | Son Charley dies during the cholera epidemic in Cincinnati |
| 1850 | | Calvin Stowe appointed to the faculty of Bowdoin College; Stowe family moves to Brunswick, Maine |
| | July | Gives birth to her last child, Charles Edward |
| | 1 August | Publishes "The Freeman's Dream: A Parable," *National Era* |
| | 18 September | Fugitive Slave Law passes as part of the Compromise of 1850 |

| | | |
|---|---|---|
| 1851 | 1 June | *Uncle Tom's Cabin* begins serialization in the *National Era* |
| 1852 | March | *Uncle Tom's Cabin; or, Life among the Lowly* published by John P. Jewett |
| | | Calvin Stowe takes a teaching position at Andover Theological Seminary; Stowe family moves to Andover, Massachusetts |
| 1853 | | Publishes *A Key to Uncle Tom's Cabin* |
| | April | Embarks on first trip to Great Britain and Europe |
| | 7 May | Presented in London with the "Affectionate and Christian Address," an antislavery petition signed by more than 500,000 British women |
| 1854 | | Publishes "An Appeal to the Women of the Free States of America, on the Present Crisis in Our Country," *Independent* |
| | | Publishes *Sunny Memories of Foreign Lands* |
| 1855 | | Republishes *The Mayflower and Miscellaneous Writings* |
| 1856 | | Publishes *Dred: A Tale of the Great Dismal Swamp* |
| | | Takes second trip to Europe and visits Lady Byron, Harriet Martineau, Charles Kingsley, and Mary Webb; meets Robert and Elizabeth Barrett Browning in Florence |
| 1857 | | Oldest son, Henry Ellis Stowe, dies by drowning in the Connecticut River while a student at Dartmouth College |
| | | Helps found *Atlantic Monthly* and begins lifelong friendships with Oliver Wendell Holmes and James Russell Lowell |
| | | Publishes "The Mourning Veil," *Atlantic Monthly* |

| | | |
|---|---|---|
| 1859 | | Publishes *The Minister's Wooing* |
| | | Takes third and final trip to Europe |
| 1860 | | Meets James and Annie Fields in Italy |
| 1861 | | Civil War begins |
| 1862 | | Publishes *Agnes of Sorrento* and *The Pearl of Orr's Island* |
| | 2 December | Meets President Abraham Lincoln in the White House |
| 1863 | 1 January | President Abraham Lincoln issues Emancipation Proclamation |
| | 10 January | Lyman Beecher dies |
| | | Publishes "Sojourner Truth, the Libyan Sibyl," *Atlantic Monthly* |
| | | Calvin Stowe retires from Andover Theological Seminary |
| 1864 | | Oversees the design and construction of the family's "Oakholm" home in Hartford, Connecticut |
| 1865 | | Publishes two collections of articles from *Atlantic Monthly: House and Home Papers* and *Little Foxes* |
| 1867 | | Visits Florida for the first time; publishes *Religious Poems* |
| 1868 | | Purchases a home in Mandarin, Florida, where the family spends their winters up to 1884 |
| 1869 | | Publishes *Oldtown Folks* |
| | | Coedits *Hearth and Home* with Ik Marvel |
| | | Begins a correspondence with George Eliot |
| | | Collaborates with Catharine Beecher on *The American Woman's Home* |
| | | Publishes "The True Story of Lady Byron's Life," *Atlantic Monthly* |

| | | |
|---|---|---|
| 1870 | | Publishes *Lady Byron Vindicated: A History of the Byron Controversy, from Its Beginnings in 1816 to the Present Time* |
| 1871 | | Publishes *Pink and White Tyranny: A Society Novel* and *My Wife and I* |
| | | Son Frederick disappears |
| 1872 | | Tours New England and the Midwest giving readings |
| 1873 | | Moves to house on Forest Street in Nook Farm area of Hartford |
| 1874 | | Publishes *Woman in Sacred History: A Series of Sketches Drawn from Scriptural, Historical, and Legendary Sources* |
| 1875 | | Publishes *We and Our Neighbors* |
| 1878 | | Publishes *Poganuc People* |
| 1882 | 14 June | Houghton, Mifflin and Company host birthday party for Stowe at William Claflin's home, "The Old Elms," in Newtonville, Massachusetts; over two hundred guests attend including Rose Terry Cooke, Oliver Wendell Holmes, William Dean Howells, Elizabeth Stuart Phelps, and John Greenleaf Whittier |
| 1886 | 6 August | Calvin Stowe dies |
| 1887 | | Daughter Georgiana May dies |
| 1889 | | Charles Edward Stowe publishes an official biography, *Life of Harriet Beecher Stowe, Compiled from Her Letters and Journals* |
| | | Florine Thayer McCray publishes *The Life-Work of the Author of "Uncle Tom's Cabin"* |
| 1896 | 1 July | Dies at home in Hartford |
| | | Houghton-Mifflin publishes *The Writings of Harriet Beecher Stowe* in sixteen volumes |

| 1897 | Annie Fields publishes *Life and Letters of Harriet Beecher Stowe* |
| 1911 | Charles Edward Stowe and Lyman Beecher Stowe publish *Harriet Beecher Stowe: The Story of Her Life* |
| 1943 | Lyman Beecher Stowe publishes *Saints, Sinners, and Beechers* |

STOWE IN HER OWN TIME

# [Memories of My Childhood in Litchfield, 1811–1824]

### Harriet Beecher Stowe

Throughout his life, Stowe's father, Lyman Beecher, carefully preserved his letters, journals, and other papers, with an eye toward eventually writing his autobiography. According to Barbara M. Cross, Beecher decided in about 1850 that he needed assistance in the preparation of his life story.[1] Six of his eleven children took notes of his reminiscences and also contributed their individual recollections, letters, and papers to Charles Beecher, who prepared the two-volume *Autobiography Correspondence, Etc., of Lyman Beecher* for publication in 1864. Stowe contributed several sections to the lengthy work. In the chapter of the *Autobiography* that follows, written in the form of a letter to her brother, she provides memories of her childhood in Litchfield, Connecticut, where her father was the pastor of the Congregational church from 1810 until 1826. In addition to offering insights into her relationship with her larger-than-life father, Stowe's account provides details about her early reading, education, and experiences at school.

DEAR BROTHER,—My earliest recollections of Litchfield are those of its beautiful scenery, which impressed and formed my mind long before I had words to give names to my emotions, or could analyze my mental processes. I remember standing often in the door of our house and looking over a distant horizon, where Mount Tom reared its round blue head against the sky, and the Great and Little Ponds, as they were called, gleamed out amid a steel-blue sea of distant pine groves. To the west of us rose a smooth-bosomed hill called Prospect Hill; and many a pensive, wondering hour have I sat at our play-room window, watching the glory of the wonderful sunsets that used to burn themselves out, amid voluminous wreathings, or castellated turrets of clouds—vaporous pageantry proper to a mountainous region.

Litchfield sunsets were famous, perhaps watched by more appreciative and intelligent eyes than the sunsets of other mountain towns around. The love and notice of nature was a custom and habit of the Litchfield people;

Lyman Beecher and Harriet Beecher Stowe, ca. 1859. Harriet Beecher Stowe Center, Hartford, Connecticut.

and always of a summer evening the way to Prospect Hill was dotted with parties of strollers who went up thither to enjoy the evening.

On the east of us lay another upland, called Chestnut Hills, whose sides were wooded with a rich growth of forest-trees; whose changes of tint and verdure, from the first misty tints of spring green, through the deepening hues of summer, into the rainbow glories of autumn, was a subject of constant remark and of pensive contemplation to us children. We heard them spoken of by older people, pointed out to visitors, and came to take pride in them as a sort of birthright.

Seated on the rough granite flag-steps of the east front door with some favorite book—if by chance we could find such a treasure—the book often fell from the hand while the eye wandered far off into those soft woody depths with endless longings and dreams—dreams of all those wild fruits, and flowers, and sylvan treasures which some Saturday afternoon's ramble had shown us lay sheltered in those enchanted depths. There were the crisp apples of the pink azalea—honeysuckle apples we called them—there were scarlet wintergreen berries; there were pink shell blossoms of trailing arbutus, and feathers of ground pine; there were blue, and white, and yellow violets, and crowsfoot, and bloodroot, and wild anemone, and other quaint forest treasures.

Between us and those woods lay the Bantam River—a small, clear, rocky stream, pursuing its way through groves of pine and birch—now so shallow that we could easily ford it by stepping from stone to stone, and again, in spots, so deep and wide as to afford bathing and swimming room for the young men and boys of the place. Many and many a happy hour we wandered up and down its tangled, rocky, and ever-changing banks, or sat under a thick pine bower, on a great granite slab called Solitary Rock, round which the clear brown waters gurgled.

At the north of the house the horizon was closed in with distant groves of chestnut and hickory, whose waving tops seemed to have mysteries of invitation and promise to our childhood. I had read, in a chance volume of Gesner's *Idyls*, of tufted groves, where were altars to Apollo, and where white-robed shepherds played on ivory flutes, and shepherdesses brought garlands to hang round the shrines, and for a long time I nourished a shadowy impression that, could I get into those distant northern groves, some of these dreams would be realized. These fairy visions were, alas! all dissolved by an actual permission to make a Saturday afternoon's excursion in these very groves, which were found to be used as goose-pastures, and to be destitute of the flowery treasures of the Chestnut Hills forests.

My father was fond of excursions with his boys into the forests about for fishing and hunting. At first I remember these only as something pertaining to father and the older boys, they being the rewards given for good conduct. I remember the regretful interest with which I watched their joyful preparations for departure. They were going to the Great Pond—to Pine Island—to that wonderful blue pine forest which I could just see on the horizon, and who knew what adventures they might meet! Then the house all day was so still; no tramping of laughing, wrestling boys—no singing and shouting; and perhaps only a long seam on a sheet to be oversewed as the sole means of beguiling the hours of absence. And then dark night would come down, and stars look out from the curtains, and innuendoes would be thrown out of children being sent to bed, and my heart would be rent with anguish at the idea of being sent off before the eventful expedition had reported itself. And then what joy to hear at a distance the tramp of feet, the shouts and laughs of older brothers; and what glad triumph when the successful party burst into the kitchen with long strings of perch, roach, pickerel, and bullheads, with waving blades of sweet-flag, and high heads of cattail, and pockets full of young wintergreen, of which a generous portion was bestowed always upon me. These were the trophies, to my eyes, brought from the land of enchantment. And then what cheerful hurrying and scurrying to and fro, and waving of lights, and what cleaning of fish in the back shed, and what calling for frying-pan and gridiron, over which father solemnly presided; for to his latest day he held the opinion that no feminine hand could broil or fry fish with that perfection of skill which belonged to himself alone, as king of woodcraft and woodland cookery.

I was always safe against being sent to bed for a happy hour or two, and patronized with many a morsel of the supper which followed, as father and brothers were generally too flushed with victory to regard very strictly dull household rules.

Somewhat later, I remember, were the expeditions for chestnuts and walnuts in the autumn, to which all we youngsters were taken. I remember the indiscriminate levy which on such occasions was made on every basket the house contained, which, in the anticipated certainty of a great harvest to bring home, were thought to be only too few. I recollect the dismay with which our second mother, the most ladylike and orderly of housekeepers, once contemplated the results of these proceedings in her well-arranged linen-room, where the contents of stocking-baskets, patch-baskets, linen-baskets, yarn-baskets, and thread-baskets were all pitched into a promiscuous heap by that omnipotent marauder, Mr. Beecher, who had accomplished all this confusion with the simple promise to bring the baskets home full of chestnuts.

[4]

What fun it was, in those golden October days, when father dared William and Edward to climb higher than he could, and shake down the glossy chestnuts! To the very last of his life, he was fond of narrating an exploit of his climbing a chestnut-tree that grew up fifty feet without branches slantwise over a precipice, and then whirling himself over the abyss to beat down the chestnuts for the children below. "That was a thing," he said, "that I wouldn't let any of the boys do." And those chestnuts were had in everlasting remembrance. I verily believe that he valued himself more on some of those exploits than even his best sermons.

My father was famous for his power of exciting family enthusiasm. Whenever he had a point to carry or work to be done, he would work the whole family up to a pitch of fervent zeal, in which the strength of each one seemed quadrupled. For instance: the wood of the family used to be brought in winter on sleds, and piled up in the yard, exactly over the spot where father wished in early spring to fix his cucumber and melon frames; for he always made it a point to have cucumbers as soon as Dr. Taylor, who lived in New Haven, and had much warmer and drier land; and he did it by dint of contrivance and cucumber frames, as aforesaid. Of course, as all this wood was to be cut, split, and carried into the wood-house before an early garden could be started, it required a miracle of generalship to get it done, considering the immense quantity required in that climate to keep an old windy castle of a house comfortable. How the axes rung, and the chips flew, and the jokes and stories flew faster; and when all was cut and split, then came the great work of wheeling in and piling; and then I, sole little girl among so many boys, was sucked into the vortex of enthusiasm by father's well-pointed declaration that he "wished Harriet was a boy, she would be more than any of them."

I remember putting on a little black coat which I thought looked more like the boys, casting needle and thread to the wind, and working almost like one possessed for a day and a half, till in the afternoon the wood was all in and piled, and the chips swept up. Then father tackled the horse into the cart, and proclaimed a grand fishing party down to Little Pond. And how we all floated among the lily-pads in our boat, christened "The Yellow Perch," and every one of us caught a string of fish, which we displayed in triumph on our return.

There were several occasions in the course of the yearly housekeeping requiring every hand in the house, which would have lagged sadly had it not been for father's inspiring talent. One of these was the apple-cutting season, in the autumn, when a barrel of cider-apple-sauce had to be made, which was to stand frozen in the milk-room, and cut out from time to time in red glaciers, which, when duly thawed, supplied the table. The work was done in the kitchen, an immense brass kettle hanging over the deep fireplace, a bright fire blazing and snapping, and all hands, children and servants, employed on the full baskets of apples and quinces which stood around. I have the image of my father still as he sat working the apple-peeler. "Come, George," he said "I'll tell you what we'll do to make the evening go off. You and I'll take turns, and see who'll tell the most out of Scott's novels;" for those were the days when the *Tales of My Landlord* and *Ivanhoe* had just appeared. And so they took them, novel by novel, reciting scenes and incidents, which kept the eyes of all the children wide open, and made the work go on without flagging.

Occasionally he would raise a point of theology on some incident narrated, and ask the opinion of one of his boys, and run a sort of tilt with him, taking up the wrong side of the question for the sake of seeing how the youngster could practice his logic. If the party on the other side did not make a fair hit at him, however, he would stop and explain to him what he ought to have said. "The argument lies so, my son; do that, and you'll trip me up." Much of his teaching to his children was in this informal way.

In regard to Scott's novels, it will be remembered that, at the time they came out, novel writing stood at so low an ebb that most serious-minded people regarded novel reading as an evil. Such a thing as a novel was not to be found in our house. And I well recollect the despairing and hungry glances with which I used to search through father's library, meeting only the same grim sentinels—Bell's *Sermons*, Bogue's *Essays*, Bonnet's *Inquiry*, Toplady on *Predestination*, Horsley's *Tracts*. There, to be sure, was Harmer on *Solomon's Song*, which I read, and nearly got by heart, because it told about the same sort of things I had once read of in the *Arabian Nights*. And there was *The State of the Clergy during the French Revolution*, which had horrible stories in it stranger than fiction. Then there was a side-closet full of documents, a weltering ocean of pamphlets, in which I dug and toiled for hours to be repaid by disinterring a delicious morsel of a *Don Quixote* that had once been a book, but was now lying in forty or fifty *dissecta membra*, amid *Calls, Appeals, Sermons, Essays, Reviews, Replies,* and *Rejoinders*. The turning up of such a fragment seemed like the rising of an enchanted island out of an ocean of mud.

Great was the light and joy, therefore, when father spoke *ex cathedra*, "George, you may read Scott's novels. I have always disapproved of novels as trash, but in these is real genius and real culture, and you may read them." And we did read them; for in one summer we went through *Ivanhoe* seven times, and were both of us able to recite many of its scenes, from beginning to end, verbatim.

One of father's favorite resorts was Aunt Esther's room, about half a minute's walk from our house. How well I remember that room! A low-studded parlor, looking out on one side into a front yard shaded with great elm-trees; on the other, down a green side-hill, under the branches of a thick apple-orchard. The floor was covered with a neat red and green carpet; the fireplace resplendent with the brightest of brass andirons; small hanging book-shelves over an old-fashioned mahogany bureau; a cushioned rocking-chair; a neat cherry tea-table; and an old-fashioned looking-glass, with a few chairs, completed the inventory. I must not forget to say that a bed was turned up against the wall, and concealed in the day time by a decorous fall of chintz drapery.

This room, always so quiet, so spotlessly neat, was a favorite retreat, not only of father, but of all us children, who were allowed, as a reward of good behavior, to go and pass an hour or two with Aunt Esther. She rented the apartment of a motherly old body, of a class whom every body in a Yankee village calls aunt. And Aunt Bull was a great favorite with all children, being always provided with a kind word and a piece of gingerbread for each and every one. Aunt Esther, too, had a deep, shady, mysterious closet in her room, most stimulating to our childish imaginations, from whence, when we went to take tea with her, came forth delicate India china, quaint old-fashioned glass, and various dainties, for the making of which she was celebrated, and some of which bear her name to this day in the family.

But Aunt Esther herself, with her sparkling hazel eyes, her keen, ready wit, and never-failing flow of anecdote and information, interested us even more than the best things she could produce from her closet. She had read on all subjects—chemistry, philosophy, physiology, but especially on natural history, where her anecdotes were inexhaustible. If any child was confined to the house by sickness, her recounting powers were a wonderful solace. I once heard a little patient say, "Only think! Aunt Esther has

[7]

told me *nineteen rat stories* all in a string." In fact, we thought there was no question we could ask her that she could not answer.

I remember once we said to her, "Aunt Esther, how came you to know so much about every sort of thing?" "Oh," said she, "you know the Bible says the works of the Lord are great, sought out of all them that have pleasure therein. Now I happened to have pleasure therein, and so I sought them out."

It was here that father came to read to her his sermons, or the articles that he was preparing for the *Christian Spectator*; for he was a man who could never be satisfied to keep any thing he wrote to himself. First he would read it to mother, and then he would say, "I think now I'll go over and read it to Esther."

It was in Aunt Esther's room that I first found a stray volume of Lord Byron's poetry, which she gave me one afternoon to appease my craving for something to read. It was the "Corsair." I shall never forget how it astonished and electrified me, and how I kept calling to Aunt Esther to hear the wonderful things that I found in it, and to ask what they could mean. "Aunt Esther, what does it mean—

'One I never loved enough to hate?'

"Oh, child, it's one of Byron's strong expressions."

I went home absorbed and wondering about Byron; and after that I listened to every thing that father and mother said at the table about him. I remember hearing father relate the account of his separation from his wife; and one day hearing him say, with a sorrowful countenance, as if announcing the death of some one very interesting to him, "My dear, Byron is dead—*gone*." After being a while silent, he said, "Oh, I'm sorry that Byron is dead. I did hope he would live to do something for Christ. What a harp he might have swept!" The whole impression made upon me by the conversation was solemn and painful.

I remember taking my basket for strawberries that afternoon, and going over to a strawberry field on Chestnut Hill. But I was too dispirited to do any thing; so I laid down among the daisies, and looked up into the blue sky, and thought of that great eternity into which Byron had entered, and wondered how it might be with his soul.

The next Sunday father preached a funeral sermon on this text: "The name of the just is as brightness, but the memory of the wicked shall rot." The main idea of the sermon was that goodness only is immortal, and that

[8]

no degree of brilliancy and genius can redeem vice from perishing. He spoke of the different English classics, and said that the impurities of Sterne and Swift had already virtually consigned them almost to oblivion. Then, after a brief sketch of Byron's career, and an estimate of his writings, he said that some things he had written would be as imperishable as brass; but that the impurities of other portions of his works, notwithstanding the beauty of the language, would in a few years sink them in oblivion. He closed with a most eloquent lamentation over the wasted life and misused powers of the great poet.

I was eleven years old at the time, and did not generally understand father's sermons, but this I understand perfectly, and it has made an impression on me that has never been effaced.

If it be recollected that the audience to whom he preached was largely composed of the students of the law school, sons of the first families from all parts of the Union, and graduates of the first colleges, and the pupils of the female school, also from the first families in all parts of the nation, and that the Byronic fever was then at its height among the young people, it will be seen how valuable may have been the moral discriminations and suggestions of such a sermon.

Father often said, in after years, that he wished he could have seen Byron, and presented to his mind his views of religious truth. He thought if Byron "could only have talked with Taylor and me, it might have got him out of his troubles;" for never did men have more utter and complete faith in the absolute verity and power of what they regarded as Gospel doctrine than my father and the ministers with whom he acted. And though he firmly believed in total depravity, yet practically he never seemed to realize that people were unbelievers for any other reason than for want of light, and that clear and able arguments would not at once put an end to skepticism.

With all that was truly great among men he felt a kindred sympathy. Genius and heroism would move him even to tears. I recollect hearing him read aloud Milton's account of Satan's marshaling his forces of fallen angels after his expulsion from heaven. The description of Satan's courage and fortitude was read with such evident sympathy as quite enlisted me in his favor, and in the passage,

> Millions of spirits, for his fault amerced
> Of heaven, and from eternal splendors flung

[9]

For his revolt, yet faithful how they stood,
Their glory wither'd; as when heaven's fire
Hath scathed the forest oaks, or mountain pines,
With singed top, their stately growth, though bare,
Stands on the blasted heath. He now prepared
To speak; whereat their doubled ranks they bend
From wing to wing, and half inclose him round
With all his peers: attention held them mute.
Thrice he essay'd, and thrice, in spite of scorn,
Tears, such as angels weep, burst forth.

On reaching this point father burst into tears himself, and the reading ended.

He had always, perhaps on the same principle, an intense admiration for Napoleon Bonaparte, which he never cared to disguise. He was wont to say that he was a glorious fellow, and ought to have succeeded. The criticisms on his moral character, ambition, unscrupulousness, etc., he used to meet by comparing him with the Bourbons whom he supplanted—"not a whit better morally, and *imbecile* to boot." Of the two, he thought it better that a wise and able bad man should reign than a stupid and weak bad man. He never altogether liked Dr. Channing's article on Napoleon. "Why rein his character up," he said, "by the strict rules of Christian perfection, when you never think of applying it to the character of any other ruler or general of the day?"

The fact is, that his sympathy with genius was so intense, especially executive genius, that it created what might almost be called a personal affection toward the great leader, and with it was blent somewhat of the anxiety of the pastor, the habitual bishop of souls, for a gifted but erratic nature. His mind was greatly exercised about the condition of the emperor's soul, and he read every memoir emanating from St. Helena with the earnest desire of shaping out of those last conversations some hope for his eternal future.

Father was very fond of music, and very susceptible to its influence; and one of the great eras of the family, in my childish recollection, is the triumphant bringing home from New Haven a fine-toned upright piano, which a fortunate accident had brought within the range of a poor country minister's means. The ark of the covenant was not brought into the tabernacle with more gladness than this magical instrument into our abode.

My older sisters had both learned to play and sing, and we had boarding in our family an accomplished performer, the charming and beautiful Louisa Wait, whose image floats through my recollection of these days like that of some marvelous little fairy, she was so small, so lovely, so lively, and sang so delightfully.

Father soon learned to accompany the piano with his violin in various psalm tunes and Scotch airs, and brothers Edward and William to perform their part on the flute. So we had often domestic concerts, which, if they did not attain to the height of artistic perfection, filled the house with gladness.

These recollections are among the most cheerful of my life. Our house rang with Scotch ballads, for which Louisa had a special taste, and the knowledge of which she introduced through all the circle of her pupils.

One of my most dedicated impressions of the family as it was in my childish days was of a great household inspired by a spirit of cheerfulness and hilarity, and of my father, though pressed and driven with business, always lending an attentive ear to any thing in the way of life and social fellowship. My oldest sister, whose whole life seemed a constant stream of mirthfulness, was his favorite and companion, and he was always more than indulgent toward her pranks and jokes. Scarcely any thing happened in the family without giving rise to some humorous bit of composition from her pen, either in prose or verse, which would be read at the table, and passed round among the social visiting circles which were frequent at our house. Among these I remember "The Complaint of the Dying Calf," which commemorated the disappearance of one of our domestic favorites, and which concluded thus:

> One short request I make to you,
> Fair ladies, ere I bid adieu:
> That for my sorrows you will feel
> When next you eat a leg of veal,
> And banish smiles, and cease to laugh,
> And think of me—a dying calf.

Another of these domestic lyrics was written to cover the retreat of a terrified domestic, who was overwhelmed by the misfortune of having broken the best dish in the minister's new service of crockery:

> Come all, and list a dismal tale!
> Ye kitchen muses, do not fail,

But join our sad loss to bewail.
High mounted on the dresser's side,
Our brown-edged platter stood with pride;
A neighboring door flew open wide,
Knock'd out its brains, and straight it died.

  Come, kindred platters, with me mourn;
  Hither, ye plates and dishes, turn;
  Knives, forks, and carvers all give ear,
  And each drop of dish-water tear.

No more with smoking roast-beef crown'd
Shall guests this noble dish surround;
No more the buttered cutlet here,
Nor tender chicken shall appear;
Roast pig no more here show his visard,
Nor goose, nor even goose's gizzard;
But broken-hearted it must go
Down to the dismal shades below;
While kitchen muses, platters, plates,
Knives, forks, and spoons upbraid the Fates;
With streaming tears cry out, "I never!
Our brown-edged platter's gone forever!"

Another ballad, at somewhat greater length, was a vast favorite among us children. It was written to celebrate the wedding of a cousin married from our house, and was so contrived as to introduce all the intimates of our circle.

Compositions of a graver cast, romantic or poetic, were also much in vogue in the literary coteries of Litchfield. The history and antiquities of the Bantam Indians formed the theme of several ballads and poetical effusions, and one of which, by sister Catharine, and two by the head teacher of the Female Academy, Mr. John P. Brace, were in the mouths and memories of us all.

The poetic compositions of this gentleman were constantly circulating among the young ladies of his school and the literati of the place, and there was a peculiar freshness of enjoyment and excitement to us in this species of native unpublished literature.

Mr. Brace was one of the most stimulating and inspiring instructors I ever knew. He was himself widely informed, an enthusiast in botany, mineralogy, and the natural sciences generally, besides being well read in English classical literature. The constant conversation which he kept up on these subjects tended more to develop the mind and inspire a love of literature than any mere routine studies. The boys were incited by his example to set up mineralogical cabinets, and my brother George tramped over the hills in the train of his teacher, with his stone-hammer on his shoulder, for many delightful hours. Many more were spent in recounting to me the stores of wisdom derived from Mr. Brace, who, he told me with pride, corresponded with geologists and botanists in Europe, exchanging specimens with them.

This school was the only one I ever knew which really carried out a thorough course of ancient and modern history. Miss Pierce herself, with great cleverness, had compiled an abridgment of ancient history, from the best sources, in four volumes, for the use of her pupils; after which, Russell's *Modern Europe*, with Coots's *Continuation*, and Ramsay's *American Revolution*, brought us down nearly to our own times.

The interest of those historical recitations with a preceptor so widely informed, and so fascinating in conversation as Mr. Brace, extended farther than the class. Much of the training and inspiration of my early days consisted, not in the things which I was supposed to be studying, but in hearing, while seated unnoticed at my desk, the conversation of Mr. Brace with the older classes. There from hour to hour I listened with eager ears to historical criticisms and discussions, or to recitations in such works as Paley's *Moral Philosophy*, Blair's *Rhetoric*, Alison's *On Taste*, all full of most awakening suggestions to my thoughts.

Mr. Brace exceeded all teachers I ever knew in the faculty of teaching composition. The constant excitement in which he kept the minds of his pupils—the wide and varied regions of thought into which he led them—formed a preparation for teaching composition, the main requisite for which, whatever people may think, is to have something which one feels interested to say.

His manner was to divide his school of about a hundred into divisions of three or four, one of which was to write every week. At the same time, he inspired an ambition by calling every week for volunteers, and there were some who volunteered to write every week.

I remember I could have been but nine years old, and my handwriting hardly formed, when the enthusiasm he inspired led me, greatly to his amusement, I believe, to volunteer to write every week.

The first week the subject of composition chosen by the class was "The Difference between the Natural and the Moral Sublime." One may smile at this for a child nine years of age; but it is the best account I can give of his manner of teaching to say that the discussion which he held in the class not only made me understand the subject as thoroughly as I do now, but so excited me that I felt sure I had something to say upon it; and that first composition, though I believe half the words were misspelled, amused him greatly.

It was not many weeks I had persevered in this way before I received a word of public commendation; for it was his custom to read all the compositions aloud before the school, and if there was a good point, it was sure to be noticed.

As you may see, our subjects were not trashy or sentimental, such as are often supposed to be the style for female schools. An incident, in my twelfth year, will show this clearly. By two years of constant practice under his training and suggestion, I had gained so far as to be appointed one of the writers for the annual exhibition—a proud distinction, as I then viewed it.

The subject assigned me was one that had been very full discussed in the school in a manner to show to the utmost Mr. Brace's peculiar power of awakening the minds of his pupils to the higher regions of thought. The question was, "Can the immortality of the soul be proved by the light of nature?"

Several of the young ladies had written strongly in the affirmative. Mr. Brace himself had written in the negative. To all these compositions and the consequent discussions I had listened, and, in view of them, chose to adopt the negative.

I remember the scene at that exhibition, to me so eventful. The hall was crowded with all the literati of Litchfield. Before them all our compositions were read aloud. When mine was read, I noticed that father, who was sitting on high by Mr. Brace, brightened and looked interested, and at the close I heard him say, "Who wrote that composition?" "*Your daughter, sir!*" was the answer. It was the proudest moment of my life. There was no mistaking father's face when he was pleased, and to have interested *him* was past all juvenile triumphs.

## Note

1.  Barbara M. Cross, ed. "Introduction," *The Autobiography of Lyman Beecher*, 2 vols. (Cambridge: Harvard University Press, 1961), 1: xi.

From *Autobiography, Correspondence, Etc., of Lyman Beecher*, ed. Charles Beecher, 2 vols. (New York: Harper and Brothers, 1864), 1: 520–537.

# From "The Girlhood of
Harriet Beecher Stowe" (1811–1832)

CHARLES EDWARD STOWE AND LYMAN BEECHER STOWE

In May 1911, Charles Edward Stowe (1850–1934) and Lyman Beecher Stowe (1880–1963), Stowe's son and grandson, published a jointly written biography, *Harriet Beecher Stowe: The Story of Her Life*. In their preface, they explained that they wished to tell "not so much what she did as what she was, and how she became what she was" (p. v). For their sources, the Stowes drew on letters, family papers, and earlier published works, such as Annie Fields's *Life and Letters of Harriet Beecher Stowe* (1897) and *Autobiography, Correspondence, Etc., of Lyman Beecher* (1864), edited by Charles Beecher. The publication of *Harriet Beecher Stowe*, designed to coincide with the centennial of Stowe's birth in 1811, was announced in a lengthy article in the Sunday *New York Times*, which included illustrations of Stowe, of her home in Brunswick, Maine, and of a memorial to Stowe and her brother Henry Ward Beecher.[1] Portions of the first two chapters of the biography were published as "The Girlhood of Harriet Beecher Stowe" in *McClure's Magazine* in May to promote the book and celebrate the centennial, as numerous other magazines and newspapers did in 1911. The article, which includes excerpts from Stowe's letters and other writings, is shaped by two close family members who provide their perspectives on the familial and cultural influences on Stowe's life. The following excerpt from the second half of the article emphasizes Stowe's religious development.

### Wonders of the "Meeting-house"

"Never shall I forget the dignity and sense of importance which swelled my mind when I was first pronounced old enough to go to meeting," writes Mrs. Stowe, in another account of those early Litchfield days. "To my childish eyes our old meeting-house was an awe-inspiring place. To me it seemed fashioned very nearly on the model of Noah's Ark and Solomon's Temple, as set forth in the pictures of my Scripture catechism, pictures which I did not doubt were authentic copies."

Harriet Beecher Stowe's birthplace, Litchfield, Connecticut. Harriet Beecher Stowe Center, Hartford, Connecticut.

### Rigors of the Sabbath

Harriet had hallowed associations connected with the thought of the old church. Early one summer morning she had been reminded that it was Sunday, the Holy Sabbath day, by the following incident. Her two younger brothers, Henry and Charles, slept together in a little trundle-bed in a corner of the nursery where she also slept. She was waked by the two little fellows chattering to each other as they lay in their bed making little sheep out of cotton pulled from the holes in the old quilt that covered them, and pasturing them on the undulating hillsides and meadows which their imagination conjured up amid the bedclothes. Suddenly Charles' eyes grew wide with fright, and he cried out, "Henry, this is wicked! It's Sunday!" There was a moment of consternation, followed by silence, as both little curly heads disappeared under the old coverlet.

[17]

## Harriet's Conversion

Yes, it was Sunday, and Harriet was trying her best to feel herself a dreadful sinner, but with very poor success. She was so healthy, and the blood raced and tingled so in her young veins. She tried to feel her sins and count them up; but the birds and the daisies and the buttercups were a constant interruption, and she went into the old meeting-house quite dissatisfied with herself. When she saw the white cloth, the shining cups, and the snowy bread of the communion-table, she hopelessly felt that the service could have nothing for a little girl—it would all be for the grown-up people, the initiated Christians. Nevertheless, when her father began to speak, she was drawn to listen by a sort of pathetic earnestness in his voice.

The Doctor was feeling very deeply, and he had chosen for his text the declaration of Jesus: "I call you not servants; but friends." His subject was Jesus as the soul-friend offered to every human being. Forgetting his doctrinal subtleties, he spoke with the simplicity and tenderness of a rich nature concerning the faithful, generous love of Christ. Deep feeling inclines to simplicity of language, and Dr. Beecher spoke in words that even a child could understand. Harriet sat absorbed; her large blue eyes gathered tears as she listened, and when the Doctor said, "Come, then, and trust your soul to this faithful friend," her little heart throbbed, "I will!" She sat through the sacramental service that followed with swelling heart and tearful eyes, and walked home filled with a new joy. She went up into her father's study, and threw herself into his arms, saying, "Father, I have given myself to Jesus, and he has taken me." He held her silently to his heart for a moment, and she felt his tears dropping on her head. "Is it so?" he said. "Then has a new flower blossomed in the kingdom this day."

## "Spiritual Experience" and the Old New England Divines

Shortly after going to Hartford to attend school, Harriet made a call upon the Rev. Dr. Hawes, her father's friend, and her spiritual adviser, which left an enduring impression upon her mind. It was her father's advice that she join the church at Hartford, as he had received a call to Boston, and the breaking up of the Litchfield home was imminent. Accordingly, accompanied by two school friends, she went, one day, to the pastor's study to consult him concerning the contemplated step. In those days much stress was placed on religious experience, and more especially on what was termed

a conviction of sin; and self-examination was carried to an extreme calcu-
lated to drive to desperation a sensitive, high-strung nature.

The good man listened to the child's simple and modest statement of her
Christian experience, and then, with an awful, though kindly, solemnity of
speech and manner, said:

"Harriet! do you feel that if the universe should be destroyed"—alarming
pause—"you could be happy with God alone?'"

After struggling in vain to fix in her mind the meaning of the sounds that
fell on her ears like the measured tolling of a funeral bell, the child of fourteen stammered out, "Yes, sir!"

"You realize, I trust, in some measure at least, the deceitfulness of your
own heart, and that, in punishment for your sins, God might justly leave
you to make yourself as miserable as you have made yourself sinful."

Having thus effectually, and to his own satisfaction, fixed the child's attention on the morbid and oversensitive workings of her own heart, the good
and truly kind-hearted man dismissed her with a fatherly benediction. He
had been alarmed at her simple and natural way of entering the kingdom.
It was not theologically sound to make short cuts to salvation. The child
went in to the conference full of peace and joy, and came out full of distress and misgivings; but the good Doctor had done his duty, as he saw it.

### Theological Struggles in the Beecher Family

It was a theological age, and in the Beecher family theology was the supreme interest. It fills their letters, as it filled their lives. Not only was the
age theological, but it was transitional, and characterized by intense intellectual activity, accompanied by emotional excitement. The winds of
doctrine were let loose, blowing first from this quarter and then from that.
Dr. Beecher spent his days in weathering theological cyclones; but the
worst of all arose in his own family, among his own children. Great as were
his intellectual powers, he was no match for his daughter Catharine and
his son Edward—the metaphysical Titans who sprang from his own loins.
It was almost in a tone of despair that this theological Samuel, who had
hewn so many heretical Agags in pieces before the lord, wrote concerning
his own daughter:

Catharine's letter will disclose the awfully interesting state of her mind. . . .
You perceive she is now handling edged tools with powerful grasp. . . . I have

at times been at my wits' ends to know what to do. . . . I conclude that nothing safe can be done, but to assert ability, and obligation, and guilt upon divine authority, throwing in at the same time as much collateral light from reason as the case admits of.

Catharine was at this time breaking out of the prison-house of the traditional orthodoxy, and her brother Edward was in many ways in sympathy with her, though not so radical as she. Dr. Beecher was contending with might and main for the traditional Calvinism; and yet, in his zeal for its defense, he often took positions that surprised and alarmed his brother ministers, seriously disturbed their dogmatic slumbers, and caused them grave doubts as to his orthodoxy.

### Tragic Death of Catharine's Betrothed

When Harriet was in her eleventh year her sister Catharine had become engaged to Professor Alexander Fisher, of Yale College. He was a young man of brilliant talents, and specially noted for his mathematical genius. As an undergraduate at Yale he distinguished himself by original and valuable contributions to mathematical astronomy. Immediately on graduation he was appointed a professor of mathematics, and was sent abroad by his alma mater to devote some time to study and the purchase of books and mathematical instruments. The ship *Albion*, on which he sailed, was wrecked on a reef off the coast of Ireland. Of the twenty-three cabin passengers, only one reached the shore. This was a man of great physical strength, and all night long he clung to the jagged rocks at the foot of the cliff, against which the sea broke, till ropes were lowered from above, and he was drawn up, limp and exhausted. He often told of the calm bravery with which Professor Fisher met his end.

Up to this time in her life, Catharine had been noted for the gaiety of her spirits and the brilliancy of her mind. An imitable story-teller and a great mimic, it seemed to be her aim to keep every one laughing. Her versatile mind and ready wit enabled her to pass brilliantly through her school days with comparatively little mental exertion, and before she was twenty-one she had become a teacher in a school for girls in New London, Connecticut. It was about this time that she met Professor Fisher, and they soon became engaged.

## *Catharine's Religion Taught That His Soul Was Lost with His Body*

When the news of his death reached her, to the crushing of earthly hopes and plans was added an agony of apprehension for his soul. He had never been formally converted; and hence, by the teachings of the times, his soul as well as his body was lost.

She wrote to her brother Edward: "It is not so much ruined hopes of this life—it is dismay and apprehension for his immortal spirit. Oh, Edward, where is he now? Are the noble faculties of such a mind doomed to everlasting woe?" Anxiously, but in vain, she searched his letters and journals for something on which she might build a hope of his eternal welfare.

Mournful contemplations awakened when I learned more of the mental exercises of him I mourned, whose destiny was forever fixed, alas, I know not where! I learned from his letters, and in other ways, as much as I could have learned from his diary. I found that, even from early childhood, he had ever been uncommonly correct and conscientious, so that his parents and family could scarcely remember of his doing anything wrong, so far as relates to outward conduct; and year after year, with persevering and unexampled effort, he sought to yield that homage of the heart to his Maker which was required, but he could not; like the friend who followed his steps, he had no strength. . . . It seemed to me that my lost friend had done all that unassisted human strength could do; and often the dreadful thought came to me that all was in vain, and that he was wailing that he ever had been born, in that dark world where hope never comes, and that I was following his steps to that dreadful scene.

### *Bereaved Girl's Struggle with Pitiless Calvinism*

Miss Beecher passed the two years following the death of Professor Fisher at Franklin, Massachusetts, at the home of his parents, where she listened to the fearless and pitiless Calvinism of Dr. Nathaniel Emmons. Her mind was too strong and buoyant to be overwhelmed and crushed by an experience that would have driven a weaker and less resolute nature to insanity.

The conventional New England Calvinism gave her no satisfactory solution of her difficulties. She was tormented with doubts. "What has the Son of God done which the meanest and most selfish creature upon earth would not have done?" she asked herself. "After making such a wretched race and placing them in such disastrous circumstances, somehow, without any sorrow or trouble, Jesus Christ had a human nature that suffered and died. If something else besides ourselves will do all the suffering, who would not save millions of wretched beings, and receive all the honor and gratitude without any of the trouble?" Yet, when such thoughts passed through her mind, she felt that it was "all pride, rebellion, and sin." So she struggled on, sometimes floundering deep in the mire of doubt, and then lifted out of it by her constitutionally buoyant spirits.

It was in this condition of mind that Catharine Beecher came to Hartford, in the winter of 1824, and opened her school. In the practical experience of teaching she found, at last, the solution of her troubles. Turning aside from doctrinal difficulties and theological quagmires, she determined "to find happiness in living to do good." She says: "It was right to pray and read the Bible, and so I prayed and read the Bible. It was right to try to save others, and so I tried to save them. In all these years I never had any fear of punishment or hope of reward."

Without ever having heard of pragmatism, she became a kind of pragmatist. She continues: "After two or three years I commenced giving instruction in mental philosophy, and at the same time began a regular course of lectures and instructions from the Bible, and was much occupied with plans for governing my school and in devising means to lead my pupils to become obedient, amiable, and pious." These "means" resulted in a code of principles for the government of her school which were nothing more nor less than systematically formulated common sense, with plenty of the "milk of human kindness" thrown in. These principles she carefully compared with the government of God, and came to the conclusion that He, in His infinitely mighty and complex task of governing the universe, was applying the same fundamental principles as she in the relatively infinitesimal and simple task of governing her school. This was her solution, and this the view of the divine nature that was for so many years preached by her brother, Henry Ward, and set forth in the writings of her sister Harriet.

### Harriet's Desire for Love

In the winter of 1829 Harriet was in Hartford again, this time assisting her sister Catharine in the school. She was now eighteen, but still morbidly introspective, sensitive, and overwrought. She apparently lived largely in her emotions. In closing one of her letters, she said: "This desire to be loved forms, I fear, the great motive for all my actions." Again, she writes to her brother Edward:

> I have been carefully reading the Book of Job, and I do not find in it the views of God you have presented to me. God seems to have stripped a dependent creature of all that renders life desirable, and then to have answered his complaints from the whirlwind; and, instead of showing mercy and pity, to have overwhelmed him by a display of his justice. From the view of God that I received from you, I should have expected that a being that sympathizes with his guilty, afflicted creatures would not have spoken thus. Yet, after all, I do believe that God is such a being as you represent him to be, and in the New Testament I find in the character of Jesus Christ a revelation of God as merciful and compassionate, in fact, just such a God as I need!

This was the vision of God that came to her at the time of her conversion. It was the confusing and perturbing influence of her father's Calvinistic theology that had dimmed that gracious vision. Out of the prison-house of Giant Despair she had been delivered by the teachings of her sister Catharine and her brother Edward.

### Religious Doubts and Fears

But, again, in the same letter we have a passage that shows that her feet are still enmeshed in the net of Calvinistic theology. She writes:

> My mind is often perplexed, and such thoughts arise in it that I cannot pray, and I become bewildered. The wonder to me is, how all ministers and all Christians can feel themselves so inexcusably sinful, when it seems to me that we all come into the world in such a way that it would be miraculous if we did not sin! Mr. Hawes always says in his prayers, 'We have nothing to offer in extenuation of any of our sins'; and I always think, when he says it, that we have every thing to offer in extenuation.
>
> The case seems to me exactly as if I had been brought into the world with such a thirst for ardent spirits that there was just a possibility but no hope that I should resist, and then my eternal happiness made to depend on my being temperate. Sometimes, when I try to confess my sins, I feel that I am more to be pitied than blamed, for I have never known the time when I have not had a temptation within me so strong that it was certain that I should not overcome it. This thought shocks me, but it comes with such force, and so appealingly, to all my consciousness, that it stifles all sense of sin.

It was such reflections and arguments as these that had aroused Dr. Beecher to despair over his daughter Catharine's spiritual condition. The fact was, he belonged to one age and his children to another. Yet the brave old man lived to sympathize with them.

### Harriet Breaks with Calvinism

Harriet at last learned to give up her introspection and morbid sensitiveness, and to live more healthily and humanly. At the age of twenty-one she was able to write thus to her friend, Georgiana May:

> The amount of the matter has been, as this inner world of mine has become worn out and untenable, I have at last concluded to come out of it and live in the eternal one, and, as F. S. once advised me, give up the pernicious habit of meditation to the first Methodist minister who would take it, and try to mix in society somewhat as other persons would.
>
> '*Horas non numero non nisi serenas*.'[2] Uncle Sam, who sits by me, has just been reading the above motto, the inscription on a sun-dial in Venice. It strikes me as having a distant relationship to what I was going to say. I have come to a firm resolution to count no hours but unclouded ones, and let all others slip out of my memory and reckoning as quickly as possible.

In this new life she was able to write to her brother Edward:

> I have never been so happy as this summer. I began it in more suffering than I ever before have felt; but there is One whom I daily thank for all that suffering, since I hope that it has brought me at last to rest entirely in Him.

So she learned to suffer and to love. To suffer and to love, and at last to rest. After five years of struggling, she returned to where she started when converted as a child of thirteen. Love became her gospel, the alpha and omega of her existence—love for her God, for her friends, and, finally, for humanity. The three words "God is love" summed up her theology.

### Notes

1. "Centenary of Birth of the Author of 'Uncle Tom's Cabin,'" *New York Times*, 16 April 1900, p. SM14.
2. I count only the hours that are serene (Latin).

From Charles Edward Stowe and Lyman Beecher Stowe, "The Girlhood of Harriet Beecher Stowe," *McClure's Magazine* 37 (1911): 28–40.

# [Stowe in Cincinnati, 1832–1836]

CHARLES EDWARD STOWE

In 1832, Lyman Beecher accepted a position as the president of Lane Theological Seminary and moved his family from Hartford, Connecticut, to Cincinnati, Ohio, a booming river town of nearly 47,000 people. Stowe, who had been a student and then a teacher at her sister Catharine Beecher's Hartford Female Seminary, went with the family, as did her sister. Catharine Beecher established the Western Female Institute, where Stowe served as a teacher and her assistant. For the next eighteen years, Cincinnati was Stowe's home. There, she began writing, and she published a textbook, *Primary Geography for Children, on an Improved Plan with Eleven Maps and Numerous Engravings* (1833). Stowe joined the Semi-Colon Club, an informal group of young people who met to read and discuss their writing, and she won a prize for her first published story, "A New England Sketch," later retitled "Uncle Lot." She met Calvin Stowe, a professor at Lane, and, after the death of his first wife, the two were married in 1836. During the Cincinnati years, Stowe gave birth to six of her seven children and continued to write when she could, publishing short articles and stories in *Godey's Lady's Book* and the *New-York Evangelist*. Her first book, *The Mayflower*, a collection of stories and sketches, was published in 1843. Living just across the Ohio River from Kentucky, a slave state, and the South, Stowe and her family became increasingly involved in the antislavery movement. The following account of Stowe's early years in Cincinnati is a chapter of *Life of Harriet Beecher Stowe* (1889) written by her son Charles Edward Stowe. Stowe helped him prepare the biography by giving him her journals and asking friends and family members to send him her letters. This chapter narrates Stowe's life as she adjusted to a new home, formed her early impressions of slavery, and began her first efforts at writing.

## Cincinnati, 1832–1836.

In 1832, after having been settled for six years over the Hanover Street Church in Boston, Dr. Beecher received and finally accepted a most urgent call to become President of Lane Theological Seminary in Cincinnati. This institution had been chartered in 1829, and in 1831 funds to the amount of

Lyman Beecher house, Walnut Hills, Cincinnati, Ohio. Harriet Beecher Stowe Center, Hartford, Connecticut.

nearly $70,000 had been promised to it provided that Dr. Beecher accepted the presidency. It was hard for this New England family to sever the ties of a lifetime and enter on so long a journey to the far distant West of those days; but being fully persuaded that their duty lay in this direction, they undertook to perform it cheerfully and willingly. With Dr. Beecher and his wife were to go Miss Catharine Beecher, who had conceived the scheme of founding in Cincinnati, then considered the capital of the West, a female college, and Harriet, who was to act as her principal assistant. In the party were also George, who was to enter Lane as a student, Isabella, James, the youngest son, and Miss Esther Beecher, the "Aunt Esther" of the children.

Before making his final decision, Dr. Beecher, accompanied by his daughter Catharine, visited Cincinnati to take a general survey of their proposed battlefield, and their impressions of the city are given in the following letter written by the latter to Harriet in Boston:—

Here we are at last at our journey's end, alive and well. We are staying with Uncle Samuel (Foote), whose establishment I will try and sketch for you. It is on a height in the upper part of the city, and commands a fine view of the whole of the lower town. The city does not impress me as being so very new. It is true everything looks neat and clean, but it is compact, and many of the houses are of brick and very handsomely built. The streets run at right angles to each other, and are wide and well paved. We reached here in three days from Wheeling, and soon felt ourselves at home. The next day father and I, with three gentlemen, walked out to Walnut Hills. The country around the city consists of a constant succession and variety of hills of all shapes and sizes, forming an extensive amphitheatre. The site of the seminary is very beautiful and picturesque, though I was disappointed to find that both river and city are hidden by intervening hills. I never saw a place so capable of being rendered a paradise by the improvements of taste as the environs of this city. Walnut Hills are so elevated and cool that people have to leave there to be sick, it is said. The seminary is located on a farm of one hundred and twenty-five acres of fine land, with groves of superb trees around it, about two miles from the city. We have finally decided on the spot where our house shall stand in case we decide to come, and you cannot (where running water or the seashore is wanting) find another more delightful spot for a residence. It is on an eminence, with a grove running up from the back to the very doors, another grove across the street in front, and fine openings through which distant hills and the richest landscapes appear.

I have become somewhat acquainted with those ladies we shall have the most to do with, and find them intelligent, New England sort of folks. Indeed, this is a New England city in all its habits, and its inhabitants are more than half from New England. The Second Church, which is the best in the city, will give father a unanimous call to be their minister, with the understanding that he will give them what time he can spare from the seminary.

I know of no place in the world where there is so fair a prospect of finding everything that makes social and domestic life pleasant. Uncle John and Uncle Samuel are just the intelligent, sociable, free, and hospitable sort of folk that everybody likes and everybody feels at home with.

The folks are very anxious to have a school on our plan set on foot here. We can have fine rooms in the city college building, which is now unoccupied, and everybody is ready to lend a helping hand. As to father, I never saw such a field of usefulness and influence as is offered to him here.

This, then, was the field of labor in which the next eighteen years of the life of Mrs. Stowe were to be passed. At this time her sister Mary was married and living in Hartford, her brothers Henry Ward and Charles were in college, while William and Edward, already licensed to preach, were preparing to follow their father to the West.

Mr. Beecher's preliminary journey to Cincinnati was undertaken in the early spring of 1832, but he was not ready to remove his family until October of that year. An interesting account of this westward journey is given by Mrs. Stowe in a letter sent back to Hartford from Cincinnati, as follows:—

Well, my dear, the great sheet is out and the letter is begun. All our family are here (in New York), and in good health.

Father is to perform to-night in the Chatham Theatre! "positively for the *last* time this season!" I don't know, I'm sure, as we shall ever get to Pittsburgh. Father is staying here begging money for the Biblical Literature professorship; the incumbent is to be C. Stowe. Last night we had a call from Arthur Tappan and Mr. Eastman. Father begged $2,000 yesterday, and now the good people are praying him to abide certain days, as he succeeds so well. They are talking of sending us off and keeping him here. I really dare not go and see Aunt Esther and mother now; they were in the depths of tribulation before at staying so long, and now,

"In the lowest depths, *another* deep!"

Father is in high spirits. He is all in his own element,—dipping into books; consulting authorities for his oration; going round here, there, everywhere; begging, borrowing, and spoiling the Egyptians; delighted with past success and confident for the future.

Wednesday. Still in New York. I believe it would kill me dead to live long in the way I have been doing since I have been here. It is a sort of agreeable delirium. There's only one thing about it, it is too *scattering*. I begin to be athirst for the waters of quietness.

Writing from Philadelphia, she adds:—

Well, we did get away from New York at last, but it was through much tribulation. The truckman carried all the family baggage to the wrong wharf, and, after waiting and waiting on board the boat, we were obliged to start without it, George remaining to look it up. Arrived here late Saturday evening,—dull, drizzling weather; poor Aunt Esther in dismay,—not a clean cap to put on,— mother in like state; all of us destitute. We went, half to Dr. Skinner's and half to Mrs. Elmes's: mother, Aunt Esther, father, and James to the former; Kate, Bella, and myself to Mr. Elmes's. They are rich, hospitable folks, and act the part of Gaius in apostolic times. . . . Our trunks came this morning. Father stood and saw them all brought into Dr. Skinner's entry, and then he swung his hat and gave a "hurrah," as any man would whose wife had not had a clean cap or ruffle for a week. Father does not succeed very well in opening purses here. Mr. Eastman says, however, that this is not of much consequence. I saw to-day a notice in the *Philadelphian* about father, setting forth how "this distinguished brother, with his large family, having torn themselves from the endearing scenes of their home," etc., etc., "were going, like Jacob," etc.,—a very scriptural and appropriate flourish. It is too much after the manner of men, or, as Paul says, speaking "as a fool." A number of the pious people of this city are coming here this evening to hold a prayer-meeting with reference to the journey and its object. For *this* I thank them.

From Downington she writes:—

Here we all are,—Noah and his wife and his sons and his daughters, with the cattle and creeping things, all dropped down in the front parlor of this tavern, about thirty miles from Philadelphia. If to-day is a fair specimen of our journey, it will be a very pleasant, obliging driver, good roads, good spirits, good dinner, fine scenery, and now and then some "psalms and hymns and spiritual songs;" for with George on board you may be sure of music of some kind. Moreover, George has provided himself with a quantity of tracts, and he and the children have kept up a regular discharge at all the wayfaring people we encountered. I tell him he is *peppering* the land with moral influence.

We are all well; all in good spirits. Just let me give you a peep into our traveling household. Behold us, then, in the front parlor of this country inn, all as much at home as if we were in Boston. Father is sitting opposite to me at this table, reading; Kate is writing a billet-doux to Mary on a sheet like this; Thomas is opposite, writing in a little journal that he keeps; Sister Bell, too, has her little record; George is waiting for a seat that he may produce his paper and write. As for me, among the multitude of my present friends, my heart still makes occasional visits to absent ones,—visits full of pleasure, and full of cause of gratitude to Him who gives us friends. I have thought of you often to-day, my G. We stopped this noon at a substantial Pennsylvania tavern, and among the flowers in the garden was a late monthly honeysuckle like the one at North Guilford. I made a spring for it, but George secured the finest bunch, which he wore in his buttonhole the rest of the noon.

This afternoon, as we were traveling, we struck up and sang "Jubilee." It put me in mind of the time when we used to ride along the rough North Guilford roads and make the air vocal as we went along. Pleasant times those. Those were blue skies, and that was a beautiful lake and noble pine-trees and rocks they were that hung over it. But those we shall look upon "na mair."

Well, my dear, there is a land where we shall not *love* and *leave*. Those skies shall never cease to shine, the waters of life we shall *never* be called upon to leave. We have here no continuing city, but we seek one to come. In such thoughts as these I desire ever to rest, and with such words as these let us "comfort one another and edify one another."

Harrisburg, Sunday evening. Mother, Aunt Esther, George, and the little folks have just gathered into Kate's room, and we have just been singing. Father has gone to preach for Mr. De Witt. To-morrow we expect to travel sixty-two miles, and in two more days shall reach Wheeling; there we shall take the steamboat to Cincinnati.

On the same journey George Beecher writes:—

We had poor horses in crossing the mountains. Our average rate for the last four days to Wheeling was forty-four miles. The journey, which takes the mail-stage forty-eight hours, took us eight days. At Wheeling we deliberated long whether to go on board a boat for Cincinnati, but the prevalence of the cholera there at last decided us to remain. While at Wheeling father preached eleven times,—nearly every evening,—and gave them the Taylorite heresy on sin and decrees to the highest notch; and what amused me most was to hear him establish it from the Confession of Faith. It went high and dry, however, above all objections, and they were delighted with it, even the old school men, since it had not been christened "heresy" in their hearing. After remaining in Wheeling eight days, we chartered a stage for Cincinnati, and started next morning.

At Granville, Ohio, we were invited to stop and attend a protracted meeting. Being in no great hurry to enter Cincinnati till the cholera had left, we consented. We spent the remainder of the week there, and I preached five times and father four. The interest was increasingly deep and solemn each day, and when we left there were forty-five cases of conversion in the town, besides those from the surrounding towns. The people were astonished at the doctrine; said they never saw the truth so plain in their lives.

Although the new-comers were cordially welcomed in Cincinnati, and everything possible was done for their comfort and to make them feel at home, they felt themselves to be strangers in a strange land. Their homesickness and yearnings for New England are set forth by the following extracts from Mrs. Stowe's answer to the first letter they received from Hartford after leaving there:—

My dear Sister (Mary),—The Hartford letter from all and sundry has just arrived, and after cutting all manner of capers expressive of thankfulness, I have skipped three stairs at a time up to the study to begin an answer. My notions of answering letters are according to the literal sense of the word; not waiting six months and then scrawling a lazy reply, but sitting down the moment you have read a letter, and telling, as Dr. Woods says, "How the subject strikes you." I wish I could be clear that the path of duty lay in talking to you this afternoon, but as I find a loud call to consider the heels of George's stockings, I must only write a word or two, and then resume my darning-needle. You don't know how anxiously we all have watched for some intelligence from Hartford. Not a day has passed when I have not been the efficient agent in getting somebody to the post-office, and every day my heart has sunk at the sound of "no letters." I felt a tremor quite sufficient for a lover when I saw your handwriting once more, so you see that in your old age you can excite quite as much emotion as did the admirable Miss Byron in her adoring Sir Charles. I hope the consideration and digestion of this fact will have its due weight in encouraging you to proceed.

The fact of our having received said letter is as yet a state secret, not to be made known till all our family circle "in full assembly meet" at the tea-table. Then what an illumination! "How we shall be edified and fructified," as that old Methodist said. It seems too bad to keep it from mother and Aunt Esther a whole afternoon, but then I have the comfort of thinking that we are consulting for their greatest happiness "on the whole," which is metaphysical benevolence.

So kind Mrs. Parsons stopped in the very midst of her pumpkin pies to think of us? Seems to me I can see her bright, cheerful face now! And then those well known handwritings! We *do* love our Hartford friends dearly; there can be, I think, no controverting that fact. Kate says that the word *love* is used in *six senses*, and I am sure in some one of them they will all come in. Well, good-by for the present.

Evening. Having finished the last hole on George's black vest, I stick in my needle and sit down to be sociable. You don't know how coming away from New England has sentimentalized us all! Never was there such an abundance of meditation on our native land, on the joys of friendship, the pains of separation. Catharine had an alarming paroxysm in Philadelphia which expended itself in "The Emigrant's Farewell." After this was sent off she felt considerably relieved. My symptoms have been of a less acute kind, but, I fear, more enduring. There! the tea-bell rings. Too bad! I was just going to say something bright. Now to take your letter and run! How they will stare when I produce it!

After tea. Well, we have had a fine time. When supper was about half over, Catharine began:

We have a dessert that we have been saving all the afternoon, and then I held up my letter. "See here, this is from Hartford!" I wish you could have seen Aunt Esther's eyes brighten, and mother's pale face all in a smile, and father, as I unfolded the letter and began. Mrs. Parsons's notice of her Thanksgiving predicament caused just a laugh, and then one or two sighs (I told you we were growing sentimental!). We did talk some of keeping it (Thanksgiving), but perhaps we should all have felt something of the text, "How shall we sing the Lord's song in a strange land?" Your praises of Aunt Esther I read twice in an audible voice, as the children made some noise the first time. I think I detected a visible blush, though she found at that time a great deal to do in spreading bread and butter for James, and shuffling his plate; and, indeed, it was rather a vehement attack on her humility, since it gave her at least "angelic perfection," if not "Adamic" (to use Methodist technics). Jamie began his Sunday-school career yesterday. The superintendent asked him how old he was. "I'm four years old now, and when *it snows very hard* I shall be five," he answered. I have just been trying to make him interpret his meaning; but he says, "Oh, I said so because I could not think of anything else to say." By the by, Mary, speaking of the temptations of cities, I have much solicitude on Jamie's account lest he should form improper intimacies, for yesterday or day before we saw him parading by the house with his arm over the neck of a great hog, apparently on the most amicable terms possible; and the other day he actually got upon the back of one, and rode some distance. So much for allowing these animals to promenade the streets, a particular in which Mrs. Cincinnati has imitated the domestic arrangements of some of her elder sisters, and a very disgusting one it is.

Our family physician is one Dr. Drake, a man of a good deal of science, theory, and reputed skill, but a sort of general mark for the opposition of all the medical cloth of the city. He is a tall, rectangular, perpendicular sort of a body, as stiff as a poker, and enunciates his prescriptions very much as though he were delivering a discourse on the doctrine of election. The other evening he was detained from visiting Kate, and he sent a very polite, ceremonious note containing a prescription, with Dr. D.'s compliments to Miss Beecher, requesting that she would take the inclosed in a little molasses at nine o'clock precisely.

The house we are at present inhabiting is the most inconvenient, ill-arranged, good-for-nothing, and altogether to be execrated affair that ever was put together. It was evidently built without a thought of a winter season. The kitchen is so disposed that it cannot be reached from any part of the house without going out into the air. Mother is actually obliged to put on a bonnet and cloak every time she goes into it. In the house are two parlors with folding doors between them. The back parlor has but one window, which opens on a veranda and has its lower half painted to keep out what little light there is. I need scarcely add that our landlord is an old bachelor and of course acted up to the light he had, though he left little enough of it for his tenants.

[32]

During this early Cincinnati life Harriet suffered much from ill-health accompanied by great mental depression; but in spite of both she labored diligently with her sister Catharine in establishing their school. They called it the Western Female Institute, and proposed to conduct it upon the college plan, with a faculty of instructors. As all these things are treated at length in letters written by Mrs. Stowe to her friend, Miss Georgiana May, we cannot do better than turn to them. In May, 1833, she writes:—

Bishop Purcell visited our school to-day and expressed himself as greatly pleased that we had opened such an one here. He spoke of my poor little geography,[1] and thanked me for the unprejudiced manner in which I had handled the Catholic question in it. I was of course flattered that he should have known anything of the book.

How I wish you could see Walnut Hills. It is about two miles from the city, and the road to it is as picturesque as you can imagine a road to be without "springs that run among the hills." Every possible variety of hill and vale of beautiful slope, and undulations of land set off by velvet richness of turf and broken up by groves and forests of every outline of foliage, make the scene Arcadian. You might ride over the same road a dozen times a day untired, for the constant variation of view caused by ascending and descending hills relieves you from all tedium. Much of the wooding is beech of a noble growth. The straight, beautiful shafts of these trees as one looks up the cool green recesses of the woods seems as though they might form very proper columns for a Dryad temple. *There*! Catharine is growling at *me* for sitting up so late; so "adieu to music, moonlight, and you." I meant to tell you an abundance of classical things that I have been thinking to-night, but "woe's me."

Since writing the above my whole time has been taken up in the labor of our new school, or wasted in the fatigue and lassitude following such labor. To-day is Sunday, and I am staying at home because I think it is time to take some efficient means to dissipate the illness and bad feelings of divers kinds that have for some time been growing upon me. At present there is and can be very little system or regularity about me. About half of my time I am scarcely alive, and a great part of the rest the slave and sport of morbid feeling and unreasonable prejudice. I have everything but good health.

I still rejoice that this letter will find you in good old Connecticut—thrice blessed—"oh, had I the wings of a dove" I would be there too. Give my love to Mary H. I remember well how gently she used to speak to and smile on that forlorn old daddy that boarded at your house one summer. It was associating with her that first put into my head the idea of saying something to people who were not agreeable, and of saying something when I had nothing to say, as is generally the case on such occasions.

Again she writes to the same friend:

Your letter, my dear G., I have just received, and read through three times. Now for my meditations upon it. What a woman of the world you are grown. How good it would be for me to be put into a place which so breaks up and precludes thought. Thought, intense emotional thought, has been my disease. How much good it might do me to be where I could not but be thoughtless. . . .

Now, Georgiana, let me copy for your delectation a list of matters that I have jotted down for consideration at a teachers' meeting to be held to-morrow night. It runneth as follows. Just hear! "About quills and paper on the floor; forming classes; drinking in the entry (cold water, mind you); giving leave to speak; recess-bell, etc., etc." "You are tired, I see," says Gilpin, "so am I," and I spare you.

I have just been hearing a class of little girls recite, and telling them a fairy story which I had to spin out as it went along, beginning with "once upon a time there was," etc., in the good old-fashioned way of stories.

Recently I have been reading the life of Madame de Stael and *Corinne*. I have felt an intense sympathy with many parts of that book, with many parts of her character. But in America feelings vehement and absorbing like hers become still more deep, morbid, and impassioned by the constant habits of self-government which the rigid forms of our society demand. They are repressed, and they burn inwardly till they burn the very soul, leaving only dust and ashes. It seems to me the intensity with which my mind has thought and felt on every subject presented to it has had this effect. It has withered and exhausted it, and though young I have no sympathy with the feelings of youth. All that is enthusiastic, all that is impassioned in admiration of nature, of writing, of character, in devotional thought and emotion, or in the emotions of affection, I have felt with vehement and absorbing intensity,—felt till my mind is exhausted, and seems to be sinking into deadness. Half of my time I am glad to remain in a listless vacancy, to busy myself with trifles, since thought is pain, and emotion is pain.

During the winter of 1833–34 the young school-teacher became so distressed at her own mental listlessness that she made a vigorous effort to throw it off. She forced herself to mingle in society, and, stimulated by the offer of a prize of fifty dollars by Mr. James Hall, editor of the *Western Monthly*, a newly established magazine, for the best short story, she entered into the competition. Her story, which was entitled "Uncle Lot," afterwards republished in the *Mayflower*, was by far the best submitted, and was awarded the prize without hesitation. This success gave a new direction to her thoughts, gave her an insight into her own ability, and so encouraged her that from that time on she devoted most of her leisure moments to writing.

Her literary efforts were further stimulated at this time by the congenial society of the Semi-Colon Club, a little social circle that met on alternate weeks at Mr. Samuel Foote's and Dr. Drake's. The name of the club originated with a roundabout and rather weak bit of logic set forth by one of its promoters. He said: "You know that in Spanish Columbus is called 'Colon.' Now he who discovers a new pleasure is certainly half as great as he who discovers a new continent. Therefore if Colon discovered a continent, we who have discovered in this club a new pleasure should at least be entitled to the name of 'Semi-Colons.'" So Semi-Colons they became and remained for some years.

At some meetings compositions were read, and at others nothing was read, but the time was passed in a general discussion of some interesting topic previously announced. Among the members of the club were Professor Stowe, unsurpassed in Biblical learning; Judge James Hall, editor of the *Western Monthly*; General Edward King; Mrs. Peters, afterwards founder of the Philadelphia School of Design; Miss Catharine Beecher; Mrs. Caroline Lee Hentz; E. P. Cranch; Dr. Drake; S. P. Chase, and many others who afterwards became prominent in their several walks of life.

In one of her letters to Miss May, Mrs. Stowe describes one of her methods for entertaining the members of the Semi-Colon as follows:—

I am wondering as to what I shall do next. I have been writing a piece to be read next Monday evening at Uncle Sam's *soirée* (the Semi-Colon). It is a letter purporting to be from Dr. Johnson. I have been stilting about in his style so long that it is a relief to me to come down to the jog of common English. Now I think of it I will just give you a history of my campaign in this circle.

My first piece was a letter from Bishop Butler, written in his outrageous style of parentheses and foggification. My second a satirical essay on the modern uses of languages. This I shall send to you, as some of the gentlemen, it seems, took a fancy to it and requested leave to put it in the *Western Magazine*, and so it is in print. It is ascribed to *Catharine*, or I don't know that I should have let it go. I have no notion of appearing in *propria personae*.

[35]

The next piece was a satire on certain members who were getting very much into the way of joking on the worn-out subjects of matrimony and old maid and old bachelorism. I therefore wrote a set of legislative enactments purporting to be from the ladies of the society, forbidding all such allusions in future. It made some sport at the time. I try not to be personal, and to be courteous, even in satire.

But I have written a piece this week that is making me some disquiet. I did not like it that there was so little that was serious and rational about the reading. So I conceived the design of writing a *set of letters*, and throwing them in, as being the letters of a friend. I wrote a letter this week for the first of the set,—easy, not very sprightly,—describing an imaginary situation, a house in the country, a gentleman and lady, Mr. and Mrs. Howard, as being pious, literary, and agreeable. I threw into the letter a number of little particulars and incidental allusions to give it the air of having been really a letter. I meant thus to give myself an opportunity for the introduction of different subjects and the discussion of different characters in future letters.

I meant to write on a great number of subjects in future. Cousin Elisabeth, only, was in the secret; Uncle Samuel and Sarah Elliot were not to know.

Yesterday morning I finished my letter, smoked it to make it look yellow, tore it to make it look old, directed it and scratched out the direction, postmarked it with red ink, sealed it and broke the seal, all this to give credibility to the fact of its being a real letter. Then I enclosed it in an envelope, stating that it was a part of a set which had incidentally fallen into my hands. This envelope was written in a scrawny, scrawly, gentleman's hand.

I put it into the office in the morning, directed to "Mrs. Samuel E. Foote," and then sent word to Sis that it was coming, so that she might be ready to enact the part.

Well, the deception took. Uncle Sam examined it and pronounced, *ex cathedra*, that it must have been a real letter. Mr. Greene (the gentleman who reads) declared that it must have come from Mrs. Hall, and elucidated the theory by spelling out the names and dates which I had erased, which, of course, he accommodated to his own tastes. But then, what makes me feel uneasy is that Elisabeth, after reading it, did not seem to be exactly satisfied. She thought it had too much sentiment, too much particularity of incident,—she did not exactly know what. She was afraid that it would be criticised unmercifully. Now Elisabeth has a tact and quickness of perception that I trust to, and her remarks have made me uneasy enough. I am unused to being criticised, and don't know how I shall bear it.

In 1833 Mrs. Stowe first had the subject of slavery brought to her personal notice by taking a trip across the river from Cincinnati into Kentucky in company with Miss Dutton, one of the associate teachers in the Western Institute. They visited an estate that afterwards figured as that of Colonel Shelby in *Uncle Tom's Cabin,* and here the young authoress first came into personal contact with the negro slaves of the South. In speaking, many years afterwards, of this visit, Miss Dutton said: "Harriet did not seem to notice anything in particular that happened, but sat much of the time as though abstracted in thought. When the negroes did funny things and cut up capers, she did not seem to pay the slightest attention to them. Afterwards, however, in reading 'Uncle Tom,' I recognized scene after scene of that visit portrayed with the most minute fidelity, and knew at once where the material for that portion of the story had been gathered."

At this time, however, Mrs. Stowe was more deeply interested in the subject of education than in that of slavery, as is shown by the following extract from one of her letters to Miss May, who was herself a teacher. She says:—

We mean to turn over the West by means of *model schools* in this, its capital. We mean to have a young lady's school of about fifty or sixty, a primary school of little girls to the same amount, and then a primary school for *boys*. We have come to the conclusion that the work of teaching will never be rightly done till it passes into *female* hands. This is especially true with regard to boys. To govern boys by moral influences requires tact and talent and versatility; it requires also the same division of labor that female education does. But men of tact, versatility, talent, and piety will not devote their lives to teaching. They must be ministers and missionaries, and all that, and while there is such a thrilling call for action in this way, every man who is merely teaching feels as if he were a Hercules with a distaff, ready to spring to the first trumpet that calls him away. As for division of labor, men must have salaries that can support wife and family, and, of course, a revenue would be required to support a requisite number of teachers if they could be found.

Then, if men have more knowledge they have less talent at communicating it, nor have they the patience, the long-suffering, and gentleness necessary to superintend the formation of character. We intend to make these principles understood, and ourselves to set the example of what females can do in this way. You see that first-rate talent is necessary for all that we mean to do, especially for the last, because here we must face down the prejudices of society and we must have exemplary success to be believed. We want original, planning minds, and you do not know how few there are among females, and how few we can command of those that exist.

During the summer of 1834 the young teacher and writer made her first visit East since leaving New England two years before. Its object was mainly to be present at the graduation of her favorite brother, Henry Ward, from Amherst College. The earlier part of this journey was performed by means of stage to Toledo, and thence by steamer to Buffalo. A pleasant bit of personal description, and also of impressions of Niagara, seen for the first time on this journey, are given in a letter sent back to Cincinnati during its progress. In it she says of her fellow-travelers:—

Then there was a portly, rosy, clever Mr. Smith, or Jones, or something the like; and a New Orleans girl looking like distraction, as far as dress is concerned, but with the prettiest language and softest intonations in the world, and one of those faces which, while you say it isn't handsome, keeps you looking all the time to see what it can be that is so pretty about it. Then there was Miss B., an independent, good-natured, do-as-I-please sort of a body, who seemed of perpetual motion from morning till night. Poor Miss D. said, when we stopped at night, "Oh, dear! I suppose Lydia will be fiddling about our room till morning, and we shall not one of us sleep." Then, by way of contrast, there was a Mr. Mitchell, the most gentlemanly, obliging man that ever changed his seat forty times a day to please a lady. Oh, yes, he could ride outside,—or, oh, certainly, he could ride inside,—he had no objection to this, or that, or the other. Indeed, it was difficult to say what could come amiss to him. He speaks in a soft, quiet manner, with something of a drawl, using very correct, well-chosen language, and pronouncing all his words with carefulness; has everything in his dress and traveling appointments *comme il faut*; and seems to think there is abundant time for everything that is to be done in this world, without, as he says, "any unnecessary excitement." Before the party had fully discovered his name he was usually designated as "the obliging gentleman," or "that gentleman who is so accommodating." Yet our friend, withal, is of Irish extraction, and I have seen him roused to talk with both hands and a dozen words in a breath. He fell into a little talk about abolition and slavery with our good Mr. Jones, a man whose mode of reasoning consists in repeating the same sentence at regular intervals as long as you choose to answer it. This man, who was finally convinced that negroes were black, used it as an irrefragable argument to all that could be said, and at last began to deduce from it that they might just as well be slaves as anything else, and so he proceeded till all the philanthropy of our friend was roused, and he sprung up all lively and oratorical and gesticulatory and indignant to my heart's content. I like to see a quiet man that can be roused.

In the same letter she gives her impressions of Niagara, as follows :—

I have seen it (Niagara) and yet live. Oh, where is your soul? Never mind, though. Let me tell, if I can, what is unutterable. Elisabeth, it is not *like* anything; it did not look like anything I expected; it did not look like a waterfall. I did not once think whether it was high or low; whether it roared or didn't roar; whether it equaled my expectations or not. My mind whirled off, it seemed to me, in a new, strange world. It seemed unearthly, like the strange, dim images in the Revelation. I thought of the great white throne; the rainbow around it; the throne in sight like unto an emerald; and oh that beautiful water rising like moonlight, falling as the soul sinks when it dies, to rise refined, spiritualized, and pure. That rainbow, breaking out, trembling, fading, and again coming like a beautiful spirit walking the waters. Oh, it is lovelier than it is great; it is like the Mind that made it: great, but so veiled in beauty that we gaze without terror. I felt as if I could have *gone over* with the waters; it would be so beautiful a death; there would be no fear in it. I felt the rock tremble under me with a sort of joy. I was so maddened that I could have gone too, if it had gone.

While at the East she was greatly affected by hearing of the death of her dear friend, Eliza Tyler, the wife of Professor Stowe. This lady was the daughter of Dr. Bennett Tyler, president of the Theological Institute of Connecticut, at East Windsor; but twenty-five years of age at the time of her death, a very beautiful woman gifted with a wonderful voice. She was also possessed of a well-stored mind and a personal magnetism that made her one of the most popular members of the Semi-Colon Club, in the proceedings of which she took an active interest.

Her death left Professor Stowe a childless widower, and his forlorn condition greatly excited the sympathy of her who had been his wife's most intimate friend. It was easy for sympathy to ripen into love, and after a short engagement Harriet E. Beecher became the wife of Professor Calvin E. Stowe.

Her last act before the wedding was to write the following note to the friend of her girlhood, Miss Georgiana May:—

*January* 6, 1836.

Well, my dear G., about half an hour more and your old friend, companion, schoolmate, sister, etc., will cease to be Hatty Beecher and change to nobody knows who. My dear, you are engaged, and pledged in a year or two to encounter a similar fate, and do you wish to know how you shall feel? Well, my dear,

I have been dreading and dreading the time, and lying awake all last week wondering how I should live through this overwhelming crisis, and lo! it has come and I feel *nothing at all.*

The wedding is to be altogether domestic; nobody present but my own brothers and sisters, and my old colleague, Mary Dutton; and as there is a sufficiency of the ministry in our family we have not even to call in the foreign aid of a minister. Sister Katy is not here, so she will not witness my departure from her care and guidance to that of another. None of my numerous friends and acquaintances who have taken such a deep interest in making the connection for me even know the day, and it will be all done and over before they know anything about it.

Well, it is really a mercy to have this entire stupidity come over one at such a time. I should be crazy to feel as I did yesterday, or indeed to feel anything at all. But I inwardly vowed that my last feelings and reflections on this subject should be yours, and as I have not got any, it is just as well to tell you *that.* Well, here comes Mr. S., so farewell, and for the last time I subscribe,

Your own

H. E. B.

## Note

1. "This geography was begun by Mrs. Stowe during the summer of 1832, while visiting her brother William at Newport, R. I. It was completed during the winter of 1833, and published by the firm of Corey, Fairbank & Webster, of Cincinnati." [Charles Edward Stowe's note.]

From Charles Edward Stowe, *Life of Harriet Beecher Stowe Compiled from Her Letters and Journals* (Boston: Houghton, Mifflin, 1889), pp. 53-77.

# [Life in Brunswick, December 1850]

## HARRIET BEECHER STOWE

In 1849, Calvin Stowe was appointed to the faculty at Bowdoin College in Brunswick, Maine, and the Stowes moved there from Cincinnati in the spring of 1850. The move was a difficult one for Stowe, who gave birth to her final child, Charles Edward, in July. Further, Stowe was recovering from illness and losses, beginning with the suicide of her brother George Beecher in 1843. But the most devastating blow had been the death of her infant son, Samuel Charles. Born in January 1848, "Charley" died of cholera in July 1849 and the Stowes buried him near Walnut Hills, their home in Cincinnati. In Brunswick, Stowe was quite occupied with her children and the new baby, setting up a household, and adjusting to life in a new place, far from her father and step-mother in Cincinnati. Letters from family members helped her, and she, in turn, wrote as frequently as she could. In her biography, *Life and Letters of Harriet Beecher Stowe* (1898), Annie Fields reprinted a letter that Stowe wrote to Sarah Buckingham Beecher, the widow of her brother George. In this letter, Stowe humorously describes the first summer in Brunswick and provides insight into both her domestic duties and her interest in returning to writing.

MY DEAR SISTER,—Is it really true that snow is on the ground and Christmas coming, and I have not written unto thee, most dear sister? No, I don't believe it! I haven't been so naughty—it's all a mistake—yes, written I must have—and written I have, too—in the nightwatches as I lay on my bed—such beautiful letters—I wish you had only received them; but by day it has been hurry, hurry, hurry, and drive, drive, drive! or else the calm of a sick-room, ever since last spring.

I put off writing when your letter first came, because I meant to write you a long letter,—a full and complete one; and so days slid by,—and became weeks,—and my little Charley came . . . etc. and etc.!!! Sarah, when I look back, I wonder at myself, not that I forget any one thing that I should remember, but that I have remembered anything. From the time that I left Cincinnati with my children to come forth to a country that I knew not

Stowe house, Brunswick, Maine. Harriet Beecher Stowe Center, Hartford, Connecticut.

of almost to the present time, it has seemed as if I could scarcely breathe, I was so pressed with care. My head dizzy with the whirl of railroads and steamboats; then ten days' sojourn in Boston, and a constant toil and hurry in buying my furniture and equipments; and then landing in Brunswick in the midst of a drizzly, inexorable north-east storm, and beginning the work of getting in order a deserted, dreary, damp old house. All day long running from one thing to another, as, for example, thus:—

"Mrs. Stowe, how shall I make this lounge, and what shall I cover the back with first?"

*Mrs. Stowe.* "With the coarse cotton in the closet."

*Woman.* "Mrs. Stowe, there isn't any more soap to clean the windows."

*Mrs. Stowe.* "Where shall I get soap?"

"Here, H., run up to the store and get two bars."

"There is a man below wants to see Mrs. Stowe about the cistern. Before you go down, Mrs. Stowe, just show me how to cover this round end of the lounge."

"There's a man up from the depot, and he says that a box has come for Mrs. Stowe, and it's coming up to the house; will you come down and see about it?"

"Mrs. Stowe, don't go till you have shown the man how to nail that carpet in the corner. He's nailed it all crooked; what shall he do? The black thread is all used up, and what shall I do about putting gimp on the back of that sofa? Mrs. Stowe, there is a man come with a lot of pails and tinware from Furbish; will you settle the bill now?"

"Mrs. Stowe, here is a letter just come from Boston inclosing that bill of lading; the man wants to know what he shall do with the goods. If you will tell me what to say, I will answer the letter for you."

"Mrs. Stowe, the meat-man is at the door. Hadn't we better get a little beefsteak, or something, for dinner?"

"Shall Hatty go to Boardman's for some more black thread?"

"Mrs. Stowe, this cushion is an inch too wide for the frame. What shall we do now?"

"Mrs. Stowe, where are the screws of the black walnut bedstead?"

"Here's a man has brought in these bills for freight. Will you settle them now?"

"Mrs. Stowe, I don't understand using this great needle. I can't make it go through the cushion; it sticks in the cotton."

[43]

Then comes a letter from my husband, saying he is sick a bed, and all but dead; don't ever expect to see his family again; wants to know how I shall manage, in case I am left a widow; knows we shall get in debt and never get out; wonders at my courage; thinks I am very sanguine; warns me to be prudent, as there won't be much to live on in case of his death, etc., etc., etc. I read the letter and poke it into the stove, and proceed. . . .

Some of my adventures were quite funny; as for example: I had in my kitchen-elect no sink, cistern, or any other water privileges, so I bought at the cotton factory two of the great hogsheads they bring oil in, which here in Brunswick are often used for cisterns, and had them brought up in triumph to my yard, and was congratulating myself on my energy, when lo and behold! it was discovered that there was no cellar door except one in the kitchen, which was truly a strait and narrow way, down a long pair of stairs. Hereupon, as saith John Bunyan, I fell into a muse,—how to get my cisterns into my cellar. In days of chivalry I might have got a knight to make me a breach through the foundation walls, but that was not to be thought of now, and my oil hogsheads, standing disconsolately in the yard, seemed to reflect no great credit on my foresight. In this strait I fell upon a real honest Yankee cooper, whom I besought, for the reputation of his craft and mine, to take my hogsheads to pieces, carry them down in staves, and set them up again, which the worthy man actually accomplished one fair summer forenoon, to the great astonishment of "us Yankees." When my man came to put up the pump, he stared very hard to see my hogsheads thus trans-lated and standing as innocent and quiet as could be in the cellar, and then I told him, in a very mild, quiet way, that I got 'em taken to pieces and put together,—just as if I had been always in the habit of doing such things. Professor Smith came down and looked very hard at them and then said, "Well, nothing can beat a willful woman." Then followed divers negotia-tions with a very clever, but (with reverence) somewhat lazy gentleman of jobs, who occupieth a carpenter's shop opposite to mine. This same John Titcomb, my very good friend, is a character peculiar to Yankeedom. He is part owner and landlord of the house I rent, and connected by birth with all the best families in town; a man of real intelligence, and good educa-tion, a great reader, and quite a thinker. Being of an ingenious turn, he does painting, gilding, staining, upholstery jobs, varnishing, all in addition to his primary trade of carpentry. But he is a man studious of ease, and fully possessed with the idea that man wants but little here below; so he boards

[44]

himself in his workshop on crackers and herring, washed down with cold water, and spends his time working, musing, reading new publications, and taking his comfort. In his shop you shall see a joiner's bench, hammers, planes, saws, gimlets, varnish, paint, picture frames, fence posts, rare old china, one or two fine portraits of his ancestry, a bookcase full of books, the tooth of a whale, an old spinning-wheel and spindle, a lady's parasol frame, a church lamp to be mended, in short, Henry says Mr. Titcomb's shop is like the ocean; there is no end to the curiosities in it.

In all my moving and fussing Mr. Titcomb has been my right-hand man. Whenever a screw was loose, a nail to be driven, a lock mended, a pane of glass set,—and these cases were manifold,—he was always on hand. But my sink was no fancy job, and I believe nothing but a very particular friendship would have moved him to undertake it. So this same sink lingered in a precarious state for some weeks, and when I had *nothing else to do*, I used to call and do what I could in the way of enlisting the good man's sympathies in its behalf.

How many times I have been in and seated myself in one of the old rocking-chairs, and talked first of the news of the day, the railroad, the last proceedings in Congress, the probabilities about the millennium, and thus brought the conversation by little and little round to my sink! . . . because, till the sink was done, the pump could not be put up, and we couldn't have any rain-water. Sometimes my courage would quite fail me to introduce the subject, and I would talk of everything else, turn and get out of the shop, and then turn back as if a thought had just struck my mind, and say:—

"Oh, Mr. Titcomb! about that sink?"

"Yes, ma'am, I was thinking about going down street this afternoon to look out stuff for it."

"Yes, sir, if you would be good enough to get it done as soon as possible; we are in great need of it."

"I think there's no hurry. I believe we are going to have a dry time now, so that you could not catch any water, and you won't need a pump at present."

These negotiations extended from the first of June to the first of July, and at last my sink was completed, and so also was a new house spout, concerning which I had had divers communings with Deacon Dunning of the Baptist church. Also during this time good Mrs. Mitchell and myself made two sofas, or lounges, a barrel chair, divers bedspreads, pillow cases, pillows, bolsters, mattresses; we painted rooms; we revarnished furniture; we—what *didn't* we do?

Then came on Mr. Stowe; and then came the eighth of July and my little Charley. I was really glad for an excuse to lie in bed, for I was full tired, I can assure you. Well, I was what folks call very comfortable for two weeks, when my nurse had to leave me. . . .

During this time I have employed my leisure hours in making up my engagements with newspaper editors. I have written more than anybody, or I myself, would have thought. I have taught an hour a day in our school, and I have read two hours every evening to the children. The children study English history in school, and I am reading Scott's historic novels in their order. To-night I finish the *Abbot*; shall begin *Kenilworth* next week; yet I am constantly pursued and haunted by the idea that I don't do anything. Since I began this note I have been called off at least a dozen times; once for the fish-man, to buy a codfish; once to see a man who had brought me some barrels of apples; once to see a book-man; then to Mrs. Upham, to see about a drawing I promised to make for her; then to nurse the baby; then into the kitchen to make a chowder for dinner; and now I am at it again, for nothing but deadly determination enables me ever to write; it is rowing against wind and tide.

I suppose you think now I have begun, I am never going to stop, and, in truth, it looks like it; but the spirit moves now and I must obey.

Christmas is coming, and our little household is all alive with preparations; every one collecting their little gifts with wonderful mystery and secrecy. . . .

To tell the truth, dear, I am getting tired; my neck and back ache, and I must come to a close.

Your ready kindness to me in the spring I felt very much; and *why* I did not have the sense to have sent you one line just by way of acknowledgment, I'm sure I don't know; I felt just as if I had, till I awoke, and behold! I had not. But, my dear, if my wits are somewhat wool-gathering and unsettled, my heart is as true as a star. I love you, and have thought of you often.

This fall I have felt often *sad*, lonesome, both very unusual feelings with me in these busy days; but the breaking way from my old home, and leaving father and mother, and coming to a strange place affected me naturally. In those sad hours my thoughts have often turned to George; I have thought with encouragement of his blessed state and hoped that I should soon be there, too. I have many warm and kind friends here, and have been treated with great attention and kindness. Brunswick is a delightful residence, and if you come East next summer, you must come to my new home. George[1] would delight to go a-fishing with the children, and see the ships, and sail in the sailboats, and all that.

Give Aunt Harriet's love to him, and tell him when he gets to be a painter to send me a picture.

Affectionately yours,
H. Stowe

## Note

1. Her brother George's only child. [Annie Fields's note.]

Letter from Harriet Beecher Stowe to Sarah Beecher, December 1850, reprinted in Annie Fields, *Life and Letters of Harriet Beecher Stowe* (Boston: Houghton, Mifflin, 1897), pp. 123–129.

# "Harriet Beecher Stowe" (1851)

## SARAH JOSEPHA HALE

Sarah Josepha Hale (1788–1879), the powerful editor of *Godey's Lady's Book*, published several of Stowe's sketches and stories in the 1830s and early 1840s. During the late 1840s, Hale began work on an encyclopedia of nearly 2,500 women writers, including excerpts from their works, *Woman's Record; or, Sketches of All Distinguished Women from "The Beginning" till A.D. 1850*, which was published in 1853. Hale wrote to Stowe, asking for information for her book as well as a portrait. Stowe, who had been writing little during the late 1840s because of her responsibilities to her young children, responded:

> I was quite amused I must say at your letter to me wholly innocent as I am of any pretensions to rank among "distinguished women"—However I read it to my tribe of little folks assembled around the evening centre table to let them know what an unexpected honour had befallen their mamma—
>
> The idea of the daguerroitype especially was quite droll—and I was diverted myself somewhat with figuring the astonishment of the children should the well known visage of their mother loom out of the pages of a book before their astonished eyes—but in sober sad news,—having reflected duly and truly on my past life, it is so thoroughly uneventful and uninteresting that I do not see how anything can be done for me in the way of a sketch. My sister Catharine has lived much more of a life—and done more that can be told of than I whose course and employments have always been retired and domestic.—The most I can think of is that I was born in Litchfield Conn—was a teacher from my fifteenth year till my marriage—that I have been mother to seven children—six of whom are now living—and that the greater portion of my time and strength has been spent in the necessary but unpoetic duties of the family—These details you can throw into two or three lines—as great a space as I should have any claim to occupy in such a company.[1]

Stowe, who was surely cheered by Hale's request for information, began writing again and, by the time the *Woman's Record* was published in 1853, she was the celebrated author of *Uncle Tom's Cabin*. Hale's positive account of Stowe, reprinted below, was followed by an excerpt from her story "The Tea-Rose." Hale, who opposed slavery but did not publish antislavery stories within the pages of *Godey's Lady's Book* in fear of offending her southern readers, would surely not have encouraged Stowe to "write more" had she known the direction Stowe's writing was about to take.

### STOWE, HARRIET BEECHER,

Was born in Litchfield, Connecticut. Daughter of the Rev. Dr. Beecher, now of Cincinnati, and sister of Miss Catharine Beecher, whose sketch we have given, the subject of our brief notice could hardly fail of enjoying great advantages of moral as well as intellectual culture. From the age of fifteen till her marriage, Miss Harriet Beecher was associated with her sister in the cares of a large female seminary. Teaching is an excellent discipline, both of the heart and mind, of a young lady; those are fortunate who, either from necessity or from a wish to do good, pass some intervening years in this praiseworthy profession before they take on themselves the responsibilities of a household of their own. Miss Harriet Beecher was thus fitted to be a congenial companion of the Rev. Calvin E. Stowe, whom she married when about twenty-one. Her husband is a man of profound learning, then the Professor of Languages and Biblical Literature in the Divinity School at Cincinnati; he is now one of the professors in Brunswick College, Maine. Mrs. Stowe has been the model of a good wife and mother; of her seven children six are living, so that the greater portion of her time, thoughts, and strength has been spent in the important duties of a family. Yet she has found time to contribute to several periodicals. Her writings are deservedly admired for their sprightly vivacity and artistic finish combined with moral sentiments of the loftiest stamp, expressed in such a familiar way, that it makes wisdom seem like a pleasant friend, instead of a grave Mentor. None of our female writers excel Mrs. Stowe in the art of entertaining her readers; the only regret is, that she does not write more. "The May-Flower," a collection of her stories, was published in 1849, and has, of course been very popular.

[49]

"The Sphere of Woman," *Godey's Lady's Book*, March 1850. Special Collections, University of Virginia Library.

## Note

1. Letter to Sarah Josepha (Buell) (Mrs. David) Hale, 10 November 1851, E. Bruce Kirkham Collection, Harriet Beecher Stowe Center, Hartford, CT.

From Sarah Josepha Buell Hale, *Woman's Record; or, Sketches of All Distinguished Women from "The Beginning" till A.D. 1850* (New York: Harper & Brothers, 1853), p. 837.

# [Letter to Gamaliel Bailey on Writing
## *Uncle Tom's Cabin*, 1851]

### Harriet Beecher Stowe

On 1 August 1850, Stowe published "The Freeman's Dream: A Parable," one of her first direct contributions to the antislavery movement, in the *National Era*, an antislavery newspaper edited by Gamaliel Bailey. She had published three other sketches in the *Era* and Bailey, wishing to encourage her, sent her $100.00, inviting her to submit additional work. When the Fugitive Slave Law was formally enacted by the United States Congress on 18 September 1850, Stowe and her family joined millions of northerners who were outraged by a law that made all a party to slavery. Her sister Isabella wrote to Stowe, pressing her to use her writing skills in the antislavery cause, and she began to think of a new story that she might write for the *Era*. In the following letter to Bailey, she outlines her plan and suggests her motivations for her new work. Two months after Bailey received Stowe's letter, he announced "the publication of a new story by Mrs. H. B. Stowe," which ultimately grew to the forty-one installments of *Uncle Tom's Cabin*, published from 5 June 1851 to 1 April 1852. The serial was read by thousands, including a young William Dean Howells, who years later recalled:

> The book that moved me most, in our stay of six months at Ashtabula, was then beginning to move the whole world more than any other book has moved it. I read it as it came out week after week in the old *National Era*, and I broke my heart over *Uncle Tom's Cabin*, as every one else did.[1]

Stowe's brief letter provides insights into her attitude toward slavery and her methods of composition as she began to write the most famous book of the nineteenth century.

The first installment of *Uncle Tom's Cabin*, in the *National Era*, 5 June 1851.
Special Collections, University of Virginia Library.

Brunswick, [Maine,] March 9 [, 1851].

Mr. Bailey,

Dear Sir:

I am at present occupied upon a story which will be a much longer one than any I have ever written, embracing a series of sketches which give the lights and shadows of the "patriarchal institution," written either from observation, incidents which have occurred in the sphere of my personal knowledge, or in the knowledge of my friends. I shall show the *best side* of the thing, and something *faintly approaching the worst.*

Up to this year I have always felt that I had no particular call to meddle with this subject, and I dreaded to expose even my own mind to the full force of its exciting power. But I feel now that the time has come when even a woman or a child who can speak a word for freedom and humanity is bound to speak. The Carthagenian women in the last peril of their state cut off their hair for bow strings to give to the defenders of their country, and such peril and shame as now hangs over this country is worse than Roman slavery, and I hope every woman who can write will not be silent. I have admired and sympathized with the free spirit of Grace Greenwood, and her letters have done my heart good.[2] My vocation is simply that of a *painter*, and my object will be to hold up in the most lifelike and graphic manner possible slavery, its reverses, changes, and the negro character, which I have had ample opportunities for studying. There is no arguing with *pictures*, and everybody is impressed by them, whether they mean to be or not.

I wrote beforehand because I know that you have much matter to arrange, and thought it might not be amiss to give you a hint. The thing may extend through three or four numbers. It will be ready in two or three weeks.

A week or two ago I sent to Mrs. Bailey a story from one of my friends for her paper, requesting also to have my name put down as a subscriber.[3] I have since heard nothing from it. Should the story not prove suitable for her purposes, she will oblige me by redirecting it to me. [Ms. illegible]

Yours with [sincere] esteem,

H. STOWE

## Notes

1. William Dean Howells, *My Literary Passions: Criticism & Fiction* (New York: Harper & Brothers, 1891), p. 50.

2. Grace Greenwood, the pseudonym of the poet and writer Sara Jane Clarke Lippin-cott (1823–1904), wrote numerous articles and sketches for the *National Era* and became increasingly involved in antislavery and other reform movements.

3. *The Friend of Youth* was a short-lived magazine for children that published mostly antislavery stories and articles, edited by Margaret L. Bailey in Washington, D.C.

Harriet Beecher Stowe to Gamaliel Bailey, 9 March 1851. Typescript copy, Rare Books and Manuscripts Department, Boston Public Library.

# From "The Story of *Uncle Tom's Cabin*"

CHARLES DUDLEY WARNER

When Stowe's *Uncle Tom's Cabin* became the runaway best seller of the nineteenth century, the reading public demanded to know more about its author as well as the circumstances in which the book was written. Stowe herself gave various accounts during her lifetime, and her friends and family members provided information as well. A neighbor of the Stowes at Nook Farm in Hartford, Connecticut, Charles Dudley Warner (1829–1900) was a journalist and novelist who also served on the editorial staff of *Harper's Magazine*. Together with his wife, Susan Lee Warner, Warner maintained a home that was a social center for writers, artists, and musicians. He became a close friend of Mark Twain's, and together they wrote *The Gilded Age* (1873), a novel about corruption in politics and business in the years following the Civil War. Warner was also friends with James Fields and his wife Annie Fields, who wrote a biography of him in 1905. After Stowe's death in 1896, Fields and Warner made an unsuccessful attempt to help Stowe's daughters keep the home at Nook Farm. In the following excerpt from an article written for the *Atlantic Monthly* in 1896, Warner provides a thoughtful commentary on the influence of the Fugitive Slave Law on the composition of *Uncle Tom's Cabin*, as well as an account of Stowe's life in the early 1850s.

ON THE 29TH OF JUNE, 1852, Henry Clay died. In that month the two great political parties, in their national conventions, had accepted as a finality all the compromise measures of 1850, and the last hours of the Kentucky statesman were brightened by the thought that his efforts had secured the perpetuity of the Union.

But on the 20th of March, 1852, there had been an event, the significance of which was not taken into account by the political conventions or by Clay, which was to test the conscience of the nation. This was the publication of *Uncle Tom's Cabin*. Was this only an "event," the advent of a new force in politics; was the book merely an abolition pamphlet, or was it a novel, one of the few great masterpieces of fiction that the world has produced? After

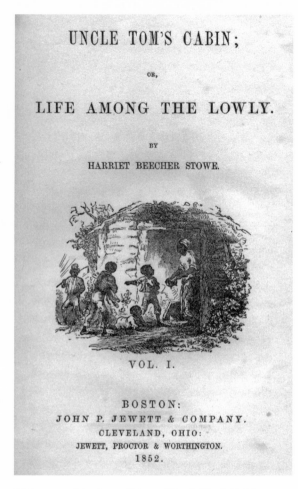

Title page of the first edition of *Uncle Tom's Cabin*
(1852). Harriet Beecher Stowe Center, Hartford,
Connecticut.

the lapse of forty-four years and the disappearance of African slavery on this
continent, it is perhaps possible to consider this question dispassionately.

The compromise of 1850 satisfied neither the North nor the South. The
admission of California as a free State was regarded by Calhoun as fatal to
the balance between the free and the slave States, and thereafter a fierce
agitation sprang up for the recovery of this loss of balance, and ultimately
for Southern preponderance, which resulted in the repeal of the Missouri
Compromise, the Kansas-Nebraska war, and the civil war. The fugitive

slave law was hateful to the North not only because it was cruel and degrading, but because it was seen to be a move formed for nationalizing slavery. It was unsatisfactory to the South because it was deemed inadequate in its provisions, and because the South did not believe the North would execute it in good faith. So unstable did the compromise seem that in less than a year after the passage of all its measures, Henry Clay and forty-four Senators and Representatives united in a manifesto declaring that they would support no man for office who was not known to be opposed to any disturbance of the settlements of the compromise. When, in February, 1851, the recaptured fugitive slave, Burns, was rescued from the United States officers in Boston, Clay urged the investment of the President with extraordinary power to enforce the law.

Henry Clay was a patriot, a typical American. The republic and its preservation were the passions of his life. Like Lincoln who was born in the State of his adoption, he was willing to make almost any sacrifice for the maintenance of the Union. He had no sympathy with the system of slavery. There is no doubt that he would have been happy in the belief that it was in the way of gradual and peaceful extinction. With him, it was always the Union before state rights and before slavery. Unlike Lincoln, he had not the clear vision to see that the republic could not endure half slave and half free. He believed that the South, appealing to the compromises of the Constitution, would sacrifice the Union before it would give up slavery, and in fear of this menace he begged the North to conquer its prejudices. We are not liable to overrate his influence as a compromising pacificator from 1832 to 1852. History will no doubt say that it was largely due to him that the war on the Union was postponed to a date when its success was impossible.

It was the fugitive slave law that brought the North face to face with slavery nationalized, and it was the fugitive slave law that produced *Uncle Tom's Cabin*. The effect of this story was immediate and electric. It went straight to the hearts of tens of thousands of people who had never before considered slavery except as a political institution for which they had no personal responsibility. What was this book, and how did it happen to produce such an effect? It is true that it struck into a time of great irritation and agitation, but in one sense there was nothing new in it. The facts had all been published. For twenty years abolition tracts, pamphlets, newspapers, and books had left little to be revealed, to those who cared to read, as to the nature of slavery or its economic aspects. The evidence was practically all in,—supplied largely by the advertisements of Southern newspapers and by the legislation of the slaveholding States,—but it did not carry conviction; that is, the sort of conviction that results in action. The subject had to be carried home to the conscience. Pamphleteering, convention-holding, sermons, had failed to do this. Even the degrading requirements of the fugitive slave law, which brought shame and humiliation, had not sufficed to fuse the public conscience, emphasize the necessity of obedience to the moral law, and compel recognition of the responsibility of the North for slavery. Evidence had not done this, passionate appeals had not done it, vituperation had not done it. What sort of presentation of the case would gain the public ear and go to the heart? If Mrs. Stowe, in all her fervor, had put forth first the facts in *A Key to Uncle Tom's Cabin*, which so buttressed her romance, the book would have had no more effect than had followed the like compilations and arraignments. What was needed? If we can discover this, we shall have the secret of this epoch-making novel.

The story of this book has often been told. It is in the nature of a dramatic incident of which the reader never tires any more than the son of Massachusetts does of the minutest details of that famous scene in the Senate Chamber when Webster replied to Hayne.

At the age of twenty-four the author was married and went to live in Cincinnati, where her husband held a chair in the Lane Theological Seminary. There for the first time she was brought into relations with the African race and saw the effects of slavery. She visited slaveholders in Kentucky and had friends among them. In some homes she saw the "patriarchal" institution at its best. The Beecher family were anti-slavery, but they had not been identified with the abolitionists, except perhaps Edward, who was associated with the murdered Lovejoy. It was long a reproach brought by the abolitionists against Henry Ward Beecher that he held entirely aloof from their movement. At Cincinnati, however, the personal aspects of the case were brought home to Mrs. Stowe. She learned the capacities and peculiarities of the negro race. They were her servants; she taught some of them; hunted fugitives applied to her; she ransomed some by her own efforts; every day there came to her knowledge stories of the hunger for freedom, of the ruthless separation of man and wife and mother and child, and of the heroic sufferings of those who ran away from the fearful doom of those "sold down South." These things crowded upon her mind and awoke her deepest compassion. But what could she do against all the laws, the political and commercial interests, the great public apathy? Relieve a case here and there, yes. But to dwell upon the gigantic evil, with no means of making head against it, was to invite insanity.

As late as 1850, when Professor Stowe was called to Bowdoin College, and the family removed to Brunswick, Maine, Mrs. Stowe had not felt impelled to the duty she afterwards undertook. "In fact, it was a sort of general impression upon her mind, as upon that of many humane people in those days, that the subject was so dark and painful a one, so involved in difficulty and obscurity, so utterly beyond human hope or help, that it was of no use to read, or think, or distress one's self about it." But when she reached New England the excitement over the fugitive slave law was at its height. There was a panic in Boston among the colored people settled there, who were daily fleeing to Canada. Every mail brought her pitiful letters from Boston, from Illinois, and elsewhere, of the terror and despair caused by the law. Still more was she impressed by the apathy of the Christian world at the North, and surely, she said, the people did not understand what the "system" was. Appeals were made to her, who had some personal knowledge of the subject, to take up her pen. The task seemed beyond her in every way. She was not strong, she was in the midst of heavy domestic cares, with a young infant, with pupils to whom she was giving daily lessons, and the limited income of the family required the strictest economy. The dependence was upon the small salary of Professor Stowe, and the few dollars she could earn by an occasional newspaper or magazine article. But the theme burned in her mind, and finally took this shape: at least she would write some sketches and show the Christian world what slavery really was, and what the system was that they were defending. She wanted to do this with entire fairness, showing all the mitigations of the "patriarchal" system, and all that individuals concerned in it could do to alleviate its misery. While pondering this she came by chance, in a volume of an anti-slavery magazine, upon the authenticated account of the escape of a woman with her child on the ice across the Ohio River from Kentucky. She began to meditate. The faithful slave husband in Kentucky, who had refused to escape from a master who trusted him, when he was about to be sold "down river," came to her as a pattern of Uncle Tom, and the scenes of the story began to form themselves in her mind. "The first part of the book ever committed to writing [this is the statement of Mrs. Stowe] was the death of Uncle Tom. This scene presented itself almost as a tangible vision to her mind while sitting at the communion-table in the little church in Brunswick. She was perfectly overcome by it, and could scarcely restrain the convulsion of tears and sobbings that shook her frame. She hastened home and wrote it, and her husband being away, read it to her two sons of ten and twelve years of age. The little fellows broke out into convulsions of weeping, one of them saying through his sobs, 'Oh, mamma, slavery is the most cursed thing in the world!' From that time the story can less be said to have been composed by her than imposed upon her. Scenes, incidents, conversations rushed upon her with a vividness and importunity that would not be denied. The book insisted upon getting itself into being, and would take no denial."

When two or three chapters were written she wrote to her friend, Dr. Bailey, of Washington, the editor of the *National Era*, to which she had contributed, that she was planning a story that might run through several numbers of the *Era*. The story was at once applied for, and thereafter weekly installments were sent on regularly, in spite of all cares and distractions. The installments were mostly written during the morning, on a little desk in a corner of the dining-room of the cottage in Brunswick, subject to all the interruptions of house-keeping, her children bursting into the room continually with the importunity of childhood. But they did not break the spell or destroy her abstraction. With a smile and a word and a motion of the hand she would wave them off, and keep on in her magician's work. Long afterwards they recalled this, dimly understood at the time, and wondered at her power of concentration. Usually at night the chapters were read to the family, who followed the story with intense feeling. The narrative ran on for nine months, exciting great interest among the limited readers of the *Era*, and gaining sympathetic words from the anti-slavery people, but without making any wide impression on the public.

We may pause here in the narrative to note two things: the story was not the work of a novice, and it was written out of abundant experience and from an immense mass of accumulated thought and material. Mrs. Stowe was in her fortieth year. She had been using her pen since she was twelve years old, in extensive correspondence, in occasional essays, in short stories and sketches, some of which appeared in a volume called *The Mayflower*, published in 1843, and for many years her writing for newspapers and periodicals had added appreciably to the small family income. She was in the maturity of her intellectual powers, she was trained in the art of writing, and she had, as Walter Scott had when he began the Waverley Novels at the age of forty-three, abundant store of materials on which to draw. To be sure, she was on fire with a moral purpose, but she had the dramatic instinct, and she felt that her object would not be reached by writing an abolition tract.

In shaping her material the author had but one purpose, to show the institution of slavery truly, just as it existed. She had visited in Kentucky; had formed the acquaintance of people who were just, upright, and generous, and yet slaveholders. She had heard their views, and appreciated their situation; she felt that justice required that their difficulties should be recognized and their virtues acknowledged. It was her object to show that the evils of slavery were the inherent evils of a bad system, and not always the fault of those who had become involved in it and were its actual administrators. Then she was convinced that the presentation of slavery alone, in its most dreadful forms, would be a picture of such unrelieved horror and darkness as nobody could be induced to look at. Of set purpose, she sought to light up the darkness by humorous and grotesque episodes, and the presentation of the milder and more amusing phases of slavery, for which her recollection of the never-failing wit and drollery of her former colored friends in Ohio gave her abundant material.

This is her own account of the process, years after. But it is evident that, whether consciously or unconsciously, she did but follow the inevitable law of all great dramatic creators and true story-tellers since literature began.

From Charles Dudley Warner, "The Story of *Uncle Tom's Cabin*," *Atlantic Monthly* 78 (1896): 311–322.

# [Autobiographical Letter to Eliza Follen, 1852]

### Harriet Beecher Stowe

In 1852, as Stowe was planning her first trip to Great Britain and Europe, she received a letter from Eliza Follen, who asked for information about her life. Follen (1787–1860) was a well-known author of books for children, including *Words of Truth* (1832) and *Little Songs for Little Boys and Girls* (1832). She also contributed articles for the *Liberty Bell*, an antislavery annual, published from 1839 to 1858. Stowe, who admired Follen's work, sent her the following autobiographical memoir. Follen received the letter while she was traveling in England and shared it with numerous friends, including George Eliot. She, in turn, wrote a friend that "the whole letter is fascinating and makes one love her."[1] Stowe's letter was copied and reprinted in newspapers and magazines, in advance of her own trip to England in 1853. The letter became famous as a major source of information about Stowe's life and was widely used in books and articles about her.

Andover Dec$^r$. 16/52

My Dear Madam,

I hasten to reply to your letter to me the more interesting that I have long been acquainted with you, and during all the nursery part of my life, made daily use of your little poems for children. I used to think sometimes in those days that I would write to you & tell you how much I was obliged to you for the pleasure which they gave us all.

So you want to know something about what sort of a woman I am—well, if this is any object, you should have statistics free of charge.

To begin then, I am a little bit of a woman—somewhat more than 40—about as thin & dry as a pinch of snuff—never very much to look at in my best days—& looking like a used up article now. I was married when I was 25 years old to a man rich in Greek & Hebrew, Latin & Arabic, & alas! rich in nothing else. When I went to housekeeping, my entire stock of china for parlour & kitchen was bought for 11 dollars, & this lasted very well for 2 years, till my brother who was married & brought in his bride to visit

Harriet Beecher Stowe, ca. 1852 to 1853, calotype possibly taken in England. Harriet Beecher Stowe Center,
Hartford, Connecticut.

me; & I found upon review that I had neither plates nor teacups enough to
set a table for my father's family, wherefore I thought it best to reinforce the
establishment by getting me a tea-set which cost 10 dollars more, & this, I
believe, formed my whole stock in trade for some years.

But then I was abundantly enriched with wealth of another kind. I had
2 little curly headed twin daughters to begin with, & my stock in this line has
gradually increased till I have been the mother of 7 children, the most beautiful of which, & the most loved, lies buried near my Cincinati residence. It
was at *his* dying bed, & at *his* grave, that I learnt what a poor slave mother
may feel when her child is torn away from her. In the depths of sorrow,

which seemed to me immeasurable, it was my only prayer to God that such anguish might not be suffered in vain! There were circumstances about his death, of such peculiar bitterness, of what might seem almost cruel suffering, that I felt I could never be consoled for it, unless it should appear that this crushing of my own heart might enable me to work out some great good to others. It was during the cholera summer, when in a circle of 5 miles around me, in the short space of 3 months, 9000 were buried, a mortality which I have never heard exceeded any where. My husband in feeble health was obliged to be absent the whole time, & I had sole charge of a family of 15 persons. He could not return to me because I would not permit it, for in many instances, where parents abroad had returned to their families in the infected atmosphere, the result had been sudden death, & the physicians warned me that if he returned it would be only to die. My poor Charley died for want of medical aid timely rendered, for in the universal confusion & despair that prevailed, it was often impossible to obtain assistance till it was too late.

I allude to this now, because I have often felt that much that is in this book had its root in the awful scenes & bitter sorrows of that summer. It has left now, I trust, no trace in my mind, except a deep compassion for the sorrowful, especially for mothers who are separated from their children.

You have probably read the article in Frazer's Magazine. It is in most respects a true history, tho' I think somewhat coloured. In looking it over, tho' I could not deny that the facts had all occurred, yet it struck me that there was more the air of romance about it than was really consistent with truth. In one respect he is mistaken. He seems to think that the Anti Slavery collision in Lane Seminary was cause of the subsequent difficulties & embarrassments, pecuniary & otherwise, which rendered our Western residence arduous & uncomfortable. In this respect he is mistaken. The facts of the case were these. When we went out there, we found an Institution organized with that looseness of design & rudeness of conception which often attends enterprizes in a new country. All conceivable & contradictory impossibilities were to be accomplished by it. It was to embrace High School, College, Theological Seminary, & manual Labour Institution all together. My father & husband found a mixed multitude to the number of 300, of all ages & sizes from High School boys to men of 28 & 30 years, all mingling together in most admired disorder; everything to be done in the future, with no buildings or accommodations of any sort do it with. They took advantage of the Anti Slavery explosion to retrench & methodize this system of housekeeping. They cut off the Preparatory School & College, because there were an abundance of better ones in the immediate vicinity, & resolved to confine themselves to the one object of preparing young men already educated, for the ministry. Of course the outward show of scholars greatly decreased, & it was said that there was but a handful of them, but there were as many theological students as there had been before, only the other departments were wanting. The object was now to get the proper buildings & endowments for a permanent Theological Institution, by which an educated, intelligent Protestant ministry should be disseminated thro' the Western valley. Then came on that great pecuniary pressure which was felt all thro' America; banks & mercantile houses were failing all over the country, & the funds of our Institution were very seriously involved. My Father's whole support was lost in the failure of a mercantile house, & he supported himself, while he performed his duties as President of the Seminary, by being at the same time Pastor of a neighboring city church. The funds of Mr. Stowe's professorship were invested in banks which either failed or suspended payment, & our yearly income was reduced to a mere pittance. Still it was thought on all hands that we must not leave the position, but struggle on with what hope we might, till the Institution should be cleared from debt. It was the hardest trial of our life at this time, to be obliged to refuse continual invitations to return to New England, whose climate was more favourable to our health, & which was endeared to us as our native land, especially as these invitations were accompanied with offers of pecuniary competence.

During these long years of struggling with poverty & sickness, & a hot debilitating climate, my children grew up around me. The nursery & the kitchen were my principal fields of labour.

Some of my friends pitying my toils, copied & sent some of my little sketches to certain liberally paying annuals, with my name. With the first money that I earned in this way, I bought a feather bed! for as I had married into poverty & without a dowry, & as my husband had only a large library of books, & a great deal of learning, this bed & pillows was thought on the whole, the most profitable investment. After this, I thought I had discovered the philosopher's stone, & when a new carpet or a mattress was going to be needed, or when at the close of the year, it began to be evident that my family accounts, like poor Dora's, *"wouldn't add up"*,[2] then I used to say to my faithful friend & factotum Anna, who shared all my joys & sorrows, "now if you'll keep the babies & attend to all the things in the house for one day, I'll write a piece, & then we shall be out of the scrape", & so I became an authoress. Very modest, at first I do assure you, & remonstrating very seriously with the friends who had thought it best to put my name to the pieces, by way of getting up a reputation, & if you ever get to see a wood cut of me, with an inordinately long nose, on the cover of all the Anti Slavery almanacs I wish you to take notice that I have been forced into it, contrary to my natural modesty by the imperative solicitations of my dear 5000 friends & the public generally.

One thing I must say with regard to my life at the West, which you will understand better than many Englishwomen could.

I lived 2 miles from the city of Cincinati, in the country, & domestic service you know, not always to be found in the city, is next to an impossibility to be obtained in the country, even by those who are willing to give the highest wages. So what was to be expected for poor me who had very little of this world's good to offer? Had it not been for my inseparable friend Anna a noble hearted English girl, who landed on our American shores in destitution & sorrow, & who clave unto me as Ruth to Naomi, I had never lived through all the toil which this uncertainty & absolute want of domestic service imposed on both; you may imagine therefore how glad I was when our Seminary property being divided into small lots, which were rented out at a low price, a number of poor families setled in our vicinity, from whom we could occasionally obtain domestic services.—About a dozen families of liberated slaves were among the number, & they became my favorite resorts in cases of emergency.—If any body wants to have a black face look handsome, let them be left as I have been, in feeble health, in oppressive, hot weather, with a sick baby in arms, & two or three other little ones in the nursery, and not a servant in the whole house to do a single turn: & then if they should see my good old aunt Frankie, coming in with her honest, bluff, black face, her long, strong arms, her chest as big & stout as a barrel, & her hilarious hearty laugh, perfectly delighted to take one's washing, & do it at a fair price, they would appreciate the beauty of black people—My cook, poor Eliza Buck (how she would stare to think of her name's going to England) was a regular epitome of slave life in herself, fat gentle, easy, loving & loveable, always calling my very modest house & door yard, "The Place" as if it had been a plantation with 700 hands on it.—Her way of arranging her kitchen was at first somewhat like Dinah's, though she imbibed our ideas more rapidly, & seemed more ready to listen to suggestions, than did that dignitary. She had lived through the whole sad story of a Virginia-raised slave's life. In her youth she must have been a very handsome mulatto girl. Her voice was sweet & her manner refined & agreeable— She was raised in a good family as nurse & sempstress. When the family became embarrassed, she was suddenly sold onto a plantation in Louisiana; She has often told me how without any warning, she was suddenly forced into a carriage, & saw her little mistress screaming & stretching her arms from the window towards her, as she was driven away. She has told me of scenes on the Louisiana plantations & how she has often been out in the night by stealth, ministering to poor slaves, who had been mangled & lacerated by the whip.—Thence she was sold again into Kentucky, & her last master was the father of all her children. On this point she always maintained a delicacy & reserve, which, though it is not at all uncommon among slave women, always appeared to me remarkable—She always called him her husband, & spoke of him with the same apparent feeling with which any woman regards her husband, & it was not till after she had lived with me some years that I discovered accidentally, the real nature of the connexion.—I shall never forget how sorry I felt for her, nor my feelings at her humble apology—"You know, Mrs. Stowe, slave women can't help themselves". She had two very pretty quadroon daughters with beautiful hair & eyes, interesting children, whom I had instructed in the family school with my children. Time would fail me to tell you all that I learnt incidentally of the working of the slave system, in the history of various slaves, who came into my family and of the *underground railroad*, which I may say ran through our barn. But I have made my labor already too long.—

You ask with regard to the remuneration which I have received for my work, here in America. Having been poor all my life, & expecting to be poor to the end of it, the idea of making anything by a book which I wrote just because I could not help it, never occurred to me. It was therefore, an agreeable surprise to receive ten thousand dollars as the first fruits of 3 months' sale. I presume as much more is now due.—Mr. Bosworth in England, the firm of Clark & Co, & Mr. Bentley have all offered to me an interest in the sales of their editions in London. I am very glad of it, both on account of the value of what they offer, & the value of the example they set in a matter, wherein, I think, justice has been too little regarded.—

I have been invited to visit Scotland, & shall probably spend the summer there & in England.—I have very much at heart, a design to erect in some of the Northern States, a normal school, for the education of coloured teachers in the United States & Canada. I have very much wished that some permanent memorial of good to the coloured race, might be erected out of the proceeds of a work, which had so unprecedented a sale.—

My own share of the profits will be less than that of the publishers either English or American, but I am willing to give largely for this purpose, & I feel no doubt that the American & English publishers, will be willing to unite with me, for nothing tends more immediately to the emancipation of the slave, than the education & elevation of the free.—

I am now writing a work which will contain perhaps an equal amount of matter with Uncle Tom's Cabin. It will contain all the facts & documents, on which that story was founded, & an immense body of facts, reports of trials, legal decisions &c &c testimony of people living in the South, which will more than confirm every statement in it & show how much more fact than fiction it is.

I must confess, that till I commenced the examinations necessary to write this, much as I thought I knew before, I had not *begun* to measure the depth of the abyss. The laws, records of courts & judicial proceedings are so incredible, as actually to make me doubt the evidence of my own eyesight, & fill me still with amazement, whenever I think of them.—It seems to me that the book cannot but be felt—& that coming upon the sensibility awakened by the other, it must do something.—

I suffer excessively in writing these things. It may truly be said I write with *heart's blood*.—Many times in writing "Uncle Tom's Cabin" I thought my health w[oul]d fail utterly, but I prayed earnestly that God would help me till I got thro'—& now I am pressed above measure, & beyond strength—This horror, this night mare, abomination! can it be *my* country! It lies like lead on my heart, it shadows my life with sorrow, the more so, that I feel, as for my own brothers, for the South—& I am pained by every horror that I am obliged to write, as one who is forced by an awful oath, to disclose in a court, some family disgrace! Many times I have thought I must die, & yet, I pray God that I may live to see something done. I shall probably be in London in May.—shall I see you?

It seems to me so odd & dream-like, that so many people want to see me—and I can't help thinking, that they will think that God hath "chosen the weak things of the world" when they do.—If I live till Spring, then I shall hope to see Shakespeare's grave & Milton's mulberry tree & the good land of my fathers—old, old England! May that day come.

Y<sup>rs</sup> affect<sup>ly</sup>

H. B. STOWE

## Notes

1. George Eliot to Mr. and Mrs. Charles Bray, 12 March 1853, *The George Eliot Letters*, edited by Gordon S. Haight, vol. 2 (New Haven: Yale University Press, 1954), p. 92.

2. Dora is David Copperfield's childlike wife in the novel *David Copperfield* (1850) by Charles Dickens.

The original letter no longer exists, and the text used here is taken from a copy in Dr. Williams's Library, London, transcribed by Dr. David Wykes, Director, Dr. Williams's Library.

# [Stowe and *Uncle Tom's Cabin*, 1853]

## Fanny Fern

As a teacher at Catharine Beecher's Hartford Female Seminary in the 1820s, Stowe met Sara Willis (1811–1872), a student who enrolled in 1827. The lively Willis quickly gained a reputation as a prankster and a rebel, and Stowe later remembered her as a "bright laughing witch of a half saint, half sinner."[1] By 1851, Willis had taken the name Fanny Fern. In the same month that she sold her first article to a popular family newspaper, the *Olive Branch*, *Uncle Tom's Cabin* began appearing in the *National Era*. In short order, Fern and Stowe became two of the most well-known writers—male or female—in the United States. Although no book of the mid-nineteenth century could match *Uncle Tom's Cabin* for sales figures, both *Fern Leaves from Fanny's Portfolio* (1853) and her novel *Ruth Hall* (1855) were best-sellers. In demand for her newspaper articles, Fern signed an exclusive contract with the *New York Ledger* and published a weekly column until her death. In May 1853, a month before the publication of her first book, Fern wrote a column for the *Olive Branch*, in defense of her old friend against the criticism of Stowe's writing style in *Uncle Tom's Cabin* and attacks generated by her enormous success, including her triumphant tour of Great Britain and Europe. With her characteristic wit and humor, Fern debunks the critics even as she playfully urges Stowe to take charge of her own career.

"Mrs. Stowe's Uncle Tom is too graphic ever to have been written by a *woman*."—[Ex.][2]

"Too graphic to be written by a woman!" D'ye hear that, Mrs. Stowe? or has English thunder stopped up your American ears? Oh, I can tell you, Mrs. "Tom Cabin" that you've got to pay "for the bridge that has carried you over." Do you suppose that you can quietly take the wind out of everybody's sails, the way you have, without having harpoons, and lampoons, and all sorts of *miss*-iles thrown after you? No indeed; every distanced scribbler is perfectly frantic; they stoutly protest your book shows no genius, which fact is unfortunately corroborated by the difficulty your

Fanny Fern (Sara Willis Parton), undated pen and ink drawing by her daughter, Ellen Eldredge Parton. Fanny Fern and Ethel Parton Papers, Sophia Smith Collection, Smith College.

publishers find in disposing of it; they are transported with rage in proportion as *you* are *translated*. Everybody whose cat ever ran through your great grandfather's entry "knows all about you," and how long it took to cut your first "wisdom tooth." Then all the bitter sectarian enemies your wide awake brothers have evoked, and who are afraid to measure lances with them, huddle into a corner to revenge by "making mouths" at their sister!

Certainly; what right had you to get an "invitation to Scotland" free gratis? or to have "Apsley House" placed at your disposal, as soon as your orthodox toes touched English ground? or to have a "silver salver" presented to you? or to have lords and ladies, and dukes and duchesses paying homage to you? or in short to raise such a little young tornado to sweep through the four quarters of the globe? *you?* nothing but a woman—an *American* woman! And a *Beecher* at that! It is perfectly insufferable—one genius in a family is enough. There's your old patriarch father—God bless him!— there's material enough in him to make a dozen ordinary men, to say nothing of "Henry Ward" who's not so great an idiot as he might be! You see you had no "call" Mrs. Tom Cabin, to drop your babies and darning-needle to immortalize your name.

Well, I hope your feminine shoulders are broad enough and strong enough to bear all the abuse your presumption will call down upon you. All the men in your family, your husband included, belong to "the cloth," and consequently can't practice pistol shooting; there's where your enemies have you, you little simpleton! that's the only objection I have to Mr. Fern's "taking orders," for I've quite a "penchant" for ministers.

I trust you are convinced by this time that "Uncle Tom's Cabin" is a "flash in the pan." I'm sorry you have lost so much money by it, but it will go to show you, that women should have their ambition bounded by a grid-iron, and a darning-needle. If you had not meddled with your husband's *divine* inkstand for such a *dark* purpose, nobody would have said you was "40 years old, and looked like an Irish woman;" don't believe they've done with you yet; for I see that every steamer tosses fresh laurels on your orthodox head, from foreign shores, and foreign powers. Poor *unfortunate* Mrs. Tom Cabin! Aint you to be pitied?

FANNY FERN

## Notes

1. Quoted in Joyce Warren, *Fanny Fern: An Independent Woman* (New Brunswick: Rutgers University Press, 1992), p. 275.

2. Fern is evidently quoting an extract from an unidentified commentary on *Uncle Tom's Cabin.*

Fanny Fern. [Stowe and *Uncle Tom's Cabin*]. *Olive Branch*, 28 May 1853, p. 3. The American Antiquarian Society.

# [Stowe at a Performance of
## *Uncle Tom's Cabin*, 1853]

FRANCIS H. UNDERWOOD

Soon after the publication of *Uncle Tom's Cabin* in book form, dramatists began work on adaptations of the novel for the stage. In the absence of a copyright law protecting the works of fiction writers, Stowe had no control over the performances, nor did she derive any profit from the various and wildly popular versions. In the fall of 1853, a young Henry James saw a version written by Henry J. Conroy and staged by P. T. Barnum at his American Museum in New York. James later saw a much longer version of the play, written by George L. Aiken and performed by the George C. Howard troupe at the National Theatre in New York.[1] Deeply impressed by the play, James wrote in his autobiography:

> Uncle Tom, instead of making even one of the cheap short cuts through the medium in which books breathe, even as fishes in water, went gaily roundabout it altogether, as if a fish, a wonderful "leaping" fish, had simply flown through the air. This feat accomplished, the surprising creature could naturally fly anywhere, and one of the first things it did was thus to flutter down on every stage, literally without exception, in America and Europe. If the amount of life represented in such a work is measurable by the ease with which representation is taken up and carried further, carried even violently furthest, the fate of Mrs. Stowe's picture was conclusive: it simply sat down wherever it lighted and made itself, so to speak, at home; thither multitudes flocked afresh and there, in each case, it rose to its height again and went, with all its vivacity and good faith, through all its motions.[2]

When the Howard troupe brought the play to Boston, Francis Underwood, an editor with Phillips, Sampson, and Company who later helped found the *Atlantic Monthly*, took Stowe to see a performance of the play. Underwood evidently wrote the following account of the evening at the invitation of Florine Thayer McCray, a neighbor of Stowe's, who included it in her biography, *The Life and Work of Harriet Beecher Stowe* (1889).

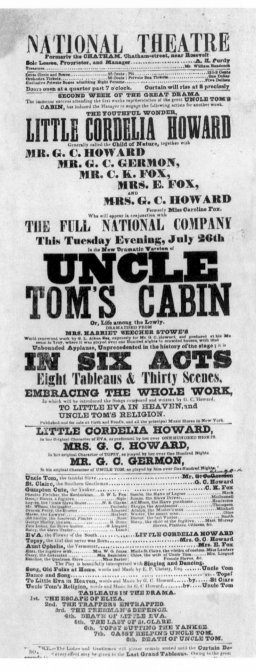

Broadside for the Aiken production of *Uncle Tom's Cabin* at the National Theatre, 26 July 1853. Harriet Beecher Stowe Center, Hartford, Connecticut.

IN THE WINTER of 1852 or 1853 a dramatic version of "Uncle Tom's Cabin" was performed at the National Theatre, Boston—a fine, large theatre, in the wrong place—that is to say, in one of the worst districts of Boston. It was burned a few years later, and never rebuilt. The dramatization was not very artistic, and the scenes introduced were generally the most ghastly ones of the painful story. Of the lightness and gayety of the book there was no sign. The actors were fairly good, but none of them remarkable, except the child who personated Eva, and the woman, (Mrs. Howard) who played Topsy.[3] Mrs. Howard was beyond comparison the best representative of the dark race I ever saw. She was a genius whose method no one could describe. In every look, gesture and tone there was an intuitive revelation of the strange, capricious and fascinating creature which Mrs. Stowe had conceived.

I asked Mrs. Stowe to go with me to see the play. She had some natural reluctance, considering the position her father had taken against the theatre, and considering the position of her husband as a preacher; but she also had some curiosity as a woman and as an author to see in flesh and blood the creations of her imagination. I think she told me she had never been in a theatre in her life. I procured the manager's box, and we entered privately, she being well muffled. She sat in the shade of the curtains of our box, and watched the play attentively. I never saw such delight upon a human face as she displayed when she first comprehended the full power of Mrs. Howard's *Topsy*. She scarcely spoke during the evening; but her expression was eloquent,—smiles and tears succeeding each other through the whole.

It must have been for her a thrilling experience to see her thoughts bodied upon the stage, at a time when any dramatic representation must have been to her so vivid. Drawn along by the threads of her own romance, and inexperienced in the deceptions of the theatre, she could not have been keenly sensible of the faults of the piece or the shortcomings of the actors.

I remember that in one scene *Topsy* came quite close to our box, with her speaking eyes full upon Mrs. Stowe's. Mrs. Stowe's face showed all her vivid and changing emotions, and the actress must surely have divined them. The glances when they met and crossed reminded me of the supreme look of Rachel when she repeated that indescribable *Helas!*[4] There was but a slight wooden barrier between the novelist and the actress—but it was enough! I think it a matter of regret that they never met.

The *Eliza* of the evening was a reasonably good actress, and skipped over the floating ice of the Ohio River with frantic agility.

The *Uncle Tom* was rather stolid—such a man as I have seen preaching among the negroes when I lived in Kentucky.

## Notes

1. Leon Edel, *Henry James: The Untried Years: 1832–1870* (Philadelphia: J. P. Lippincott, 1953), pp. 101–102; details about the performance are taken from Thomas F. Gossett, *Uncle Tom's Cabin and American Culture* (Dallas: Southern Methodist University Press, 1985), pp. 260–269; 274–275. See also Eric Lott, *Love and Theft: Blackface Minstrelsy and the American Working Class* (New York: Oxford University Press, 1993), pp. 211–233.

2. Henry James, *A Small Boy and Others* (New York: Charles Scribner's Sons, 1913), pp. 159–160.

3. Caroline Emily Fox Howard (1829–1908), the wife of the director of the troupe, was a well-known actress. Her cousin was George L. Aiken, commissioned by her husband to write a dramatic version of *Uncle Tom's Cabin*.

4. Rachel, the French actor Élisabeth Rachel Félix (1821–1858), was an international celebrity known for her performances in French tragedies. Her most famous role was in Jean Racine's *Phédre*, about a woman involved in a love triangle who commits suicide at the end of the play.

From Florine Thayer McCray, *The Life-Work of the Author of "Uncle Tom's Cabin"* (New York: Funk & Wagnalls, 1889), pp. 121–123.

# [Stowe and the Success of *Uncle Tom's Cabin*]

## J. C. DERBY

Throughout her life, Stowe was friendly with the editors and publishers of her books. James Cephas Derby (1818–1892) began his career as an apprentice to a publishing firm in Auburn, New York, and eventually formed his own company, J. C. Derby & Company. In 1848, he formed another company, Derby & Miller, and moved to New York City, where he published a variety of books, including biographies, histories, and school books. Derby encouraged the popular Fanny Fern to collect her newspaper articles, and he published her best-selling *Fern Leaves from Fanny's Portfolio* (1853). He published Stowe's *The Minister's Wooing* in 1859. Derby, who knew Stowe and her family well, included the following chapter on her success in his lengthy autobiography, *Fifty Years Among Authors, Books and Publishers* (1884). The recollection includes extensive quotations from Stowe's brother Henry Ward Beecher and discusses, at some length, the publication of *Uncle Tom's Cabin* and the impact of the novel on Stowe and her family in the 1850s.

THIS MOST FAMOUS WRITER of the Beecher family, and author of the most celebrated work of fiction ever published in America or indeed in the world during the present century, first became well known as an author in 1852, when the world-renowned *Uncle Tom's Cabin* first appeared as a serial in the *National Era*, an anti-slavery paper then published in Washington.

It was afterwards issued in two volumes in book form by John P. Jewett & Co. The sale of nearly a half million of copies in this country alone in five years, is without a parallel; this was more than thirty years ago, and its sale has continued unabated, many thousands being sold annually. That the interest in the story of Uncle Tom does not readily die out, is manifested by the continual representations in the theatres, for which it has often been dramatized. The sale of *Uncle Tom's Cabin* in foreign countries is thus graphically described in a long article published in the *Edinburgh Review*, of April, 1855.

[77]

Illustration for "Harriet Beecher Stowe" in *Our Famous Women* (1884), edited by Elizabeth Stuart Phelps. Love Library, University of Nebraska, Lincoln.

The first London edition was published in May, 1852, and was not large; for the European popularity of a picture of negro life was doubted. But in the following September the London publishers furnished to one house 10,000 copies per day for about four weeks, and had to employ 1,000 persons in preparing copies to supply the general demand. We cannot follow it beyond 1852; but at that time, more than a million copies had been sold in England, probably ten times as many as have been sold of any other work, except the Bible and Prayer Book. In France, "Uncle Tom" still covers the shop-windows of the Boulevards, and one publisher alone, Eustance Barba, has sent out five different editions in different forms. Before the end of 1852, it had been translated into Italian, Swedish, Danish, Dutch, Flemish, German, Polish and Magyar. There are two different Dutch and twelve different German translations, and the Italian translation enjoys the honor of the Pope's prohibition. It has been dramatized in twenty different forms and acted in every capital in Europe and in the free States of America.

The sales abroad have been so large that they cannot be computed, and on them no copyright returns have ever been received by the author. She has, however, something which she values more than the copyright, and that is, in addition to the place assigned her in English literature by the most eminent critics in the world, the letters and addresses which she has received from foreign states, cities and towns as noted below.

The following statement appears in a bibliographical account prefixed to a late edition of *Uncle Tom's Cabin*, published by Houghton, Mifflin & Co.

The next step in the history of "Uncle Tom" was a meeting at Stafford House, when Lord Shaftesbury recommended to the women of England, the sending of an "affectionate and Christian address to the women of America." This address, composed by Lord Shaftesbury, was taken in hand for signatures by energetic canvassers in all parts of England, and also among resident English on the Continent. The demand for signatures went as far as the City of Jerusalem. When they were all collected, the document was forwarded to the care of Mrs. Stowe in America, with a letter from Lord Carlisle, recommending it to her to be presented to the ladies of America in such way as she should see fit.

It was exhibited first at the Boston Anti-Slavery fair and now remains in its solid oak case in Mrs. Stowe's possession, a lasting monument of the feeling called forth by "Uncle Tom's Cabin." It is in twenty-six thick folio volumes, solidly bound in morocco with the American eagle on each. On the first page of the first volume is the address beautifully illuminated on vellum, and following, the subscriber's names, filling the volumes. There are five hundred and sixty-two thousand four hundred and forty-eight names of women of every rank of life, from the nearest in rank to the throne of England to the wives and daughters of the humblest artisan and laborer.

During a recent visit to Mrs. Stowe at her beautiful Hartford home, I was favored with an opportunity to examine the treasures above referred to. I was also both interested and amazed to see the different editions of *Uncle Tom's Cabin*. Besides the thirty-five different editions of that work in London and Edinburgh, there were nineteen translations in different languages, in which Uncle Tom appears under the following curious titles. It is called in French, "La Case de l'Oncle Tom;" in German, "Oncle Tom's Hütte;" in Danish, "Onkel Tomas;" in Dutch, "De Negerhut;" in Flemish, "De hut van Onkel Tom;" in Hungarian, "Tama's Batya;" in Italian, "La Capanno delo Zio Tommaso;" in Polish, "Chata Wuga Tomasza;" in Portugese, "A Cabana do Pai Thomas;" in Spanish, "La Cabana del Tio Tomas;" in Russian, "Khishina dyadi Toma;" in Swedish, "Onkel Tom's Stuga."

*Blackwood's Magazine*, in an article of more than thirty pages, devoted to the examination of the literary merits of *Uncle Tom's Cabin*, viewing it solely as a work of art, thus summed up its opinion of the author:

> Mrs. Stowe is unquestionably a woman of genius, and that is a word we always use charily, regarding genius as a thing per se different from talent, in its highest development, altogether, and in kind. Quickness, shrewdness, energy, intensity, may and frequently do accompany, but do not constitute genius. Its divine spark is the direct and special gift of God; we cannot completely analyze it, though we may detect its presence and the nature of many of its attributes, by its action; and the skill of high criticism is requisite in order to distinguish between the feats of genius and the operation of talent. Now, we imagine that no person of genius can read *Uncle Tom's Cabin* and not feel in glowing contact with genius—generally gentle and tender, but capable of rising with its theme into very high regions of dramatic power. This Mrs. Stowe had done several times in the work before us—exhibiting a passion, an intensity, a subtle delicacy of perception, a melting tenderness, which are as far out of reach of mere talent, however well trained and experienced, as the prismatic colors are out of reach of the born blind. But the genius of Mrs. Stowe is of that kind which instinctively addresses itself to the affections; and though most at home with the gentler, it can be yet fearlessly familiar with the fiercest passions which can

agitate and rend the human breast. With the one she can exhibit an exquisite tenderness and sympathy; watching the other, however, with stern but calm scrutiny and delineating both with a truth and simplicity in the one case touching, in the other really terrible.

Mrs. Stowe once said to me, while speaking of her brother, "Henry wrote me he wouldn't read *Uncle Tom's Cabin*, but he couldn't help it." And said he, "If you ever write such another book, I will kill you, if I have to go around the world to find you. You have taken more out of me than a whole year of preaching. I wish that all the slaveholders in the South and all the Northern sympathizers with them were shut up for a century and obliged to read 'Uncle Tom's Cabin.' I will say this for Henry. I never heard him speak a cross word in all my life. I have been very intimate with him and have seen him under very trying circumstances. He is the sweetest tempered person, although he is my brother; he is a mighty fellow and all feeling. When he is angry he doesn't say anything; he shuts his mouth and sits still. Henry doesn't look like the traditional idea of the saints, but he is one. Those saints were generally rolling up their eyes and wearing long faces. He doesn't do anything of that kind. He jokes and says good-natured things. I think good-nature is a virtue. I consider that God loves good-natured people."

At the garden party given in honor of Mrs. Stowe to commemorate her seventieth birthday, in June, 1882, I had the pleasure of hearing Oliver Wendell Holmes refer to these different editions of *Uncle Tom's Cabin* in foreign languages, in the following felicitous lines:

> If every tongue that speaks her praise,
> For whom I shape my tinkling phrase,
>     Were summoned to the table,
> The vocal chorus that would meet,
> Of mingled accents, harsh or sweet,
> From every land and tribe, would beat
>     The polyglots of Babel.
>
> Briton and Frenchman, Swede and Dane,
> Turk, Spaniard, Tartar of Ukraine,
>     Hidalgo, Cossack, Cadi,

High Dutchman and Low Dutchman too,
The Russian serf, the Polish Jew,
Arab, Armenian and Mantchoo,
    Would shout, "We know the lady!"

Mr. Beecher, on the occasion referred to above, in his eloquent and feeling remarks, said:

> I don't know whether it is in good taste for any other member of my father's family to join in the laudation of Mrs. Stowe, but if it is, I am a very proper one to do it. I know that for a long time after the publication of *Uncle Tom's Cabin* there were a great many very wise people who said they knew that she never wrote it herself, but that I did. The matter at last became so scandalous that I determined to put an end to it, and therefore I wrote "Norwood." That killed the thing dead. . . .[1]
>
> Now, I think we might have a good experience meeting here this afternoon, if every one would tell under what circumstances he read the book, and how he acted. I can still remember plainly the circumstances under which I finished it. I had got well into the second volume. It was Thursday. Sunday was looming up before me, and at the rate at which I was going there would not be time to finish it before Sunday, and I could never preach till I finished it. So I set myself to it and determined to finish it at once. I had got a considerable way into the second volume, and I recommended my wife to go to bed. I didn't want anybody down there. I soon began to cry. Then I went and shut all the doors, for I did not want any one to see me. Then I sat down to it and finished it that night, for I knew that only in that way should I be able to preach on Sunday. I know that many of you must have read it something as I did at that time.

In one of my conversations with Rev. Henry Ward Beecher, I asked him to tell me how Mrs. Stowe came to write the book. He replied, "Sister Harriet said to me one day, 'Have you ever seen the *National Era*?' (It was an anti-slavery paper established in Washington.) I said, 'No, I don't see it, but I can.' She said, 'Dr. Bailey, the editor, has sent a request to me to write him a story. I am going to send him one I think that will run through three or four of the papers.' That was the beginning of *Uncle Tom's Cabin*. Instead of running through three or four papers, it ran through about fifty, nearly a year. It produced such an effect that it was soon published in book form. It had got up to the point where it could be published in book form. Her publisher, John P. Jewett, was very anxious she should put it into one volume and not by any means into two, and he got me to write to her. I accordingly wrote, 'You know what difficulty there is in laying before the public any matter that is prejudicial to slavery. You have succeeded in this story, and if you do not make it too long, I think it will be a book that will have an important influence.' She never answered my letter and never said a word, but went on writing until she got to the end."

"Some one said to Mrs. Stowe one day, 'I don't see how you could have suffered Eva to die.' 'Well,' said she, 'I was sick in bed three days after her death.' The story was written every week and read in the family before it went off. Some of them said it was exactly like a history going on in some neighboring family and the news being brought over to them every day of how they were getting on. When Eva died, the house was as still and solemn as at a funeral."

"Mrs. Stowe always speaks of that book as not being hers. Sometimes people would speak to her of working up something else, and would say, 'You know how it was with "Uncle Tom's Cabin"'. 'Well,' she would answer, 'that wasn't mine, that was given to me.'"

"The persons in her story were not real, living characters, except so far as to give her a hint. There was a man said to be the original of Uncle Tom, who pleased her very much, and may have contributed one or two ideas. For one accustomed to writing fiction, only one or two hints are needed, and the whole scene pictures itself. Many of the characters in 'Uncle Tom's Cabin' were suggested by the people in her own house."

"There was one character named 'Sam,' who is represented early in the story as ingeniously assisting the escape of Eliza. The original of Sam was a very curious fellow. At one time he was convicted of stealing and was put in prison at Columbus. He afterwards came back to see us, and said he had been in the service of the State for a year or two. On making inquiries we found he had been in the state prison. Mrs. Stowe once said, 'I always have been sorry I let Sam die off, but I had nothing for him to do. Topsy had an original. She was just such a creature as is described in "Uncle Tom's Cabin". She lived on Walnut Hill, Cincinnati. Her name was Celeste.'"

"Mrs. Stowe's conversations about negro people, when she is in a narrative mood, are equal to anything in 'Uncle Tom's Cabin.' Sojourner Truth once gave Mrs. Stowe an account of her life. It is a most extraordinary narrative of events which never could have occurred anywhere except among these American negroes. Mrs. Stowe's recital of this story is very touching. When she was in Rome she related it to Mrs. Browning and the sculptor

Story, at the house of the former. They were so struck with it, that parties were afterwards formed there to hear her give narrative accounts of some of these negro characters. I have sometimes thought she narrated better than she wrote."

After this, I said, "Mr. Beecher, this is very interesting. Tell me more about your sister's habits while writing." He went on to say: "Harriet Stowe's habits in those days were peculiar. She would owl about all day, go to look at a picture, get a book, and sit down in a corner and read; if anyone talked to her she couldn't hear what was said and did not know. In the afternoon she would go to sleep. About five or six o'clock she would begin to twinkle and look around and perhaps make some comical remark. Towards evening she would commence to talk for two or three hours, and her conversation was perfectly fascinating. She had a wonderful memory. She could recite pretty much all of the English classics, among others passages from Goldsmith, Dryden, Shakspeare and Milton. I don't mean that she could recite the whole of their poems, but passages that would come in pat. If one was talking about anything and should say, 'How does that run?' she would catch the note and recite it. So with the Bible; she could recite it almost from beginning to end."

"I remember at one time when she was a child, so young as to subject to discipline, her mother for some reason, boxed her ears and refused to give her any supper. She went out into the garden and picked a lot of quince blossoms and brought them up into the chamber where I was, I believe, in equal disgrace, and commenced pulling off the petals and eating them, saying: 'I will have some supper.'" [. . .]

In the year 1859, my firm became the publishers of her next book, entitled, *The Minister's Wooing*, which many consider her best work next after Uncle Tom. In an unpublished letter of Archbishop Whateley, he pronounces *The Minister's Wooing* to be superior, from a literary point of view, to anything Mrs. Stowe has ever written. Mr. Gladstone also wrote that "he had just been reading the book and expressed himself much delighted with it. He considered it one of the most charming pictures of Puritan life possible, and he thought the different characters were differentiated remarkably well."

In another letter to Professor Stowe, Dean Alford wrote: "I read *The Minister's Wooing* with interest and pleasure. You will allow me to say that I like it best of all Mrs. Stowe's tales. The picture which it gives of the

Calvinistic Life of New England is most interesting and informing." Professor Stowe himself is the author of a very able work on the origin of the Bible, and several theological works.

## Note

1. Derby's ellipses.

From J. C. Derby, *Fifty Years Among Authors, Books and Publishers* (New York: G. W. Carleton & Co., 1884), pp. 452–460.

# [First Meeting with Stowe, 1853]

## FREDERICK DOUGLASS

Stowe's first contact with Frederick Douglass came in a famous letter she wrote to him in July 1851. Asking if he could provide information for the "series of articles that I am furnishing for the *Era* under the title of 'Uncle Tom's Cabin or Life among the lowly,'" she wrote. "In the course of my story, the scene will fall upon a cotton plantation—I am very desirous to gain information from one who has been an actual labourer on one—& it occurred to me that in the circle of your acquaintance there might be one who would be able to communicate to me some such information as I desire."[1] Although there is no record of Douglass's response to this letter, he was a cautious admirer of *Uncle Tom's Cabin*, and the two began to correspond and developed a long friendship. As Douglass explains in this section from his third autobiography, the *Life and Times of Frederick Douglass* (1881), Stowe invited him to visit her shortly before she traveled to Great Britain in 1853. In addition to recording his impressions of her, Douglass also reveals his frustrations with Stowe. He had hoped that she would help fund an industrial school for black men with some of the proceeds of her books and contributions from British antislavery activists. Although she later contributed money to his periodical, *Frederick Douglass's Paper*, Stowe was not interested in helping with his school, much to Douglass's disappointment.

IN THE MIDST of these fugitive slave troubles came the book known as *Uncle Tom's Cabin*, a work of marvelous depth and power. Nothing could have better suited the moral and humane requirements of the hour. Its effect was amazing, instantaneous, and universal. No book on the subject of slavery had so generally and favorably touched the American heart. It combined all the power and pathos of preceding publications of the kind, and was hailed by many as an inspired production. Mrs. Stowe at once became an object of interest and admiration. She had made fortune and fame at home, and had awakened a deep interest abroad. Eminent persons in England roused to anti-slavery enthusiasm by her *Uncle Tom's Cabin*, invited her to visit that country, and promised to give her a testimonial. Mrs. Stowe

Frederick Douglass, frontispiece of *My Bondage and My Freedom*
(1855). Love Library, University of Nebraska, Lincoln.

accepted the invitation and the proffered testimonial. Before sailing for
England, however, she invited me from Rochester, N. Y., to spend a day
at her house in Andover, Mass. Delighted with an opportunity to become
personally acquainted with the gifted authoress, I lost no time in making
my way to Andover. I was received at her home with genuine cordiality.
There was no contradiction between the author and her book. Mrs. Stowe
appeared in conversation equally as well as she appeared in her writing.
She made to me a nice little speech in announcing her object in sending
for me. "I have invited you here," she said, "because I wish to confer with
you as to what can be done for the free colored people of the country. I
am going to England and expect to have a considerable sum of money
placed in my hands, and I intend to use it in some way, for the permanent

improvement of the free colored people, and especially for that class which has become free by their own exertions. In what way I can do this most successfully is the subject I wish to talk with you about. In any event I desire to have some monument rise after *Uncle Tom's Cabin*, which shall show that it produced more than a transient influence." She said several plans had been suggested, among others an educational institution pure and simple, but that she thought favorably of the establishment of an industrial school; and she desired me to express my views as to what I thought would be the best plan to help the free colored people. I was not slow to tell Mrs. Stowe all I knew and had thought on the subject. As to a purely educational institution, I agreed with her that it did not meet our necessities. I argued against expending money in that way. I was also opposed to an ordinary industrial school where pupils should merely earn the means of obtaining an education in books. There were such schools, already. What I thought of as best was rather a series of workshops, where colored people could learn some of the handicrafts, learn to work in iron, wood, and leather, and where a plain English education could also be taught. I argued that the want of money was the root of all evil to the colored people. They were shut out from all lucrative employments and compelled to be merely barbers, waiters, coachmen and the like at wages so low that they could lay up little or nothing. Their poverty kept them ignorant and their ignorance kept them degraded. We needed more to learn how to make a good living than to learn Latin and Greek. After listening to me at considerable length, she was good enough to tell me that she favored my views, and would devote the money she expected to receive abroad to meeting the want I had described as the most important; by establishing an institution in which colored youth should learn trades as well as to read, write, and count. When about to leave Andover, Mrs. Stowe asked me to put my views on the subject in the form of a letter, so that she could take it to England with her and show it to her friends there, that they might see to what their contributions were to be devoted. I acceded to her request and wrote her the following letter for the purpose named.

ROCHESTER, March 8, 1853.

MY DEAR MRS. STOWE:

You kindly informed me, when at your house a fortnight ago, that you designed to do something which should permanently contribute to the improvement and elevation of the free colored people in the United States. You especially expressed an interest in such of this class as had become free by their own exertions, and desired most of all to be of service to them. In what manner and by what means you can assist this class most successfully, is the subject upon which you have done me the honor to ask my opinion. . . . I assert, then, that poverty, ignorance, and degradation are the combined evils; or in other words, these constitute the social disease of the free colored people of the United States.

To deliver them from this triple malady is to improve and elevate them, by which I mean simply to put them on an equal footing with their white fellow-countrymen in the sacred right to "Life, Liberty, and the pursuit of happiness." I am for no fancied or artificial elevation, but only ask fair play. How shall this be obtained? I answer, first, not by establishing for our use high schools and colleges. Such institutions are, in my judgment, beyond our immediate occasions and are not adapted to our present most pressing wants. High schools and colleges are excellent institutions, and will in due season be greatly subservient to our progress; but they are the result, as well as they are the demand, of a point of progress which we as a people have not yet attained. Accustomed as we have been to the rougher and harder modes of living, and of gaining a livelihood, we cannot and we ought not to hope that in a single leap from our low condition, we can reach that of Ministers, Lawyers, Doctors, Editors, Merchants, etc. These will doubtless be attained by us; but this will only be when we have patiently and laboriously, and I may add successfully, mastered and passed through the intermediate gradations of agriculture and the mechanic arts. Besides, there are (and perhaps this is a better reason for my view of the case) numerous institutions of learning in this country, already thrown open to colored youth. To my thinking, there are quite as many facilities now afforded to the colored people as they can spare the time, from the sterner duties of life, to judiciously appropriate. In their present condition of poverty, they cannot spare their sons and daughters two or three years at boarding-schools or colleges, to say nothing of finding the means to sustain them while at such institutions. I take it, therefore, that we are well provided for in this respect; and that it may be fairly inferred from the fact, that the facilities for our education, so far as schools and colleges in the Free States are concerned, will increase quite in proportion with our future wants. Colleges have been open to colored youth in this country during the last dozen years. Yet few, comparatively, have acquired a classical education; and even this few have found themselves educated far above a living condition there being no methods by which they could turn their learning to account. Several of this latter class have entered the ministry; but you need not be told that an educated people is needed to sustain an educated ministry. There must be a certain amount of cultivation among the people, to sustain such a ministry. At present we have not that cultivation amongst us; and, therefore, we value in the preacher strong lungs rather than high learning. I do not say that educated ministers are not needed amongst us, far from it! I wish there were more of them! but to increase their number is not the largest benefit you can bestow upon us.

We have two or three colored lawyers in this country; and I rejoice in the fact; for it affords very gratifying evidence of our progress. Yet it must be confessed that, in point of success, our lawyers are as great failures as our ministers. White people will not employ them to the obvious embarrassment of their causes, and the blacks, taking their cue from the whites, have not sufficient confidence in their abilities to employ them. Hence educated colored men, among the colored people, are at a very great discount. It would seem that education and emigration go together with us, for as soon as a man rises amongst us, capable, by his genius and learning, to do us great service, just so soon he finds that he can serve himself better by going elsewhere. In proof of this, I might instance the Russwurms, the Garnetts, the Wards, the Crummells, and others, all men of superior ability and attainments, and capable of removing mountains of prejudice against their race, by their simple presence in the country; but these gentlemen, finding themselves embarrassed here by the peculiar disadvantages to which I have referred, disadvantages in part growing out of their education, being repelled by ignorance on the one hand, and prejudice on the other, and having no taste to continue a contest against such odds, have sought more congenial climes, where they can live more peaceable and quiet lives. I regret their election, but I cannot blame them; for with an equal amount of education, and the hard lot which was theirs, I might follow their example. . . .

There is little reason to hope that any considerable number of the free colored people will ever be induced to leave this country, even if such a thing were desirable. The black man (unlike the Indian) loves civilization. He does not make very great progress in civilization himself, but he likes to be in the midst of it, and prefers to share its most galling evils, to encountering barbarism. Then the love of country, the dread of isolation, the lack of adventurous spirit, and the thought of seeming to desert their "brethren in bonds," are a powerful check upon all schemes of colonization, which look to the removal of the colored people, without the slaves. The truth is, dear madam, we are here, and here we are likely to remain. Individuals emigrate—nations never. We have grown up with this republic, and I see nothing in her character, or even in the character of the American people, as yet, which compels the belief that we must leave the United States. If, then, we are to remain here, the question for the wise and good is precisely that which you have submitted to me—namely: What can be done to improve the condition of the free people of color in the United States? The plan which I humbly submit in answer to this inquiry (and in the hope that it may find favor with you, and with the many friends of humanity who honor, love and coöporate with you) is the establishment in Rochester, N. Y., or in some other part of the United States equally favorable to such an enterprise, of an INDUSTRIAL COLLEGE in which shall be taught several important branches of the mechanic arts. This college shall be open to colored youth. I will pass over the details of such an institution as I propose. . . . Never having had a day's schooling in all my life, I may not be expected to map out the details of a plan so comprehensive as that involved in the idea of a college. I repeat, then, that I leave the organization and administration of the institution to the superior wisdom of yourself and the friends who second your noble efforts. The argument in favor of an Industrial College (a college to be conducted by the best men, and the best workmen which the mechanic arts can afford; a college where colored youth can be instructed to use their hands, as well as their heads; where they can be put in possession of the means of getting a living whether their lot in after life may be cast among civilized or uncivilized men; whether they choose to stay here, or prefer to return to the land of their fathers) is briefly this: Prejudice against the free colored people in the United States has shown itself nowhere so invincible as among mechanics. The farmer and the professional man cherish no feeling so bitter as that cherished by these. The latter would starve us out of the country entirely. At this moment I can more easily get my son into a lawyer's office to study law than I can into a blacksmith's shop to blow the bellows and to wield the sledge-hammer. Denied the means of learning useful trades, we are pressed into the narrowest limits to obtain a livelihood. In times past we have been the hewers of wood and drawers of water for American society, and we once enjoyed a monopoly in menial employments, but this is so no longer. Even these employments are rapidly passing away out of our hands. The fact is (every day begins with the lesson, and ends with the lesson) that colored men must learn trades; must find new employments; new modes of usefulness to society, or that they must decay under the pressing wants to which their condition is rapidly bringing them.

We must become mechanics; we must build as well as live in houses; we must make as well as use furniture; we must construct bridges as well as pass over them, before we can properly live or be respected by our fellow men. We need mechanics as well as ministers. We need workers in iron, clay, and leather. We have orators, authors, and other professional men, but these reach only a certain class, and get respect for our race in certain select circles. To live here as we ought we must fasten ourselves to our countrymen through their every-day, cardinal wants. We must not only be able to black boots, but to make them. At present we are, in the northern States, unknown as mechanics. We give no proof of genius or skill at the county, State, or national fairs. We are unknown at any of the great exhibitions of the industry of our fellow-citizens, and being unknown, we are unconsidered.

The fact that we make no show of our ability is held conclusive of our inability to make any, hence all the indifference and contempt with which incapacity is regarded fall upon us, and that too when we have had no means of disproving the infamous opinion of our natural inferiority. I have, during the last dozen years, denied before the Americans that we are an inferior race; but this has been done by arguments based upon admitted principles rather than by the presentation of facts. Now, firmly believing, as I do, that there are skill, invention, power, industry, and real mechanical genius among the colored people, which will bear favorable testimony for them, and which only need the means to develop them, I am decidedly in favor of the establishment of such a college as I have mentioned. The benefits of such an institution would not be confined to the Northern States, nor to the free colored people. They would extend over the whole Union. The slave not less than the freeman would be benefited by such an institution. It must be confessed that the most powerful argument now used by the southern slaveholder, and the one most soothing to his conscience, is that derived from the low condition of the free colored people of the North. I have long felt that too little attention has been given by our truest friends in this country to removing this stumbling-block out of the way of the slave's liberation.

The most telling, the most killing refutation of slavery is the presentation of an industrious, enterprising, thrifty, and intelligent free black population. Such a population I believe would rise in the Northern States under the fostering care of such a college as that supposed.

To show that we are capable of becoming mechanics I might adduce any amount of testimony; but, dear madam, I need not ring the changes on such a proposition. There is no question in the mind of any unprejudiced person that the Negro is capable of making a good mechanic. Indeed, even those who cherish the bitterest feelings toward us have admitted that the apprehension that negroes might be employed in their stead dictated the policy of excluding them from trades altogether. But I will not dwell upon this point, as I fear I have already trespassed too long upon your precious time, and written more than I ought to expect you to read. Allow me to say in conclusion that I believe every intelligent colored man in America will approve and rejoice at the establishment of some such institution as that now suggested. There are many respectable colored men, fathers of large families, having boys nearly grown up, whose minds are tossed by day and by night with the anxious inquiry, What shall I do with my boys? Such an institution would meet the wants of such persons. Then, too, the establishment of such an institution would be in character with the eminently practical philanthropy of your transatlantic friends. America could scarcely object to it as an attempt to agitate the public mind on the subject of slavery, or to dissolve the Union. It could not be tortured into a cause for hard words by the American people, but the noble and good of all classes would see in the effort an excellent motive, a benevolent object, temperately, wisely, and practically manifested.

Wishing you, dear madam, renewed health, a pleasant passage and safe return to your native land.

I am, most truly, your grateful friend,

FREDERICK DOUGLASS.

I was not only requested to write the foregoing letter for the purpose indicated, but I was also asked, with admirable foresight, to see and ascertain, as far as possible, the views of the free colored people themselves in respect to the proposed measure for their benefit. This I was able to do in July, 1853, at the largest and most enlightened colored convention that, up to that time, had ever assembled in this country. This convention warmly approved the plan of a manual labor school, as already described, and expressed high appreciation of the wisdom and benevolence of Mrs. Stowe. This convention was held in Rochester, N. Y., and will long be remembered there for the surprise and gratification it caused our friends in that city. They were not looking for such exhibition of enlightened zeal and ability as were there displayed in speeches, addresses, and resolutions; and in the conduct of the business for which it had assembled. Its proceedings attracted wide-spread attention at home and abroad.

While Mrs. Stowe was abroad, she was attacked by the pro-slavery press of our country so persistently and vigorously, for receiving money for her own private use, that the Rev. Henry Ward Beecher felt called upon to notice and reply to them in the columns of the New York *Independent*, of which he was then the editor. He denied that Mrs. Stowe was gathering British gold for herself, and referred her assailants to me, if they would learn what she intended to do with the money. In answer to her maligners, I denounced their accusations as groundless, and assured the public through the columns of my paper, that the testimonial then being raised in England by Mrs. Stowe, would be sacredly devoted to the establishment of an industrial school for colored youth. This announcement was circulated by other journals, and the attacks ceased. Nobody could well object to such application of money, received from any source, at home or abroad. After her return to this country, I called again on Mrs. Stowe, and was much disappointed to learn from her that she had reconsidered her plan for the industrial school. I have never been able to see any force in the reasons for this change. It is enough, however, to say that they were sufficient for her, and that she no doubt acted conscientiously, though her change of purpose was a great disappointment, and placed me in an awkward position before the colored people of this country, as well as to friends abroad, to whom I had given assurances that the money would be appropriated in the manner I have described.

## Note

1. Harriet Beecher Stowe to Frederick Douglass, 9 July 1851; quoted by permission of the E. Bruce Kickham Collection, Harriet Beecher Stowe Center, Hartford, CT.

From Frederick Douglass, *Life and Times of Frederick Douglass* (Hartford, CT: Park Publishing Co., 1881), pp. 289–296.

# [Letters about Stowe, 1852–1853]

## HARRIET JACOBS

Although Stowe helped a number of former slaves, her response to a request for assistance from Harriet Jacobs (1813–1897) reveals the contradictory attitudes shared by many white, middle-class women in the nineteenth century. Born a slave, Jacobs escaped by living in hiding for seven years and then making her way to the North, where she worked as a domestic servant for the writer Nathaniel P. Willis and his wife, Cornelia Grinnell Willis. In 1852, Cornelia Willis arranged to buy Jacobs and her children from their former mistress and also arranged for their emancipation. Now a free woman, Jacobs began to think of writing the story of her own life and received strong encouragement from Amy Post (1802–1889), a woman's rights and antislavery activist. Jacobs hoped that her life story would aid the antislavery movement, but she was uncertain of how to go about it and whether she wanted to tell her story herself, especially since she had never been married to her children's father.[1] Post, who knew all the details of Jacobs's life, offered to contact Stowe, now famous for *Uncle Tom's Cabin*, who might be interested in helping Jacobs publish her life story. Jacobs wrote out a sketch of her life, and Post sent it in a letter to Stowe.

In the meantime, Jacobs and Cornelia Willis (who did not know the details of Jacobs's children's parentage) learned in a newspaper about Stowe's impending departure for England. Jacobs was eager to help her daughter, Louisa, find a position, perhaps in the antislavery movement, and thought Stowe would find the young woman useful in her antislavery activities. She asked Willis to write to Stowe, asking the famous writer to include Louisa on the trip. Jacobs, who also hoped that Louisa might be able to interest Stowe in helping her publish her story, had saved money from her wages and planned to pay Louisa's expenses herself. Stowe responded to Willis's letter, flatly rejecting the idea of taking Louisa because she feared that such an experience would spoil her. Further, Stowe included Post's original letter with Jacobs's sketch and asked Willis to verify the details so that she might use some of Jacobs's story in her *A Key to Uncle Tom's Cabin*, which she was completing before her departure for England. Jacobs was outraged when Willis told her of Stowe's response, angered by Stowe's insensitivity in revealing the private details of her life to Willis, her rejection of Louisa, and her apparent desire to incorporate details about Jacobs's life into her own book. Willis wrote Stowe, asking her not to use Jacobs's story but offering to provide factual informa-tion. Jacobs also wrote to Stowe, offering to provide details about slavery for her *Key* but not her full story. But Stowe did not respond. As Jacobs wrote to Post in October 1853, "Mrs Stowe never answered any of my letters after I refused to have my history in her key. Perhaps its for the best. At least I will try and think so." [2] Ultimately, Jacobs told her own story in *Incidents in the Life of a Slave Girl* (1861).

In the following letters to Post, written in great agitation and haste, Jacobs reveals her assessment of Stowe's actions and attitudes. In the texts, which I have transcribed from the original manuscripts, I have incorporated Jacobs's few deletions and interlineations. To aid in reading, I have inserted in square brackets letters she inadvertently omitted from words and silently added ter-minal punctuation and capitalization, but I have not otherwise altered her punctuation or spelling.

Cornwall Orrange Co.[3]

My Dear Friend

Yours of the 24 was recieved on the 27th and my pen will fail to describe my greatful feelings on reading it. Although you could never be forgotten yet you do not know how much itt cheers my sad heart and how much I ap-preciate a word of sympathy and friendship from those I love for you little know how much I have had to pass through since we last meet. But it is a blessing that we can say a word in this way to each other. Many far more deserving than myself has been debared from this privilege.

I answered Mrs Hallowell kind letter which I hope she recieved. I wrote Mrs Bush also but I recieved a letter yesterday by the way of New York from her. Will you please say that I had written? I am sorry to have given her so much trouble but I have been unfortunate twice and I thought this would be more sure to come to hand. My best love to her. I am glad her hopes were realised in a sweet little Daughter and hope she may be blessed in having her health and strength restored before she leaves our shores. I am sorry to hear Dear little Willie looks so delicate. I should dearly love to see him and oh my dear friend how much I would prise a few hours with you at this

Harriet Jacobs, 1894. By permission.

present time but we poor mortals must always strive to teach our hearts submission to our circumstances. It is a hard lesson but it is a blessing to those who truly practice it.

Your proposal to me has been thought over and over again but not with out some most painful rememberances. Dear Amy if it was the life of a Heroine with no degradation associated with it. Far better to have been one of the starving poor of Ireland whose bones had to bleach on the highways than to have been a slave with the curse of slavery stamped upon yourself and Children. Your purity of heart and kindly sympathies won me at one time to speak of my children. It is the only words that has passed my lips since I left my Mothers door. I had determined to let others think as they pleased but my lips should be sealed and no one had a right to question me. For this reason when I first came North I avoided the Antislavery people as much as possible because I felt that I could not be honest and tell the whole truth. Often have I gone to my poor Brother with my grieved and mortified spirits. He would mingle his tears with mine while he would advise me to do what was right. My conscience approved it but my stubborn pride would not yeild. I have tried for the last two years to conquer it and I feel that God has helped me or I never would consent to give my past life to any one for I would not do it with out giving the whole truth. If it could help save another from my fate it would be selfish and unchristian in me to keep it back. Situated as I am I do not see any way that I could put it forward. Mrs Willis thinks it would do much good in Mrs Stowe hand but I could not ask her to take any step. Mr W is too proslavery he would tell me that it was very wrong and that I was trying to do harm or perhaps he was sorry for me to undertake it while I was in his family. Mrs Willis thinks if [it] is not done in my day it will [be] a good legacy for my children to do it after my death but now is the time when their is so much excitement everywhere. Mrs Hallowell said in her letter that you thought of going to New York in the course of a few weeks. If you will let me know when I will meet you there. I can give you my Ideas much better than write them.

If the Antislavery society could prapare this I would be willing to exert my self in any way that they thought best for the welfare of the cause.

They do not know me. They have heard of me as John Jacobs sister.

My dear friend would you be willing to make this proposal? I would rather have you do it than any one else. You could do it better. I should be happier in remembering it was you. If Mrs Stowe would undertake it I should like to be with her a Month. I should want the History of my childhood and the first five years in one volume and the next three and my home in the northern states in the secont. Besids I could give her some fine sketches for her pen on slavery. Give my love to your dear Husband and sons. Kiss Willie for me. Love to all. God bless. Yours Harriet

Feby 14th [1853]

My Dear Friend

I recieved your kind letter yesterday. If silence is expressive of ones deep feeling then in this way I must ask you to recieve the emotions of what my heart and pen cannot express hoping the time is not far distant when we may see each other. But I must tell you what I am trying to accomplish. Having seen the notice in the paper of Mrs Stowe intention to visit England I felt there would not be much hope of coming before her for some time and I thought if I could get her to take Louisa with her she might get interested enough. If she could do nothing herself she might help Louisa to do something. Besides I thought Louisa would be a very good representative of a Southern Slave. She has improved much in her studies and I think that she has energy enough to do something for the cause. She only needs to to be put in the field. I told my Ideas to Mrs Willis. She thought they were good and offered to write Mrs Stowe. She wrote last Tuesday asking her protection and if she would place her in some Antislavery family unless her services could be useful to her which I would perfer myself intending to pay her expenses there. The letter was directed as yours. When it is answered you shall know dear Amy. Since I have no fear of my name coming before those whom I have lived in dread of I can not be happy without trying to be useful in some way. I had a kind note from dear Sarah saying that she would be in New york on the 20th and wished to know our street and number. I am going down to see her and Mrs Bush and if Mrs B do not sail on the 20th will you drop me a line to let me know? I send an answer to Sarah to day also as she will not be there unless Mrs B sails. I shall be more than glad to see you all.[4]

April 4th [1853]

My Dear friend

I steal this moment to scratch you a few lines. I should have writen you before but I have been waiting with the hope of having some thing to tell you from our friend Mrs Stowe. But as it is I hardly know where to begin for my thoughts come rushing down with such a spirit of rivalry each wishing to be told you first so that they fill my heart and make my eyes dim therefore my silence must express to you what my poor pen is not capable of doing. But you know dear Amy that I have a heart towards you filled with love and gratitude for all the interest you have so kindly shown in my behalf. I wish that I could sit by you and talk instead of writing but that pleasure is denied and I am thankful for this. Mrs Stowe recieved your letter and Mrs Willis. She said it would be much care to her to take Louisa as she went by invitation it would not be right and she was afraid that if her situation as a Slave should be known it would subject her to much petting and patronizing which would be more pleasing to a young Girl than useful and the English was very apt to do it and sh[e] was very much opposed to it with this class of people. I will leave the rest for you to solve but remem[ber] that I mene to pay Louisa expenses. Your letter she sent to Mrs Willis asking might she trouble her so far as to ask if this most extraordinary event was true in all its bearings and if she might use it in her key. I had never opend my lips to Mrs Willis concerning my Children. In the Charitableness of her own heart she sympathised with me and never asked their origin. My suffering she knew. It embarrassed me at first but I told her the truth but we both thought it was wrong in Mrs Stowe to have sent you[r] letter. She might have written to enquire if she liked. Mrs Willis wrote her a very kind letter beging that she would not use any of the facts in he[r] key saying that I wished it to be a history of my life entirely by its s[e]lf which would do more good and it needed no romance but if she wanted some facts for her book that I would be most happy to give her some. She never answered the letter. She wrote again and I wrote twice with no better success. It was not Lady like to treat Mrs Willis so. She would not have done it to any one. I think she did not like my objection. I cant help it.[5]

## Notes

1. For a detailed discussion of the circumstances surrounding Jacobs's writing of her narrative, see Jean Fagan Yellin, *Harriet Jacobs: A Life* (New York: Basic Books, 2004), pp. 117–136; see also Joan Hedrick, *Harriet Beecher Stowe: A Life* (Oxford: Oxford University Press, 1994), pp. 248–249.

2. Harriet Jacobs to Amy Post, 9 October [1853], Department of Rare Books & Special Collections, University of Rochester Library.

3. When Jacobs wrote this letter, in late 1852 or early 1853, she was working for Cornelia Willis and her husband, the prominent writer and publisher Nathaniel P. Willis, who had residences in New York City and Cornwall, a town north of the city in rural Orange County.

4. The letter ends here and is unsigned.

5. The letter ends here and is unsigned.

Harriet Jacobs to Amy Post, (undated [1852?]); 14 February [1853]; and 4 April [1853], all at the Department of Rare Books & Special Collections, University of Rochester Library.

# [Stowe in Liverpool, 13 April 1853]

### Anonymous

On 1 April 1853, Stowe, her husband Calvin, her brother Charles, her sister-in-law Sarah Buckingham Beecher, and Sarah's brother William and son George sailed for Liverpool, England, the first stop on a tour of Great Britain and Europe. Stowe was the triumphant author of *Uncle Tom's Cabin*, expressly invited to England to receive an antislavery petition, "An Affectionate and Christian Address of Many Thousands of Women of Great Britain and Ireland to Their Sisters the Women of the United States of America," signed by over half a million women, and to attend a series of antislavery events. Throughout the journey, Stowe and the others kept journals and sent frequent letters home to family members and friends to record their impressions of their trip. When Stowe returned to the United States, she assembled her travel letters and published them in two volumes, *Sunny Memories of Foreign Lands* (1854). Calvin Stowe wrote the introduction for the book, which was followed by several accounts from unnamed newspapers designed to give readers contextual information about the events—the "general tone and spirit of the meetings," as he described it. The following account describes a public meeting in Liverpool where Stowe was an honored guest on 13 April 1853. The account includes the text of her speech, which was read by Calvin Stowe since Stowe did not give public speeches at that time.

THE CHAIRMAN, (A. HODGSON, Esq.,) in opening the proceedings, thus addressed Mrs. Beecher Stowe:

The modesty of our English ladies, which, like your own, shrinks instinctively from unnecessary publicity, has devolved on me, as one of the trustees of the Liverpool Association, the gratifying office of tendering to you, at their request, a slight testimonial of their gratitude and respect. We had hoped almost to the last moment that Mrs. Cropper would have represented, on this day, the ladies with whom she has cooperated, and among whom she has taken a distinguished lead in the great work which you had the honor and the happiness to originate. But she has felt with you that the path most grateful and most congenial to female exertion, even in its widest and most elevated range, is still

[102]

Portrait of Harriet Beecher Stowe and Calvin Ellis Stowe, ca. 1852. The Schlesinger Library, Radcliffe Institute, Harvard University.

a retired and a shady path; and you have taught us that the voice which most effectually kindles enthusiasm in millions is the still small voice which comes forth from the sanctuary of a woman's breast, and from the retirement of a woman's closet—the simple but unequivocal expression of her unfaltering faith, and the evidence of her generous and unshrinking self-devotion. In the same spirit,

[103]

and as deeply impressed with the retired character of female exertion, the ladies who have so warmly greeted your arrival in this country have still felt it entirely consistent with the most sensitive delicacy to make a public response to your appeal, and to hail with acclamation your thrilling protest against those outrages on our common nature which circumstances have forced on your observation. They engage in no political discussion, they embark in no public controversy; but when an intrepid sister appeals to the instincts of women of every color and of every clime against a system which sanctions the violation of the fondest affections and the disruption of the tenderest ties; which snatches the clinging wife from the agonized husband, and the child from the breast of its fainting mother; which leaves the young and innocent female a helpless and almost inevitable victim of a licentiousness controlled by no law and checked by no public opinion,—it is surely as feminine as it is Christian to sympathize with her in her perilous task, and to rejoice that she has shed such a vivid light on enormities which can exist only while unknown or unbelieved. We acknowledge with regret and shame that that fatal system was introduced into America by Great Britain; but having in our colonies returned from our devious paths, we may without presumption, in the spirit of friendly suggestion, implore our honored transatlantic friends to do the same. The ladies of Great Britain have been admonished by their fair sisters in America, (and I am sure they are bound to take the admonition in good part,) that there are social evils in our own country demanding our special vigilance and care. This is most true; but it is also true that the deepest sympathies and most strenuous efforts are directed, in the first instance, to the evils which exist among ourselves, and that the rays of benevolence which flash across the Atlantic are often but the indication of the intensity of the bright flame which is shedding light and heat on all in its immediate vicinity. I believe this is the case with most of those who have taken a prominent part in this great movement. I am sure it is preeminently the case with respect to many of those by whom you are surrounded; and I hardly know a more miserable fallacy, by which sensible men allow themselves to be deluded, than that which assumes that every emotion of sympathy which is kindled by objects abroad is abstracted from our sympathies at home. All experience points to a directly opposite conclusion; and surely the divine command, "to go into all the world, and preach the gospel to every creature," should put to shame and silence the specious but transparent selfishness which would contract the limits of human sympathy, and veil itself under the garb of superior sagacity. But I must not detain you by any further observations. Allow me, in the name of the associated ladies, to present you with this small memorial of great regard, and to tender to you their and my best wishes for your health and happiness while you are sojourning among us, for the blessing of God on your children during your absence, and for your safe return to your native country when your mission shall be accomplished. I have just been requested to state the following particulars: In December last, a few ladies met in this place to consider the best plan of obtaining signatures in Liverpool to an address to the women of America on the subject of negro slavery, in substance coinciding with the one so nobly proposed and carried forward by Lord Shaftesbury. At this meeting it was suggested that it would be a sincere gratification to many if some testimonial could be presented to Mrs. Stowe which would indicate the sense, almost universally entertained, that she had been the instrument in the hands of God of arousing the slumbering sympathies of this country in behalf of the suffering slave. It was felt desirable to render the expression of such a feeling as general as possible; and to effect this it was resolved that a subscription should be set on foot, consisting of contributions of one penny and upwards, with a view to raise a testimonial, to be presented to Mrs. Stowe by the ladies of Liverpool, as an expression of their grateful appreciation of her valuable services in the cause of the negro, and as a token of admiration for the genius and of high esteem for the philanthropy and Christian feeling which animate her great work, *Uncle Tom's Cabin.* It ought, perhaps, to be added, that some friends, not residents of Liverpool, have united in this tribute. As many of the ladies connected with the effort to obtain signatures to the address may not be aware of the whole number appended, they may be interested in knowing that they amounted in all to twenty-one thousand nine hundred and fifty-three. Of these, twenty thousand nine hundred and thirty-six were obtained by ladies in Liverpool, from their friends either in this neighborhood or at a distance; and one thousand and seventeen were sent to the committee in London from other parts, by those who preferred our form of address. The total number of signatures from all parts of the kingdom to Lord Shaftesbury's address was upwards of five hundred thousand.

PROFESSOR STOWE then said,

On behalf of Mrs. Stowe I will read from her pen the response to your generous offering: "It is impossible for me to express the feelings of my heart at the kind and generous manner in which I have been received upon English shores. Just when I had begun to realize that a whole wide ocean lay between me and all that is dearest to me, I found most unexpectedly a home and friends waiting to receive me here. I have had not an hour in which to know the heart of a stranger. I have been made to feel at home since the first moment of landing, and wherever I have looked I have seen only the faces of friends. It is with deep feeling that I have found myself on ground that has been consecrated and made holy by the prayers and efforts of those who first commenced the struggle for that sacred cause which has proved so successful in England, and which I have a solemn assurance will yet be successful in my own country. It is a touching thought that here so many have given all that they have, and are, in behalf of oppressed humanity. It is touching to remember that one of the noblest men which England has ever produced now lies stricken under the heavy hand of disease, through a last labor of love in this cause. May God grant us all to feel that nothing is too dear or precious to be given in a work for which such men have lived, and labored, and suffered. No great good is ever wrought out for the human race without the suffering of great hearts. They who would serve their fellow-men are ever reminded that the Captain of their salvation was made perfect through suffering. I gratefully accept the offering confided to my care, and trust it may be so employed that the blessing of many 'who are ready to perish' will return upon your heads. Let me ask those—those fathers and mothers in Israel—who have lived and prayed many years for this cause, that as they prayed for their own country in the hour of her struggle, so they will pray now for ours. Love and prayer can hurt no one, can offend no one, and prayer is a real power. If the hearts of all the real Christians of England are poured out in prayer, it will be felt through the heart of the whole American church. Let us all look upward, from our own feebleness and darkness, to Him of whom it is said, 'He shall not fail nor be discouraged till he have set judgment in the earth. To him, the only wise God our Saviour, be glory and majesty, dominion and power, both now and ever. Amen.'"—These are the words, my friends, which Mrs. Stowe has written, and I cannot forbear to add a few words of my own. It was our intention, as the invitation to visit Great Britain came from Glasgow, to make our first landing there. But it was ordered by Providence that we should land here; and surely there is no place in the kingdom where a landing could be more appropriate, and where the reception could have been more cordial. [Hear, hear!] It was wholly unexpected by us, I can assure you. We knew that there were friendly hearts here, for we had received abundant testimonials to that effect from letters which had come to us across the Atlantic—letters wholly unexpected, and which filled our souls with surprise; but we had no thought that there was such a feeling throughout England, and we scarcely know how to conduct ourselves under it, for we are not accustomed to this kind of receptions. In our own country, unhappily, we are very much divided, and the preponderance of feeling expressed is in the other direction, entirely in opposition, and not in favor. [Hear, hear!] We knew that this city had been the scene of some of the greatest, most disinterested, and most powerful efforts in behalf of emancipation. The name of Clarkson was indissolubly associated with this place, for here he came to make his investigations, and here he was in danger of his life, and here he was protected by friends who stood by him through the whole struggle. The names of Cropper, and of Stephen, and of many others in this city, were very familiar to us—[Hear, hear!]—and it was in connection with this city that we received what to our feelings was a most effective testimonial, an unexpected letter from Lord Denman, whom we have always venerated. When I was in England in 1836, there were no two persons whom I more desired to see than the Duke of Wellington and Lord Denman; and soon I sought admission to the House of Lords, where I had the pleasure both of seeing and hearing England's great captain; and I found my way to the Court of Queen's Bench, where I had the pleasure of seeing and hearing England's great judge. But how unexpected was all this to us! When that book was written, in sorrow, and in sadness, and obscurity, and with the heart almost broken in the view of the sufferings which it described, and the still greater sufferings which it dared not describe, there was no expectation of any thing but the prayers of the sufferers and the blessing of God, who has said that the seed which is buried in the earth shall spring up in his own good time; and though it may be long buried, it will still at length come forth and bear fruit. We never could believe that slavery in our land would be a perpetual curse; but we felt, and felt deeply, that there must be a terrible struggle before we could be delivered from it, and that there must be suffering and martyrdom in this cause, as in every other great cause; for a struggle of eighteen years had taught us its strength. And, under God, we rely very much on the Christian public of Great Britain; for every expression of feeling from the wise and good of this land, with whatever petulance it may be met by some, goes to the heart of the American people. [Hear, hear!] You must not judge of the American people by the expressions which have come across the Atlantic in reference to the subject. Nine tenths of the American people, I think, are, in opinion at least, with you on this great subject; [Hear, hear!] but there is a tremendous pressure brought to bear upon all who are in favor of emancipation. The whole political power, the whole money power, almost the whole ecclesiastical power is wielded in defence of slavery, protecting it from all aggression; and it is as much as a man's reputation is worth to utter a syllable boldly and openly on the other side. Let me say to the ladies who have been active in getting up the address on the subject of slavery, that you have been doing a great and glorious work, and a work most appropriate for you to do; for in slavery it is woman that suffers most intensely, and the suffering woman has a claim upon the sympathy of her sisters in other lands. This address will produce a powerful impression throughout the country. There are ladies already of the highest character in the nation pondering how they shall make a suitable response, and what they shall do in reference to it that will be acceptable to the ladies of the United Kingdom, or will be profitable to the slave; and in due season you will see that the hearts of American women are alive to this matter, as well as the hearts of the women of this country. [Hear, hear!] Such was the mighty influence brought to bear upon every thing that threatened slavery, that had it not been for the decided expression on this side of the Atlantic in reference to the work which has exerted, under God, so much influence, there is every reason to fear that it would have been crushed and put under foot, as many other efforts for the overthrow of slavery have been in the United States. But it is impossible; the unanimous voice of Christendom prohibits it; and it shows that God has a work to accomplish, and that he has just commenced it. There are social evils in England. Undoubtedly there are; but the difference between the social evils in England and this great evil of slavery in the United States is just here: In England, the power of the government and the power of Christian sympathy are exerted for the removal of those evils. Look at the committees of inquiry in Parliament, look at the amount of information collected with regard to the suffering poor in their reports, and see how ready the government of Great Britain is to enter into those inquiries, and to remove those evils. Look at the benevolent institutions of the United Kingdom, and see how active all these are in administering relief; and then see the condition of slavery in the United States, where the whole power of the government is used in the contrary direction, where every influence is brought to bear to prevent any mitigation of the evil, and where every voice that is lifted to plead for a mitigation is drowned in vituperation and abuse from those who are determined that the evil shall not be mitigated. This is the difference: England repents and reforms. America refuses to repent and reform. It is said, "Let each country take care of itself, and let the ladies of England attend to their own business." Now I have always found that those who labor at home are those who labor abroad; [Hear, hear!] and those who say, "Let us do the work at home," are those who do no work of good either at home or abroad. [Hear, hear!] It was just so when the great missionary effort came up in the United States. They said, "We have a great territory here. Let us send missionaries to our own territories. Why should we send missionaries across the ocean?" But those who sent missionaries across the ocean were those who sent missionaries in the United States; and those who did not send missionaries across the ocean were those who sent missionaries nowhere. [Hear, hear!] They who say, "Charity begins at home," are generally those who have no charity; and when I see a lady whose name is signed to this address, I am sure to find a lady who is exercising her benevolence at home. Let me thank you for all the interest you have manifested and for all the kindness which we have received at your hands, which we shall ever remember, both with gratitude to you and to God our Father.

The REV. C. M. BIRRELL afterwards made a few remarks in proposing a vote of thanks to the ladies who had contributed the testimonial which had been presented to the distinguished writer of *Uncle Tom's Cabin*. He said it was most delightful to hear of the great good which that remarkable volume had done, and, he humbly believed, by God's special inspiration and guidance, was doing, in the United States of America. It was not confined to the United States of America. The volume was going forth over the whole earth, and great good was resulting, directly and indirectly, by God's providence, from it. He was told a few days ago, by a gentleman fully conversant with the facts, that an edition of *Uncle Tom*, circulated in Belgium, had created an earnest desire on the part of the people to read the Bible, so frequently quoted in that beautiful work, and that in consequence of it a great run had been made upon the Bible Society's depositories in that kingdom. [Hear, hear!] The priests of the church of Rome, true to their instinct, in endeavoring to maintain the position which they could not otherwise hold, had published another edition, from which, they had entirely excluded all reference to the word of God. [Hear, hear!] He had been also told that at St. Petersburg an edition of *Uncle Tom* had been translated into the Russian tongue, and that it was being distributed, by command of the emperor, throughout the whole of that vast empire. It was true that the circulation of the work there did not spring from a special desire on the part of the emperor to give liberty to the people of Russia, but because he wished to create a third power in the empire, to act upon the nobles; he wished to cause them to set free their serfs, in order that a third power might be created in the empire to serve as a check upon them. But whatever was the cause, let us thank God, the Author of all gifts, for what is done.

Sir GEORGE STEPHEN seconded the motion of thanks to the ladies, observing that he had peculiar reasons for doing so. He supposed that he was one of the oldest laborers in this cause. Thirty years ago he found that the work of one lady was equal to that of fifty men; and now we had the work of one lady which was equal to that of all the male sex. [Applause.]

From Harriet Beecher Stowe, *Sunny Memories of Foreign Lands*, vol. 1 (Boston: Phillips, Sampson, and Co., 1854), pp. xvi–xxi.

# [Diary Entry for 14 April 1853]

## Charles Beecher

Among those who accompanied Stowe and her husband Calvin on their first tour of Great Britain and Europe in 1853 was her brother Charles Beecher (1815–1900). Stowe invited him to join her on the journey, in part to organize their many engagements and handle travel arrangements. Beecher kept a detailed journal from their departure in April through their return to the United States in September. His journal primarily describes the events they attended as well as the people they met, but Beecher often wrote humorously of the difficulties of nineteenth-century travel. In this entry, Beecher provides his views on the event Stowe and her party had attended in Liverpool on 13 April 1853, as well as an admiring account of his sister's ability to handle her newfound celebrity.

Thursday, April 14, 1853

GLASGOW. Twelve night

Wrote notes and diary this morning till half-past eleven and out in carriage to the presentation [Liverpool, Wednesday, April 13]. About 200 ladies were assembled in a small room. Mr. Hodgson made a speech, Hatty, sitting on his right facing the meeting, and Stowe on his left. Hatty looks exactly right. Still, timid, modest, yet self-possessed and apparently feeling rather funny on the whole. I love to look at her. She seems surrounded and shielded by higher powers. It is a privilege to be near her. Nor do I wonder that people follow her and strive to get near her. There is nothing to repel and everything to win. Stowe also never appeared so to advantage. His clear and crisp style, his perfect frankness, great knowledge of facts and readiness, and fund of anecdote, and, withal, his right, thorough genial feeling make him a favorite at once. And his words in this highly oxygenated atmosphere of public excitement are like red-hot steel.

His speech in answer (after reading Hatty's) was the best yet. And I think will create some sensation in the United States. I do not forget, nor does he, nor Hatty, that every word we say here we must meet at home. We are ready and the Lord be the judge. The sum presented to Hatty was 130 pounds or $650. It was in Bank of England notes, enclosed in a beautifully embossed gold *porte-monnaie*, one side of which had a beautiful enamel picture. Her name and the date were engraved on it.[1]

Immediately after, we (through much tribulation of shaking hands, etc.) made our way to the railroad station and entered our car. The cars are not like ours in America. Tell Fred they are like three coaches fastened, end to end, into one. Each coach is finished off with six seats so that three of the inmates must ride backward. The back, sides, and seat are stuffed. The baggage is put on top or stowed under the seat. For a *family* where there are women and children along, it is just the thing. But for common travel it is unsociable. Our party just filled one coach. Stowe grumbled that here we six Yankees were shut up together and not a single Englishman to tell us about the country. But we got on pleasurably enough. A basket of provisions furnished by Mrs. Cropper seemed to have an excellent effect upon the spirits of the party. Our route lay through Lancashire, Westmorland, and Cumberland counties in England and Dumfries and Lanark in Scotland. The principal towns were Wigan, Preston, Lancaster, and Carlisle. At Lancaster Stowe quoted the line "John o' Gaunt, time-honored Lancaster." It was the first *walled* town we had seen. At Carlisle, associations thronged thick. Scots, from *Redgauntlet* and from *Guy Mannering*, were conned over among us.[2] And when we saw a real bona fide castle and walls of strength, we *felt*, you don't know! Stowe was in ecstasy about a church, a splendid old Gothic in which Paley preached. Paley, you know, of "evident" memory. Stowe said he was a jolly old fellow as ever lived.[3]

All between the great places we kept a sharp look out for ruins and old houses. And Stowe constantly informed us that there was an old house, here was a square tower, there was an ancient church, which things our lesser wisdom could in no wise gainsay, especially as we saw with our own eyes that the houses were *old*, the ruins ruined, and the tower square. Nevertheless, our professor felicitated himself hugely on his lore and grew fa-ce-ti-ous. We even had a lesson in psalmody, he pupil and I teacher. And we came within an ace of the wry-mouthed family. And we had several stories of a singular point and pith. Just as we crossed the border into bonny Scotland, the demonstrations of interest at each stopping place grew more striking. For example, at Lockerbie, the first town in Scotland, it was really affecting to see the crowd of simple bonny Scots lasses and lads that gathered around the door. Hatty seemed drawn to them by a strong attraction, and they to her. It did not seem like mere lionizing, like mere praise or admiration. It looked like *Love*. And so it was—mutual love. For Hatty is not proud nor vain, but her heart, like our blessed Savior's, seems all love. This draws the common people to her with an irresistible magnetism.

Now it so happened that we had been dozing a little. Stowe with his embroidered skullcap on, looking for all the world like a foolscap, and I (not to be outdone in *that* line) with a white silk handkerchief tied round my jaw. As we woke up, "Charles, Charles, take that off," Sarah whispered. I snatched it off as if it had been a hot plaster.

"Stowe, Stowe," I said, "pull that off!" And off he snatched it as if it had been a mosquito, and both our snatches were so quick that you couldn't say Jack Robinson between. Then, as we moved away, the crowd gave a huzza, and Stowe suddenly bethought him that Hatty ought to wave her white handkerchief; but not being used to that sort of thing, she had not one ready.

"Here," said Stowe, "here's one." Hatty snatched it and was just going to wave it.

"Oh, stop," said Sarah. "It's a *towel*!"

And Hatty sat down and we all roared with laughter. A merry set, the next car must have thought us. Then we sang "Auld Lang Syne," "Bonie Doon," "Scots Wha Hae," "Dundee," and "Dunlaps-creek." All through Lanarkshire, we rode after dark, *furnaces* blazing like beacons in every direction. It was a singular sight. At half-past ten we reached Glasgow, and there was a crowd waiting. Mr. Paton got Hatty and Stowe into a carriage and drove off, the crowd following and cheering.[4] Dr. Robson took Sarah and Georgy, William, and me, and we all rendezvoused at Paton's.[5] Then I came here (to Dr. Robson's), and Sarah and William and Georgy went to the Queen's Hotel. Dr. Robson is an Independent, I believe. His house five minutes from Hatty's place. And a large and splendid one. *Splendid* to me at least. My bedroom (which was designed for me and my wife) has a high ceiling, heavy mahogany furniture, and a closet with every convenience known in the plumber's art. Paton's, where Hatty is, is the most splendid house I have yet seen, e.g., two beautiful marble pillars in the hall just by the front door.

[112]

## Notes

1. CB is confused here. The *porte-monnaie* with the money was given to HBS by the antislavery society in Glasgow on April 15, 1853 [Van Why and French's note].

2. Novels by Sir Walter Scott, 1771–1832, a favorite author of HBS and her family [Van Why and French's note].

3. William Paley, 1743–1805, archdeacon of Carlisle and author of *Evidences of Christianity*, 1794 [Van Why and French's note].

4. Mr. Paton, a bailie (or municipal magistrate), was the first to suggest HBS visit Europe. He served as her host in Glasgow and presided at the tea sponsored by the local antislavery society [Van Why and French's note].

5. Dr. Robson, an Independent Presbyterian minister, served as host to CB in Glasgow [Van Why and French's note].

Charles Beecher, *Harriet Beecher Stowe in Europe: The Journal of Charles Beecher*, edited by Joseph S. Van Why and Earl French (Hartford, CT: The Stowe-Day Foundation, 1986), pp. 30–33.

# [Stowe in London, May 1853]

SARAH PUGH

---

Sarah Pugh (1800–1884) was a Virginia-born Quaker, teacher, and reformer. Along with Elizabeth Cady Stanton and other American antislavery activists, Pugh attended the British and Foreign Anti-Slavery Society general conference in London in 1840. In the United States she helped establish antislavery organizations, and after returning to England in 1861, she served as an advisor to antislavery and women's suffrage organizations. In England, Pugh knew a great many activists, including William Wells Brown, an escaped slave who had become a prominent orator, writer, and abolitionist; and William and Ellen Craft, who helped each other escape from slavery in Georgia and in 1850 fled to England, where William Craft eventually published *Running a Thousand Miles for Freedom* (1860). When the Stowes visited London, Pugh attended some of the same events, recording her impressions in her diary for May 1853.

---

—THE MEETING IN Exeter Hall was a large one, and in many respects great, though the speaking was nothing to boast of, either as to manner or matter. The sight of such an immense mass of human beings is of itself imposing. The Duchess of Sutherland was cheered on entering. When Mrs. Stowe appeared the house came down in rounds of applause; three British cheers were called for and given most heartily. The Duchess took her hand with a look of affection; they stood up together, Mrs. Stowe with calm, unpretending dignity. Soon after Professor Stowe made his speech, late in the evening, Mrs. Stowe withdrew, again cheered.

5th mo. 19th.
—Yesterday we attended the annual meeting of the Unitarian Association. Henry Crabb Robinson, an elderly gentleman of high standing in the literary world, not as an author, but their companion and friend, was in the chair. He made some interesting remarks in connection with the subject of American slavery, which was brought up by a resolution asking their brethren

of a common faith in America to act in this matter as became their high profession. He said that early in life he ceased to be a Trinitarian, but he had never connected himself with the Unitarians, as he shared the feeling, common in the world, that, though as a society they stood high in intellect and learning, they were not warm in Christian feeling. When staying with Thomas Clarkson he read an address of the Unitarians in England to their brethren in America on the subject of slavery; they both felt and said, "This is instinct with vital Christianity," and from that day he was satisfied to join the society. In reference to slaveholders and the apologists of the Fugitive Slave Law occupying the pulpit, he feared that, like the ancient tradition, "no grass would grow where their feet had pressed." To one who did not think the association the place and time for the discussion of American slavery, quoting Solomon, "There is a time for everything under the sun," he replied that Paul had said there are some things which "in season and out of season" may be spoken, and was not St. Paul higher authority than Solomon?

I called on Cornelius Hanbury, Plough Court, Lombard Street, the house and place of business so long identified with the name of William Allen. It was interesting to walk through the plain, venerable mansion, and to dine from the same table which had fed so many worthies now gone to their rest. It was Yearly Meeting time, but on Seventh-day there is no public meeting; the family were at their place at Stoke Newington. Cornelius Hanbury was there; received me politely and kindly, and urged my staying to dine and attend a meeting of the Free Produce Association in the afternoon. Some dozen friends dined with us. The meeting, held in Devonshire House, was a women's meeting, though a few men were present,—Eli Jones, John Candler, Dykes Alexander, Joseph Sturge. Professor Stowe and Harriet Beecher Stowe were present a short time; both spoke, she in confirmation of her husband's views, and relating a few pleasant incidents in a simple manner.

5th mo. 25th.
—Yesterday, with William Wells Brown, I breakfasted with some friends at the veritable inn of which the Wicksteeds spoke. In the heart of London, in a quiet, clean court, is a large house where at this time one hundred Friends are accommodated. Large rooms handsomely furnished, three of them opening into each other, in the largest a table at which fifty could be

seated, two in the next, accommodating as many more; at one of these we sat with our friends. A chapter was read ere we commenced our pleasant social repast. There were some fine-looking young men at our table, and altogether a "goodlie" company.

In the evening the British and Foreign Anti-Slavery Society gave a soirée to Mrs. Stowe in Willis's rooms; about a thousand persons present, half of them Friends. On a raised platform at one end of the room sat Joseph Sturge, Chairman, the committee and their wives, with Mrs. Stowe and her husband. Samuel Bowley read an address to her, to which Mr. Stowe replied. The company were then invited to walk by the platform, in the front of which she sat, to pay their respects. They were asked, on account of her feeble health, to excuse her shaking hands with them. She bowed pleasantly to persons as they passed, and to some she was particularly introduced, among them William and Ellen Craft, William Wells Brown, and Edward Matthews, these being mentioned in the "Key." The company separated in different rooms for refreshments; tea, coffee, etc., in one room, meats, salads, ices, etc., in another; Mrs. Stowe and her party with the committee in a small room. All was over soon after ten o'clock.

From Sarah Pugh, *Memorial of Sarah Pugh: A Tribute of Respect from Her Cousins* (Philadelphia: J. B. Lippincott & Co., 1888), pp. 79–81.

# [Impressions of Stowe]

## Elizabeth Barrett Browning

On her second trip to Europe in 1856–1857, Stowe visited a number of famous writers and people, including the poets Robert Browning (1812–1889) and Elizabeth Barrett Browning (1806–1861). When Stowe was touring Italy, she called on them at their home, Casa Guidi, in Florence. Barrett Browning supported a number of reform movements, including antislavery, and her poem "Runaway Slave at Pilgrim's Point" had appeared in the Boston antislavery annual the *Liberty Bell* in 1848. She had been greatly impressed with *Uncle Tom's Cabin* when she first read it in 1853. In a letter to her friend, Eliza Anne Harris Ogilvy, she called Stowe "a woman of remarkable largeness of mind & heart."[1] Although Barrett Browning did not admire Stowe's later work, she enjoyed meeting her and their subsequent correspondence. In the following letters and fragments of letters written to her friends Mary Russell Mitford, Anna Brownell Jameson, and Euphrasia Fanny Haworth, Barrett Browning describes her impressions of Stowe, her gratitude for their friendship, and the consolation Stowe provided her after the death of her sister, Henrietta.

To Miss Mitford

Florence: March 15, [1853].

[. . .] You don't say a word to me of Mrs. Beecher Stowe. How did her book impress you? No woman ever had such a success, such a fame; no man ever had, in a single book. For my part I rejoice greatly in it. It is an individual glory full of healthy influence and benediction to the world.

To Mrs. Jameson

Florence: April 12, [1853].

[. . . ] Not read Mrs. Stowe's book! But you *must*. Her book is quite a sign of the times, and has otherwise and intrinsically considerable power. For myself, I rejoice in the success, both as a woman and a human being. Oh, and is it possible that you think a woman has no business with questions

Elizabeth Barrett Browning, undated. Library of Congress, Prints and Photographs Division.

like the question of slavery? Then she had better use a pen no more. She had better subside into slavery and concubinage herself, I think, as in the times of old, shut herself up with the Penelopes in the "women's apartment," and take no rank among thinkers and speakers. Certainly you are not in earnest in these things. A difficult question—yes! All virtue is difficult. England found it difficult. France found it difficult. But we did not make ourselves an armchair of our sins. As for America, I honor America in much; but I would not be an American for the world while she wears that shameful scar upon her brow. The address of the New President exasperates me. Observe, I am an abolitionist, not to the fanatical degree, because I hold that compensation should be given by the North to the South, as in England. The States should unite in buying off this national disgrace. [. . .]

Ba.

To Miss Mitford
Florence: December 11, 1854.
[. . .] Do you hear from Mr. Kingsley? and, if so, how is his wife? I am reading now Mrs. Stowe's "Sunny Memories," and like the naturalness and simplicity of the book much, in spite of the provincialism of the tone of mind and education, and the really wretched writing. It's quite wonderful that a woman who has written a book to make the world ring should write so abominably. [. . .]

Your ever affectionate<br>Ba.

To Mrs. Jameson
Florence: April 9 [1857].
[. . . ] Mrs. Stowe has just arrived, and called here yesterday and this morning, when Robert took her to see the salvators at the end of our street. I like her better than I thought I should—that is, I find more refinement in her voice and manner—no rampant Americanisms. Very simple and gentle, with a sweet voice; undesirous of shining or *poser*-ing, so it seems to me. Never did lioness roar more softly (that is quite certain); and the temptations of a sudden enormous popularity should be estimated, in doing her full justice. She is nice-looking, too; and there's something strong and copious and characteristic in her dusky wavy hair. For the rest, the brow has not very large capacity; and the mouth wants something both in frankness and sensitiveness, I should say. But what can one see in a morning visit? I must wait for another opportunity. She spends to-morrow evening with us, and talks of remaining in Florence till the end of the next week—so I shall see and hear more. Her books are not so much to me, I confess, as the fact is, that she above all women (yes, and men of the age) has moved the world—and *for good*. [. . .]

Your ever affectionate<br>Ba.

To Miss E. F. Haworth

[Rome: autumn 1860.]

[. . .] Do you know, the first thing from without which did me the least good was a letter from America, from dear Mrs. Stowe. Since we parted here in the spring, neither of us had written, and she had not the least idea of my being unhappy for any reason. In fact, her thought was to congratulate me on public affairs (knowing how keenly I felt about them), but her letter dwelt at length upon spiritualism. She had heard, she said, for the fifth time from her boy (the one who was drowned in that awful manner through carrying out a college jest) without any seeking on her part. She gave me a minute account of a late manifestation, not seeming to have a doubt in respect to the verity and identity of the spirit. In fact, secret things were told, reference to private papers made, the evidence was considered most satisfying. And she says that all of the communications descriptive of the *state* of that Spirit, though coming from very different mediums (some high Calvinists and others low infidels) tallied exactly. She spoke very calmly about it, with no dogmatism, but with the strongest disposition to receive the facts of the subject with all their bearings, and at whatever loss of orthodoxy or sacrifice of reputation for common sense. I have a high appreciation of her power of forming opinions, let me add to this. It is one of the most vital and growing minds I ever knew. Besides the inventive, the critical and analytical faculties are strong with her. How many women do you know who are *religious*, and yet analyse point by point what they believe in? She lives in the midst of the traditional churches, and is full of reverence by nature; and yet if you knew how fearlessly that woman has torn up the old cerements and taken note of what is a dead letter within, yet preserved her faith in essential spiritual truth, you would feel more admiration for her than even for writing "Uncle Tom." There are quantities of irreverent women and men who profess infidelity. But this is a woman of another order, observe, devout yet brave in the outlook for truth, and considering, not whether a thing be *sound*, but whether it be true. Her views are Swedenborgian on some points, beyond him where he departs from orthodoxy on one or two points, adhering to the orthodox creed on certain others. She used to come to me last winter and open out to me very freely, and I was much interested in the character of her intellect. Dr. Manning tried his converting power on her. "It might have answered," she said, "if one side of her mind had not confuted what the other side was receptive of." In fact, she caught at all the beauty and truth and good of the Roman Catholic symbolism, saw what was better in it than Protestantism, and also, just as clearly, what was worse. She admired Manning immensely, and was very keen and quick in all her admirations; had no national any more than ecclesiastical prejudices; didn't take up Anglo-Saxon outcries of superiority in morals and the rest, which makes me so sick from American and English mouths. By the way (I must tell Sarianna *that* for M. Milsand!) a clever Englishwoman (married to a Frenchman) told Robert the other day that she believed in "a special hell for the Anglo-Saxon race on account of its hypocrisy." [. . .]

Your affectionate as ever

BA.

To Miss E. F. Haworth
126 Via Felice, Rome:
Tuesday, [about January 1861].

You really astonish me, dearest Fanny, so much by your letter, that I must reply to it at once. I ask myself under what new influence (strictly clerical) is she now, that she should write so? And has she forgotten me, never read "Aurora Leigh," never heard of me or from me that, before "Spiritualism" came up in America, I have been called orthodox by infidels, and heterodox by church-people; and gone on predicting to such persons as came near enough to me in speculative liberty of opinion to justify my speaking, that the present churches were in course of dissolution, and would have to be followed by a reconstruction of Christian essential verity into other than these middle-age scholastic forms. Believing in Christ's divinity, which is the life of Christianity, I believed this. Otherwise, if the end were here—if we were to be covered over and tucked in with the Thirty-nine Articles or the like, and good-night to us for a sound sleep in "sound doctrine"—I should fear for a revealed religion incapable of expansion according to the needs of man. What comes from God has life in it, and certainly from all the growth of living things, spiritual growth cannot be excepted. But I shun religious controversy—it is useless. I never "disturb anybody's mind," as it is called—let those sleep who can. If I had not known that *your* mind was broken up rather broadly by truths out of Swedenborg, I should not have mooted the subject, be sure. (Have you given up Swedenborg? this by the way.) Having done so, I am anxious to set you right about Mrs. Stowe. As the author of the most successful book printed by man or woman, perhaps

I a little under-rated her. The book has genius, but did not strike *me* as it did some other readers. Her "Sunny Memories," I liked very little. When she came to us in Florence some years ago, I did not think I should like her, nor did Robert, but we were both of us surprised and charmed with her simplicity and earnestness. At Rome last year she brought her inner nature more in contact with mine, and I, who had looked for what one usually finds in women, was startled into much admiration and sympathy by finding in her a largeness and fearlessness of thought which, coming out of a clerical and puritan *cul-de-sac*, and combined with the most devout and reverent emotions, really is fine. So you think that since "Uncle Tom" she has turned infidel, because of her interest in Spiritualism. Her last words to me when we parted, were, "Those who love the Lord Jesus Christ never see one another for the last time." That's the attitude of the mind which you stigmatise as corrupting. [. . .]

Your ever affectionate

BA.

## Note

1. "To Mrs. David Ogilvy" 12 September [1860], *Elizabeth Barrett Browning's Letters to Mrs. David Ogilvy 1849–1861 with Recollections by Mrs. Ogilvy*, edited by Peter N. Heydon and Philip Kelley (New York: Quadrangle, the New York Times Book Co., and the Browning Institute, 1973), p. 160.

Elizabeth Barrett Browning, *The Letters of Elizabeth Barrett Browning*, edited by Frederic G. Kenyon (New York: Macmillan, 1899), pp. 107, 110–111, 183, 258–259, 408–410, 420–421.

# [Recollections of Stowe at Andover]

## Elizabeth Stuart Phelps

In 1852, Calvin Stowe accepted a position at the Andover Theological Seminary, and the Stowe family lived in Andover, Massachusetts, until his retirement in 1864. When she was first at Andover, Stowe saw *Uncle Tom's Cabin* through production as a novel and found herself an international celebrity. The following years there were extremely productive ones for her. She published six more books, including *A Key to Uncle Tom's Cabin* (1853); traveled to Europe three times; became a founder of the *Atlantic Monthly*; and met President Abraham Lincoln at the White House during the Civil War. At the same time, Stowe was immersed in her family life. One of her neighbors was the young Elizabeth Stuart Phelps (1844–1911), who became the prolific writer of nearly sixty books, including her best-selling novel *The Gates Ajar* (1868). In *Chapters from a Life* (1896), first published as a serial in *McClure's Magazine*, Phelps chronicles her life as a writer, reminiscing about a host of famous American writers, including Henry Wadsworth Longfellow, John Greenleaf Whittier, Lucy Larcom, Lydia Maria Child, and her longtime friend, Stowe. In this chapter, Phelps remembers Stowe as she first knew her: as a professor's wife, deeply engaged mother, manager of a busy household, successful writer, and helpful mentor.

ONE PREËMINENT FIGURE moving gently for a few years upon the Andover stage, I had almost omitted from the reminiscences of the Hill,—I suppose because in truth she never seemed to me to be of Andover, or its life akin to hers. I refer to the greatest of American women, Harriet Beecher Stowe.

To the stranger visiting Andover for a day, there will long be pointed out, as one of the "sights" of the Hill, the house occupied by Mrs. Stowe during the time of her husband's professorship in the Seminary. After she disappeared from among us, that home of genius met a varied fate. I wonder, do houses feel their ascents and declines of fortune as dogs do, or horses? One sometimes fancies that they may, if only through the movement of that odic force whose mysterious existence science cannot deny, and speculation would not. Next a man's book or his child, what can be so invested

Portrait of Elizabeth Stuart Phelps, ca. 1880. The Schlesinger Library, Radcliffe Institute, Harvard University.

with himself as the house he lives in? Saturated with humanity as they are, who knows how far sentience may develop under observant roofs and in conscious rooms long possessed by human action and endurance?

Mrs. Stowe's house, still retaining the popular name of Uncle Tom's Cabin, became for a while a club devoted to the honorable ends of boarding theologies. At the present time the Trustees' hotel is in the building, which has suffered many dreary practical changes. The house is of stone, and in the day of its distinguished occupant was a charming place. As a house, it is very difficult; but Mrs. Stowe has always had the home-touch in a beautiful degree.

In fact, my chief impression of those years when we had the rich opportunity of her vicinity consists in occasional glimpses of lovely interiors, over which presided a sweet and quiet presence, as unlike the eidolon which Andover Seminary seemed to have created for itself of this great and gracious lady, as a spirit is unlike an old-time agitator. To tell the truth,— which perhaps is not necessary—I dimly suspected then, and I have been sure of it since, that the privilege of neighborhood was but scantily appreciated in Andover in the case of this eminent woman. Why, I do not know. She gave no offense, that I can recall, to the peculiar preferences of the place; the fact that she was rumored to have leanings towards the Episcopal Church did not prevent her from dutifully occupying with her family her husband's pew in the old chapel; it was far to the front, and her ecclesiastical delinquencies would have been only too visible, had they existed. A tradition that she visited the theatre in Boston when she felt like it, sometimes passed solemnly from lip to lip; but this is the most serious criticism upon her which I can remember.

I have since found suspicion blossoming into a belief that the vagueness of arithmetic which led to an insufficient estimate of Mrs. Stowe's value, or at least to a certain bluntness in our sense of the honor which she did to Andover by living among us, sprung from the fact that she was a woman.

Andover was a heavily masculine place. She was used to eminent men, and to men who thought they were, or meant to be, or were thought to be by the ladies of their families, and the pillars of their denomination. At the subject of eminent women the Hill had not arrived. I have sometimes wondered what would have been the fate even of my mother, had she lived to work her power to its bloom. And Mrs. Stowe's fame was clearly a fact so apart from the traditions and from the ideals, that Andover was puzzled by it. The best of her good men were too feudal in their views of women in those days, to understand a life like Mrs. Stowe's. It should be remembered that we have moved on since then, so fast and so far, that it is almost as hard now for us to understand the perplexity with which intelligent, even instructed men, used to consider the phenomenon of a superior woman, as it was then for such men to understand such a woman at all. Let us offer to them the width of sympathy and fineness of perception which they did not always know how to offer to the woman.

My personal remembrances of Mrs. Stowe are those of a young girl whom she entertained at intervals, always delightfully, in the long parlor running the width of the stone house, whose deep embrasured window-seats seemed to me only less wonderful than the soft and brightly-colored, rather worldly-looking pillows with which these attractive nooks were generously filled. There were flowers always, and a bower of ivy made summer of the eternal Andover winters in the stone house; and there were merry girls and boys,—Mrs. Stowe was the most unselfish and loving of mothers,—and there were always dogs; big and little, curly and straight; but in some form, dog-life with its gracious reaction on the gentleness and kindness of family life abounded in her house. It was an open, hospitable house, human and hearty and happy, and I have always remembered it affectionately.

An amusing instance of the spirit of the stone house comes back to me from some faraway day, when I found myself schoolmate to Mrs. Stowe's youngest daughter. This little descendent of genius and of philanthropy was bidden to write a composition—an order which she resolutely refused for some time to obey. But the power above her persisted, and one day, the child brought in a slip of paper a few inches long, on which were inscribed these words only: "Slavery is the greatest curse of human nature."

*Uncle Tom's Cabin* was not written in the stone house at Andover. But there the awful inscription of a great grief was cut into the quivering flesh and blood of a mother's heart. The sudden and violent death of a favorite son—which made of *The Minister's Wooing* an immortal outcry to mothers bereaved—occurred, if I am not wrong, while Mrs. Stowe was among us. I never pass the house without thinking what those stone walls have known and kept of that chrism of personal anguish through which a great soul passed in learning how to offer consolation to the suffering of the world.

One of the prettiest pictures which I have of Mrs. Stowe is framed in the everglades of Florida. Her home at Magnolia offered a guest-room in which one could pass a night of such quiet as Paradise might envy. The house, I remember, was built about a great live-oak, and the trunk of the tree grew into the room; the walls being cleverly adjusted to the contour of the bark. Through the open windows the leaves drifted silently, falling about the room, the floor, the bed, as they pleased. One slept like a hamadryad, and waked like a bird in a bough.

Into this nest of green and peace, I had (I remember it with shame and contrition) the hardness of heart and bluntness of courtesy to intrude a pile of proof-sheets. It was my first book of verses. The volume was in press. I was in misery of doubt about the venture. In the State of Florida my hostess was the only accessible person whose judgment could help me; and fate had thrown me on her sweet charity with my galleys. The publishers at the North, a thousand miles away, were hurrying me. There was not a day to lose, if I had made a grave blunder; and I mercilessly read the verses to her, beseeching her advice and criticism.

It would be hard to forget the sweetness, the patience, and the frankness with which she gave herself to my cruel request. I remember how she curled herself up on the bed beside me, like a girl, with her feet crossed under her, and listened gently. The live-oak leaves fell softly about us, and the St. John's River showed in glimpses, calm, coffee-colored, and indifferent, between the boughs. The utter silence of a Florida wilderness compassed us. My own voice sounded intrusive and foreign to me as I read. Nothing could exceed her kindness or her wisdom as a critic. I had made one rather serious mistake in one of the poems,—a fault in taste which I had overlooked. She called my attention to it so explicitly, yet so delicately, that I could have thanked her with tears. "A sweeter woman ne'er drew breath" than she was to me that day.

The last time that I saw Mrs. Stowe was on the occasion of her seventieth birthday; when, at the country seat of Governor and Mrs. Claflin, in Newtonville, her publishers, Messrs. Houghton, Mifflin and Company, tendered her a reception,—I think she called it a birthday party.

It fell to me to go out to the breakfast with Doctor Holmes, who always loved and appreciated Mrs. Stowe, and who seemed to enjoy himself like a happy boy all day. His tribute, written for the day, was one of the best of his famous occasional poems; and he did me the honor to read my own unimportant verses for me—a thing which I found it impossible to do for myself—with such grace and fervor as almost made me feel as if I had written something of Doctor Holmes's. It was a unique sensation; and, though one of the most humbling of life, yet one of the most agreeable.

Mrs. Stowe's appearance that day—one of her last, I think, in public—was a memorable one. Her dignity, her repose, a certain dreaminess and aloofness of manner characteristic of her, blended gently with her look of peace and unmistakable happiness. Crowded with honors as her life had been, I have fancied that this, among her latest, in her quiet years, and so full of the tenderness of personal friendship, had especial meanings to her, and gave her deep pleasure. Among our literary people no one of consequence omitted to do honor to the foremost woman of America: there were possibly one or two exceptions, of the school which does not call *Uncle Tom's Cabin* literature unless it is obliged to; but they were scarcely missed.

The most beautiful story which I ever heard about Mrs. Stowe I have asked no permission to share with the readers of these papers, and yet I feel sure that no one who loves and honors her could refuse it; for I believe that if the whole of it were told, it might live to enhance the nobility of her name and fame as long as Uncle Tom himself. It was told me, as such things go, from lip to lip of personal friends who take pride in cherishing the sweetest thoughts and facts about those whom they love and revere.

During the latter part of her life Mrs. Stowe has been one of those devout Christian believers whose consecration takes high forms. She has placed faith in prayer, and given herself to the kind of dedication which exercises and cultivates it. There came a time in her history when one who was very dear to her seemed about to sink away from the faith in which she trusted, and to which life and sorrow had taught her to cling as only those who have suffered, and doubted, and accepted, can.

This prospect was a crushing grief to her, and she set herself resolutely to avert the calamity if, and while, she could. Letter after letter—some of them thirty pages long—found its way from her pen to the foreign town in which German rationalism was doing its worst for the soul she loved. She set the full force of her intellect intelligently to work upon this conflict. She read, she reasoned, she wrote, she argued, she pleaded. Months passed in a struggle whose usefulness seemed a pitiable hope, to be frustrated in the effort.

Then she laid aside her strong pen, and turned to her great faith. As the season of the sacred holiday approached, she shut herself into her room, secluding herself from all but God, and prayed, as only such a believer—as only such a woman—may. As she had set the full force of her intellect, so now she set the full power of her faith to work upon her soul's desire. One may not dwell in words upon that sacred battle. But the beautiful part of the story, as I have been told it, is, that a few weeks after this a letter reached her, saying only: "At Christmas time a light came to me. I see things differently now. I see my way to accept the faith of my fathers;—and the belief in Christianity which is everything to you has become reasonable and possible to me at last."

From Elizabeth Stuart Phelps, *Chapters from a Life* (Boston: Houghton, Mifflin, 1896), pp. 131–140.

# [Stowe and the *Atlantic Monthly* Dinner, 1859]

### Thomas Wentworth Higginson

The *Atlantic Monthly* was founded in 1857 as a literary and cultural magazine that also engaged political issues. One of the founders, Francis Underwood, observed that he "desired to bring the literary influence of New England to aid the anti-slavery cause," though he wished to place the primary emphasis of the magazine on the literary.[1] He had first proposed the idea of a magazine to John Jewett, the publisher of *Uncle Tom's Cabin*, but Jewett withdrew because his company was overextended. With the encouragement of Stowe, Underwood proposed the magazine to her new publisher, Phillips, Sampson, and Company. A number of other literary luminaries, including Oliver Wendell Holmes, Ralph Waldo Emerson, Henry Wadsworth Longfellow, and James Russell Lowell, who became the first editor, were eager to participate. The inaugural issue, which appeared in November 1857, included Stowe's story "The Mourning Veil." For the first two years of the magazine, the publishers sponsored monthly dinners for editors and contributors. On the single occasion in which women were invited, only Stowe and Harriet Prescott Spofford attended. "Mrs. Stowe had demurred at first, and only consented upon the stipulation that there should be no wine on the table," Underwood recalled. "Cigars were, of course, out of the question. The condition was agreed to, for all were desirous of doing honor to the woman who had taken such a distinguished part in the great question of the day."[2] The minister, reformer, and writer Thomas Wentworth Higginson (1823–1911) was also involved in the founding of the *Atlantic*. In this excerpt from his autobiographical *Cheerful Yesterdays* (1899), Higginson provides a humorous account of how Stowe's presence altered the usual atmosphere of the men's dinner.

DURING THE FIRST YEAR of the magazine under Phillips & Sampson's management, there were monthly dinners, in or near Boston, under the general ship of Francis H. Underwood, the office editor, and John C. Wyman, then his assistant. The most notable of these gatherings was undoubtedly that held at the Revere House, on occasion of Mrs. Stowe's projected departure for Europe. It was the only one to which ladies were invited, and the

Thomas Wentworth Higginson, undated. Prints and Photographs Division, Library of Congress.

invitation was accepted with a good deal of hesitation by Mrs. Stowe, and with a distinct guarantee that no wine should be furnished for the guests. Other feminine contributors were invited, but for various reasons no ladies appeared except Mrs. Stowe and Miss Harriet Prescott (now Mrs. Spofford), who had already won fame by a story called "In a Cellar," the scene of which was laid in Paris, and which was so thoroughly French in all its appointments that it was suspected of being a translation from that language, although much inquiry failed to reveal the supposed original. It may be well to add that the honest young author had so little appreciation of the high compliment thus paid her that she indignantly proposed to withdraw her manuscript in consequence. These two ladies arrived promptly, and the gentlemen were kept waiting, not greatly to their minds, in the hope that other fair contributors would appear. When at last it was decided to proceed without further delay, Dr. Holmes and I were detailed to escort the ladies to the dining-room: he as the head of the party, and I as the only one who knew the younger lady. As we went up stairs the vivacious Autocrat said to me, "Can I venture it? Do you suppose that Mrs. Stowe disapproves of me very much?"—he being then subject to severe criticism from the more conservative theologians. The lady was gracious, however, and seemed glad to be rescued at last from her wearisome waiting. She came downstairs wearing a green wreath, of which Longfellow says in his diary (July 9, 1859) that he "thought it very becoming."[3]

We seated ourselves at table, Mrs. Stowe at Lowell's right, and Miss Prescott at Holmes's, I next to her, Edmund Quincy next to me. Dr. Stowe was at Holmes's left, Whittier at his; and Longfellow, Underwood, John Wyman, and others were present. I said at once to Miss Prescott, "This is a new edition of *Evelina, or a Young Lady's Entrance into the World*. Begin at the beginning: what did you and Mrs. Stowe talk about for three quarters of an hour?" She answered demurely, "Nothing, except that she once asked me what o'clock it was, and I told her I didn't know." There could hardly be a better illustration of that curious mixture of *mauvaise honte*[4] and indifference which often marred the outward manners of that remarkable woman. It is very likely that she had not been introduced to her companion, and perhaps had never heard her name; but imagine any kindly or gracious person of middle age making no effort to relieve the shyness of a young girl stranded with herself during three quarters of an hour of enforced seclusion!

The modest entertainment proceeded; conversation set in, but there was a visible awkwardness, partly from the presence of two ladies, one of whom was rather silent by reason of youth, and the other by temperament; and moreover, the thawing influence of wine was wanting. There were probably no men of the party, except Whittier and myself, who did not habitually drink it, and various little jokes began to circle sotto voce at the table; a suggestion, for instance, from Longfellow, that Miss Prescott might be asked to send down into her Cellar for the wine she had described so well, since Mrs. Stowe would allow none abovestairs. Soon, however, a change came over the aspect of affairs. My neighbor on the right, Edmund Quincy, called a waiter mysteriously, and giving him his glass of water remained tranquilly while it was being replenished. It came back suffused with a rosy hue. Some one else followed his example, and presently the "conscious water" was blushing at various points around the board, although I doubt whether Holmes, with water-drinkers two deep on each side of him, got really his share of the coveted beverage. If he had, it might have modified the course of his talk, for I remember that he devoted himself largely to demonstrating to Dr. Stowe that all swearing doubtless originated in the free use made by the pulpit of sacred words and phrases; while Lowell, at the other end of the table, was maintaining for Mrs Stowe's benefit that *Tom Jones* was the best novel ever written. This line of discussion may have been lively, but was not marked by eminent tact; and Whittier, indeed, told me afterwards that Dr. and Mrs. Stowe agreed in saying to him that while the company at the club was no doubt distinguished, the conversation was not quite what they had been led to expect. Yet Dr. Stowe was of a kindly nature and perhaps was not seriously disturbed even when Holmes assured him that there were in Boston whole families not perceptibly affected by Adam's fall; as for instance, the family of Ware.[5]

## Notes

1. Francis Underwood, *The Poet and the Man: Recollections and Appreciations of James Russell Lowell* (Boston: Lee and Shepard, 1893), p. 48.

2. Underwood, p. 56.

3. Longfellow's diary entry for 9 July 1859 reads: "Dined with the Atlantic Club at the Revere. Mrs. Stowe was there with a green wreath on her head, which I thought very becoming. Also Miss Prescott, who wrote the story 'In a Cellar.' The others were, Mr. Stowe, with his patriarchal gray beard, Lowell, Holmes, Whittier, Underwood, Higginson, etc. One of the publishers of the Magazine is a good teller of funny stories." *Life of Henry Wadsworth Longfellow with Extracts from his Journals and Correspondence*, vol. 2, edited by Samuel Longfellow (Boston: Houghton, Mifflin, 1891), p. 387.

4. Bashfulness (French).

5. The Ware family included a number of ministers, including Henry Ware (1764–1845), a member of the Harvard Divinity School and teacher of Ralph Waldo Emerson. In his "Divinity School Address" (1838), Emerson famously took issue with the conservative Unitarian theology of his former teacher.

Thomas Wentworth Higginson, *Cheerful Yesterdays* (New York: Macmillan, 1898), pp. 176–180.

# "Days with Mrs. Stowe"

## ANNIE ADAMS FIELDS

Annie Adams Fields (1834–1915) was Stowe's closest personal friend.[1] She and her husband, the publisher James T. Fields, met Stowe in Italy in early 1860. Stowe was on her third and final trip to Europe, and the Fieldses were touring Italy before returning to Boston, where James Fields was to become editor of the *Atlantic Monthly*. Stowe and Fields called on one another frequently while they remained in Florence, and Stowe arranged her own return to the United States on the same ship with them. Nathaniel and Sophia Hawthorne were also on board, but Stowe spent most of her time with the Fieldses. Back in New England in the summer of 1860, Stowe relied on James Fields as her editor and publisher, and for the rest of her life she relied on Annie Fields for friendship, advice, and even editorial assistance. Her choice was a good one. Fields was among the most influential women in Boston during the nineteenth century. She was friendly with Hawthorne, Ralph Waldo Emerson, and Henry Wadsworth Longfellow. She helped the careers of a number of women writers, including Rebecca Harding Davis, Willa Cather, Lucy Larcom, and Sarah Orne Jewett, with whom Annie Fields lived in partnership after James died in 1881. Fields, who wrote poems, essays, novels, and biographies, included a chapter on Stowe in her *Authors and Friends* (1896) and published *The Life and Letters of Harriet Beecher Stowe* (1897), still an important resource for information on Stowe. The following selection is from an article published in the *Atlantic Monthly* in 1896, excerpted from the chapter on Stowe in Fields's *Authors and Friends*.

FLORENCE, THE CITY of charms and flowers, was the spot where I first met Mrs. Stowe. She was delighting herself in the fascinations of that lovely place. Not alone every day but every second as it passed was full of eager interest to her. She could say with Thoreau, "I moments live who lived but years." We had both been invited to a large reception, on a certain evening, in one of the old palaces on the Arno. There were music and dancing, and there were lively groups of ladies and gentlemen strolling from room to room, contrasting somewhat strangely in their gayety with the solemn

Annie Adams Fields, 1861. The Metropolitan Museum of Art, gift of I. N. Phelps Stokes, Edward S. Hawes, Alice Mary Hawes, and Marion Augusta Hawes, 1937 (37.14.27). Copy Photography © The Metropolitan Museum of Art.

pictures hanging on the walls, and a sense of shadowy presence which seems to haunt those dusky interiors. An odd discrepancy between the modern company and the surroundings, a weird mingling of the past and the present, made any apparition appear possible, and left room only for a faint thrill of surprise when a voice by my side said, "There is Mrs. Stowe." In a moment she approached and I was presented to her, and after a brief pause she passed on. All this was natural enough, but a wave of intense disappointment swept over me. Why had I found no words to express or even indicate the feeling that had choked me? Was the fault mine? Oh, yes, I said to myself, for I could not conceive it to be otherwise, and I looked upon my opportunity, the gift of the gods, as utterly and forever wasted. I was depressed and sorrowing over the vanishing of a presence I might perhaps never meet again, and no glamour of light, or music or pictures or friendly voices could recall any pleasure to my heart. Meanwhile, the unconscious object of all this disturbance was strolling quietly along, leaning on the arm of a friend, hardly ever speaking, followed by a group of traveling companions, and entirely absorbed in the gay scene around her. She was a small woman; and her pretty curling hair and far-away dreaming eyes, and her way of becoming occupied in what interested her until she forgot everything else for the time, all these I first began to see and understand as I gazed after her retreating figure.

Mrs. Stowe's personal appearance has received scant justice and no mercy at the hand of the photographer. She was always herself, during her triumphal visit to England after the publication of *Uncle Tom*: "The general topic of remark on meeting me seems to be that I am not so bad looking as they were afraid I was; and I do assure you, when I have seen the things that are put up on the shop windows here with my name under them, I have been lost in wondering imagination at the boundless loving-kindness of my English and Scottish friends in keeping up such a warm heart for such a Gorgon. I should think that the Sphinx in the London Museum might have sat for most of them. I am going to make a collection of these portraits to bring home to you. There is a great variety of them, and they will be useful, like the Irishman's guideboard which showed 'where the road did not go.'" I remember once accompanying her to a reception at a well-known house in Boston, where, before the evening was over, the hostess drew me aside, saying, "Why did you never tell me that Mrs. Stowe was beautiful?" And indeed, when I observed her in the full ardor of conversation, with her heightened color, her eyes shining and awake, but filled with great softness, her abundant curling hair rippling naturally about her head and falling a little at the sides (as in the portrait by Richmond), I quite agreed with the lady of the house. Nor was that the first time her beauty had been revealed to me, but she was seldom seen to be beautiful by the great world, and the pleasure of this recognition was very great to those who loved her.

She was never afflicted with a personal consciousness of her reputation, nor was she trammeled by it. The sense that a great work had been accomplished through her only made her more humble, and her shy, absent-minded ways were continually throwing her admirers into confusion. Late in life (when her failing powers made it impossible for her to speak as one living in a world which she seemed to have left far behind) she was accosted, I was told, in the garden of her country retreat, in the twilight one evening, by a good old retired sea captain who was her neighbor for the time. "When I was younger," said he respectfully, holding his hat in his hand while he spoke, "I read with a great deal of satisfaction and instruction *Uncle Tom's Cabin*. The story impressed me very much, and I am happy to shake hands with you, Mrs. Stowe, who wrote it." "I did not write it," answered the white-haired old lady gently, as she shook the captain's hand. "You didn't?" he ejaculated in amazement. "Why, who did, then?" "God wrote it," she replied simply. "I merely did his dictation." "Amen," said the captain reverently, as he walked thoughtfully away.

This was the expression in age of what lay at the foundation of her life. She always spoke and behaved as if she recognized herself to be an instrument breathed upon by the Divine Spirit. When we consider how this idea absorbed her to the prejudice of what appeared to others a wholesome exercise of human will and judgment, it is not wonderful that the world was offended when she once made conclusions contrary to the opinion of the public, and thought best to publish them.

Mrs. Stowe was a delightful talker. She loved to gather a small circle of friends around a fireside, when she easily took the lead in fun and story telling. This was her own ground, and upon it she was not to be outdone. "Let me put my feet upon the fender," she would say, "and I can talk till all is blue."

It appeared to those who listened most frequently to her conversation that a large part of the charm of her tales was often lost in the writing down; yet with all her unusual powers she was an excellent listener herself. Her natural modesty was such that she took keen pleasure in gathering fresh thought and inspiration from the conversation of others. Nor did the universal homage she received from high and low leave any unworthy impression upon her self-esteem. She was grateful and pleased and humble, and the only visible effect produced upon her was the heightened pleasure she received from the opportunities of knowing men and women who excited her love and admiration. Her name was a kind of sacred talisman, especially in New and Old England. It was a banner which had led men to battle against slavery. Therefore it was often a cause of surprise and social embarrassment when the bearer of this name proved to be sometimes too modest, and sometimes too absent-minded, to remember that anything was expected of her or anything arranged for her special entertainment.

It was my good fortune to be in Mrs. Stowe's company once in Rome when she came unexpectedly face to face with an exhibition of the general feeling of reverence and gratitude towards herself. We had gone together to the rooms of the brothers Castellani, the world-famous workers in gold. The collection of antique gems and the beautiful reproductions of them were new to us. Mrs. Stowe was full of enthusiasm, and we lingered long over the wonderful things which the brothers brought forward to show. Among them was the head of an Egyptian slave carved in black onyx. It was an admirable work of art, and while we were enjoying it one of them said to Mrs. Stowe, "Madam, we know what you have been to the poor slave. We ourselves are but poor slaves still in Italy: you feel for us; will you keep this gem as a slight recognition of what you have done?" She took the jewel in silence; but when we looked for some response, her eyes were filled with tears, and it was impossible for her to speak.

When the hours of her European play-day grew near the end, she began to lay plans for returning home in the steamer with those who had become dear to her, and in one of her notes of that period she wrote to me:—"On the strength of having heard that you were going home in the Europa June 16th, we also have engaged passage therein for that time, and hope that we shall not be disappointed.... It must be true, we can't have it otherwise.... Our Southern Italy trip was a glory—it was a rose—a nightingale—all, in short, that one ever dreams; but alas! It is over."

It was a delightful voyage homeward in every sense. At that period a voyage was no little matter of six days, but a good fourteen days of sitting together on deck in pleasant summer weather, and having time enough and to spare. Hawthorne and his family also concluded to join the party. Mrs. Hawthorne, who was always the romancer in conversation, filled the evening hours by weaving magic webs of her fancies, until we looked upon her as a second Scheherazade, and the day the head was to be cut off was the day we should come to shore. "Oh," said Hawthorne, "I wish we might never get there." But the good ship moved steadily as fate. Meanwhile, Mrs. Stowe often took her turn at entertaining the little group. She was seldom tired of relating stories of New England life and her early experiences.

When the ship came to shore, Mrs. Stowe and her daughters went at once to Andover, where Professor Stowe had remained at his post during their long absence in Europe. She went also with equal directness to her writing-desk; and though there are seldom any dates upon her letters, the following note must have been written shortly after her return:—

MY DEAR MR. FIELDS,—"Agnes of Sorrento" was conceived on the spot,—a spontaneous tribute to the exceeding loveliness and beauty of all things there. One bright evening, as I was entering the old gateway, I saw a beautiful young girl sitting in its shadow selling oranges. She was my Agnes. Walking that same evening through the somber depths of the gorge, I met "Old Elsie," walking erect and tall, with her piercing black eyes, Roman nose, and silver hair,—walking with determination in every step, and spinning like one of the Fates glittering silver flax from a distaff she carried in her hands.

A few days after, our party, being weather-bound at Salerno, had resort to all our talents to pass the time, and songs and stories were the fashion of the day. The first chapter was my contribution to that entertainment. The story was voted into existence by the voices of all that party, and by none more enthusiastically than by one young voice which will never be heard on earth more. It was kept in mind and expanded and narrated as we went on to Rome over a track that the pilgrim Agnes is to travel. To me, therefore, it is fragrant with love of Italy and memory of some of the brightest hours of life. [. . .]

## Note

1. Rita K. Gollin, *Annie Adams Fields: Woman of Letters* (Amherst: University of Massachusetts Press, 2002), p. 135.

From Annie Fields, "Days with Mrs. Stowe," *Atlantic Monthly* 78 (1896): 145–147.

# [An Evening with Stowe in 1861]

## Lydia Maria Child

The editor and writer Lydia Maria Child (1802–1880) first became known for writing *Hobomok* (1824), a historical novel about a Puritan woman's marriage to an Indian. She subsequently founded and edited the first magazine for children, the *Juvenile Miscellany*; wrote a popular household manual, *The Frugal Housewife*; and enjoyed a considerable literary reputation by the early 1830s. Her antislavery views and especially the publication of *An Appeal in Favor of That Class of Americans Called Africans* (1833) earned her praise from abolitionists such as William Lloyd Garrison but damaged her standing among the conservative literary establishment in Boston. With her husband, David Lee Child, she moved to New York in 1841 and became the editor of the *National Anti-Slavery Standard*. A prolific author of articles and stories, Child was committed to antislavery and other reforms, including rights for women and Native Americans. She admired *Uncle Tom's Cabin*, calling it a "truly great work" that "has also done much to command respect for the faculties of women."[1] Child and Stowe were friendly for most of their adult lives. One of Child's closest friends was Sarah Blake Sturgis Shaw, the wife of Francis G. Shaw and the mother of Colonel Robert Gould Shaw, the white commander of the 54th Massachusetts Volunteer Infantry, the first regiment of black troops organized in a Northern state. In the following letter written to Shaw on 21 July 1861, Child describes an evening spent with the Stowes at a party and their conversation about politics; William H. Seward, Abraham Lincoln's Secretary of State; and the early stages of the Civil War.

Wayland, July 21ˢᵗ, 1861.

Darling Friend,

I have indited ever so many letters to you in my thoughts, but, partly owing to the inertia of increasing years, and partly owing to perpetual anxiety and doubt about public affairs, I have not taken "pen in hand to tell you that I am well and hope that you are enjoying the same blessing." That

Copy of a drawn portrait of Lydia
Maria Child, ca. 1850. The Schles-
inger Library, Radcliffe Institute,
Harvard University.

is pretty much *all* I have too tell, except that last week I performed the
extraordinary feat of going, in outspread fashionable garments, to a stylish
party in Weston, where over a hundred people were assembled. Mrs. Stowe
was there, and she and I got into a corner, and, with few interruptions, succeeded in ignoring the party. I paid no attention to any of the strangers,
except one Bell-Everett malignant[2] who came with prancing horses, and
chariot lined with white, making the air resound with orders to his coach-
man. He had a thin, hard face, and skinny clutching hands, like a beast of
prey.[3] He looked so much like a slave-holder, that I could not help drawing
down my lip-corners every time he passed near me. It was a great triumph
of politeness that I did not accompany the gesture with a movement of
my foot.

Mrs. Stowe's habitual stiffness of manner vanished the moment we spoke
together. We dived at once into public affairs, and I found faith and hope
stronger than anxiety in her mind. She has no more faith in politicians than
I have; and most especially does she distrust that selfish diplomat, William

H. Seward, who exerts so much ingenuity to say what he does *not* mean. It is a pity The Delphic Oracle has fallen into disuse. He would be invaluable to the priests in writing responses that might be turned *any* way, according as circumstances required. Sarah, let nobody ever induce you to trust that man! If he does not do the cause of freedom an irreparable mischief, it will merely be because the spirit of the people holds him upright so that he has no *temptation* to lean or crawl. I do not say this because I am rabid, or entirely one-sided. I recognize the usefulness of expediency; but its legitimate province is to choose between wise and unwise *modes of advancing principles*. To *compromise principles* is *never* expediency, however *appearances* may, for a time, indicate the contrary; and the politician who is willing to compromise *principle* is never a statesman, in any true and large sense of the word. Such men as Seward are capable of doing great mischief to noble young souls. Distinctions between right and wrong get all enveloped in fog by such diplomatic influence. Mrs. Stowe agreed with me in thinking that the spirit of the people would render it *politic* for him to walk straight. God and the people we *can* rely upon; the people, because God is now moving them. Thus far, events have been wonderfully over-ruled. They so plainly indicate the Divine *intention*, that I cannot be otherwise than hopeful about the result. If God *has* determined to deliver these people from the house of bondage, William H. Seward will be no more than a fly on his chariot wheels. So let him go!

I was extremely pleased with Mrs. Stowe, and also with Professor Stowe. I noticed in her continual indications of *Puritan* education. She said she had been convinced that slavery would be overthrown, ever since our Chief Justice passed *under the chain*, to enter the Court House; it was one of those *signs*, such as God inspired the old *Prophets* to enact, to reveal to the people the depth of their degradation and, from that time to the present, she thought the hand of God had been very remarkably and peculiarly manifest in the ordering of events. The conviction that all this could not be for *nothing*, she said, was the foundation of her faith that Pharaoh would be swamped and Israel was to go free. I am surprised to find how indifferent I am to the drowning of Pharaoh's hosts, provided the Israelites get on dry, firm ground. The fact is my Christian patience and forbearance are utterly exhausted. Every now and then, I sincerely *try* to get a fresh stock; but then comes along some Col. Cowden, or Col. Jones, and fills me with such wrath, that I want to behead half the world. How such incidents deprive the war of its moral dignity! In view of such things, no wonder the English press speaks of North and South as if it were "six of one and half a dozen of the other." But I believe the hearts of the *soldiers* are right. God bless him who *refused* to obey orders to arrest fugitive slaves! I was rejoiced to see that the officers did not *dare* to *repeat* the orders. I am trying to find out that soldier's name. It ought to be engraved on white marble, in letters of gold.

I suppose you may have some curiosity to know how I came to be in the midst of a large party, the first time these twenty-five years. It was the Golden Wedding of Alpheus Bigelow Esq. of Weston. He is a distant relative of Mr. Child, and has been very attentive to him ever since he was a young man. They have tried to get me to their house for the last eight years, that I have lived within three miles of them; and, at last, I yielded to the urgent solicitations of the good old lady, because it was her Golden Wedding, and she was thoroughly anti-slavery. I happened to have a spic-spam new light silk, brown & white, in which I made a very respectable figure. I thought I shouldn't know how to behave; but after I got there, I forgot all about it, which is the surest way to behave well. As for the slight gestures I made at the Bell Everett malignant, I don't think anybody noticed them. I merely indulged in them for the satisfaction of my own mind.

I wish you would let me publish, in the Traveller, the anecdote you told me about Mr. Shaw's father's parting request to his grandsons about intemperance and slavery. If published with his name it would have great weight, and do great good in helping on public opinion at this time; but I will not do it, of course, without permission from you and Frank. I send you the extract from your letter, which I took the liberty to publish. In *that* case, no *persons* were mentioned, but I now want to use the *name* of Robert G. Shaw.

You don't know how my mind was relieved by your visit. I was *so* glad to see you looking so well! For several days after you were gone, it seemed as if otto of rose had be spilled in the house. The fragrance will never entirely depart. There never was such a profitable investment of capital as the strawberries you brought. I dispensed them to two aged neighbors, and four poor invalids, and made them all happy. Rich people never know how good anything can taste. I hope that makes you suitably uneasy at your own unfortunate condition.[4]

## Notes

1. Lydia Maria Child to Sarah Blake Sturgis Shaw, 5 September 1852, *Letters of Lydia Maria Child with a Biographical Introduction*, edited by John Greenleaf Whittier (Boston: Houghton, Mifflin, and Co., 1883), p. 280.

2. John Bell, a Tennessee slaveholder, and Edward Everett, a well-known Massachusetts politician, ran for President and Vice-President on the Constitutional Union Party in the election of 1860 and lost to the Republican ticket of Abraham Lincoln and Hannibal Hamlin.

3. Child wrote the following in the left margin of the first page: "Have you read *Silas Marner?* Those *Adam Bede* books are wonderfully great. How deeply you must feel the death of your friend Mrs. Browning! What a great and glorious woman she was!"

4. Child wrote the closing lines in the margin of the third page of the letter: "Remember me with great affection to Frank, and believe me always your loving old friend Mariquita—". Child often signed her letters to Shaw as "Mariquita" and sometimes "Mariechen." Child added another line in the margin of the fifth page of the letter: "Mr. Child united with in [*sic*] blessings on you and all your house."

Lydia Maria Child to [Sarah Blake (Sturgis) Shaw], 21 July 1861, bM S Am 1417 (78), The Houghton Library, Harvard University.

# [Lunch with Stowe, August 1862]

## Lucy Larcom

Born in Beverly, Massachusetts, Lucy Larcom (1824–1893) went to work in a textile mill in nearby Lowell at the age of eleven. She began her writing career by contributing to the *Lowell Offering*, a monthly literary magazine written and published by women working at the mills from 1840 to 1845. Toward the end of her life, Larcom wrote about her experiences in her autobiography, *A New England Girlhood* (1889). Larcom also trained as a teacher and taught at schools in Illinois and Massachusetts. She published poetry in a variety of periodicals and anthologies and was included in Rufus W. Griswold's influential volume *The Female Poets of America* (1849). Larcom became friendly with Annie Fields in 1861, about the same time that Fields and Stowe began their friendship. Larcom was one of the many women writers Fields helped, and Stowe published Larcom's work in the magazine *Hearth and Home* that she coedited from 1868 to 1869. In this entry for her diary in August 1862, Larcom describes her first meeting with Stowe at her home in Andover, Massachusetts.

August 10. This week has been a more remarkable one than any in my life, I believe, in the way of seeing people I have heard of, and had some little curiosity about. Last Thursday was spent at Andover, and one of the golden days it was. The day itself was one of shine and shadow just rightly blended; and the place, the well-known Hill of the students, was in its glory. After sitting awhile in church, where the learned Professors, Park, Phelps, and Stowe, sat in state (I wonder if Professors dread anniversaries and conspicuous positions as we boarding-school teachers do!) we went up the hill to accept an invitation to lunch with Mrs. Harriet Beecher Stowe. It was beautiful as a page from one of her own story books.

Mrs. Stowe herself I liked, and her house and garden were just such as an authoress like her ought to have. It all had what I imagine to be an English look, the old stone house, with its wild vines and trees brought into shape in picturesque walks, and its cool refreshment-room looking off over the

Stowe house, "Stone Cabin," Andover, Massachusetts, ca. 1890. Harriet Beecher Stowe Center, Hartford, Connecticut.

river, the city, and the far hills, to the mountains; the arrangement of the table, too, showing so much of the poetess. I could not have called upon Mrs. Stowe formally; as it was, nothing could have been much pleasanter, of that kind.

Then before I left I called upon some old friends; a call which finished the day very delightfully; for there, besides the cordiality of really well-bred people, I saw one of the sweetest specimens of girlhood that can be shown in New England, I fancy. Beauty does not often fascinate me, in its common acceptation; but where there is soul in a young, sweet face— modesty and intelligence that greet you like the fragrance of a rosebud before it is well opened—it is so rare a thing in these "Young America" days that it makes me a little extravagant in admiration, perhaps.

Saturday I spent at Amesbury; it was not quite like other visits, for two other visitors were there; yet I enjoyed one of them especially; an educated mulatto girl, refined, lady-like in every respect, and a standing reply to those who talk of the "inferiority of the colored race." It is seldom that I see any one who attracts me so much, whose acquaintance I so much desire, just from first sight. She would like to teach at Port Royal, but the government will not permit. Ah, well! my book ends with no prospect of the war's end. Three hundred thousand recruits have just been raised, and as many more are to be drafted.

Many talk as if there never was a darker time than now. We have no unity of purpose; the watchword is "Fight for the Government!" but that is an abstraction the many cannot comprehend. If they would say, "Fight for Liberty—your own liberty, and that of every American," there would be an impetus given to the contest that, on our side, "drags its slow length along." This is an extreme opinion, our law-abiding people say, but I believe we shall come to worse extremes before the war ends.

From *Lucy Larcom: Life, Letters, and Diary*, edited by Daniel Dulany Addison (Boston: Houghton, Mifflin, 1894), pp. 146–147.

# [Stowe and President Abraham Lincoln,
2 December 1862]

CHARLES EDWARD STOWE AND LYMAN BEECHER STOWE

Perhaps the most enduring story about Stowe's life is her meeting with President Abraham Lincoln during the Civil War. According to Joan Hedrick, on 2 December 1862, Stowe, her daughter Hatty, and her sister Isabella Beecher Hooker, accompanied by Senator and Mrs. Henry Wilson of Massachusetts, went to tea at the White House, at the invitation of Mary Todd Lincoln.[1] Stowe had traveled to Washington in November for the express purpose of lobbying the President to issue the Emancipation Proclamation and to visit her son, Frederick, then a soldier serving in a regiment in Washington. As Hedrick explains, Stowe never wrote an account of the meeting, simply noting in a letter to her husband, Calvin: "I had a real funny interview with the President introduced by Henry Wilson, the particulars of which I will tell you."[2] In her account of the meeting, Annie Fields wrote:

> It was left for others to speak of her interview with President Lincoln. Her daughter was told that when the President heard her name he seized her hand, saying, "Is this the little woman who made this great war?" He then led her apart to a seat in the window, where they were withdrawn from other guests, and undisturbed. No one but those two souls will ever know what waves of thought and feeling swept over them in that brief hour.[3]

Nonetheless, family members provided recollections that have been reprinted as facts ever since. In 1911, Stowe's son and grandson, Charles Edward Stowe and Lyman Beecher Stowe, gave the fullest accounts of the meeting. One appeared in a brief paragraph at the end of "How Mrs. Stowe Wrote 'Uncle Tom's Cabin,'" published in *McClure's Magazine* in April 1911. In their centennial biography, *Harriet Beecher Stowe: The Story of Her Life*, they gave the following account of the famous story.

MRS. STOWE, in telling of her interview with Lincoln at this time, dwelt particularly on the rustic pleasantry with which that great man received her. She was introduced into a cosy room where the President had been seated

Illustration for "How Mrs. Stowe Wrote 'Uncle Tom's Cabin,'" by Charles Edward Stowe and Lyman Beecher Stowe, *McClure's Magazine*, April 1911. Love Library, University of Nebraska, Lincoln.

before an open fire, for the day was damp and chilly. It was Mr. Seward[4] who introduced her, and Mr. Lincoln rose awkwardly from his chair, saying, "Why, Mrs. Stowe, right glad to see you!" Then with a humorous twinkle in his eye, he said, "So you're the little woman who wrote the book that made this great war! Sit down, please," he added, as he seated himself once more before the fire, meditatively warming his immense hands over the smouldering embers by first extending the palms, and then turning his wrists so that the grateful warmth reached the backs of his hands. The first thing he said was, "I do love an open fire. I always had one to home." Mrs. Stowe particularly remarked on the expression "to home." "Mr. Lincoln," said Mrs. Stowe, "I want to ask you about your views on emancipation." It was on that subject that the conversation turned. Mrs. Stowe, like so many others at this time, had failed to grasp Lincoln's farsighted statesmanship. "Mr. Lincoln has been too slow," she said, speaking of what she called his "Confiscation Bill." "He should have done it sooner, and with an impulse. . . ." Bismarck has said something to the effect that a statesman who should permit himself to be guided exclusively by abstract moral considerations in his public acts would be like a man taking a long pole in his mouth and trying to run through a thick woods on a dark night. Would it have been for the best interests of humanity to have had a John Brown or a Garrison in Lincoln's place in those critical moments of the Civil War?

At this period Mrs. Stowe's interest in literature was overwhelmed by the intensity with which she entered into the great struggle that was going on about her. She wrote to the *Independent*, "The agitations and mental excitements of the war have in the case of the writer, as in the case of many others, used up the time and strength that would have been devoted to authorship. Who could write on stories that had a son to send to battle, with Washington beleaguered, and the whole country shaken as with an earthquake?"

### Notes

1. Joan Hedrick, *Harriet Beecher Stowe: A Life* (Oxford: Oxford University Press, 1994), p. 305.

2. Quoted in Hedrick, p. 306.

3. Annie Fields, *Authors and Friends* (Boston: Houghton Mifflin, 1896), p. 81.

4. In her letter to her husband, Stowe wrote that Senator Henry Wilson introduced her, not William H. Seward, Lincoln's Secretary of State.

From Charles Edward Stowe and Lyman Beecher Stowe, *Harriet Beecher Stowe: The Story of Her Life* (Boston: Houghton Mifflin Co., 1911), pp. 202–204.

# [Impressions of Stowe in 1867]

### GAIL HAMILTON

Gail Hamilton was the pseudonym of Mary Abigail Dodge (1833–1896). After graduating from the Ipswich Female Seminary, she taught school for a few years, including a position at the Hartford Female Seminary, founded by Stowe's sister Catharine Beecher. In 1856, Dodge began her writing career by sending some of her poems to Gamaliel Bailey, editor of the *National Era*, in which *Uncle Tom's Cabin* had been serialized. Bailey was impressed with her work and she moved to Washington, working as a governess to his children and writing for the *Era* and several other periodicals. Single by choice, Dodge lived an independent life and frequently wrote about women's rights and responsibilities. She became friendly with Annie Fields and with her husband, James, who became her publisher and who introduced her to a variety of New England writers. Dodge admired Stowe and viewed her career as a model.[1] Throughout her own long career, Dodge advocated for equal pay and equal treatment for women writers. After Stowe read Hamilton's *Woman's Wrongs: A Counter-Irritant* (1868), she wrote to Fanny Fern: "If you haven't *read it*, before you are a day older—Its decidedly the brightest, cleanest healthiest noblest kind of a book—Do you know her? She is a trump—a real original—healthy—largehearted & simple indeed & good as she can be."[2] Stowe and Dodge became friends, corresponding and visiting one another. In this entry from her diary, Dodge describes her first meeting with Stowe.

June 17, 1867

Just as we were sitting down to dinner the bell rang, and Professor and Mrs. Stowe appeared at the door. They had ridden from Andover to Georgetown, and from G. here, and were to go back to G. to dinner at five. They stayed till near four o'clock. The first half hour I did not like her. After she came out to her lunch she glowed up and was very simple, natural, agreeable, and entertaining. About half an hour before she went away she

Gail Hamilton (Mary Abigail Dodge), frontispiece of
*Gail Hamilton's Life in Letters* (1901). Love Library,
University of Nebraska, Lincoln.

gave out again and was silent, but I understood it and did not mind. He
rallied her and declared she had not come up to his expectations. She told
me coming out that the fact was she had talked just as much as she could,
but of course as she had come twenty-five miles she was tired. She is plain
at first sight, but not after five minutes. Her face is very attractive and her
smile charming and sometimes very expressive. When she was silent it said
a great deal. She said Professor Stowe was gone to Canada before she got
home from Florida and she had not seen the critter since February. They
are not going to sell their Hartford house, but only going to Florida, winters. She says he has been round at a great rate trading on female sensibili-
ties over going to Florida, and making people think he was the most abused
man in the world. They are evidently very happy together.

## Notes

1. Susan Coultrap-McQuin, *Doing Literary Business: American Women Writers in the Nineteenth Century* (Chapel Hill: University of North Carolina Press, 1990), p. 108.

2. Quoted in Joan Hedrick, *Harriet Beecher Stowe: A Life* (Oxford: Oxford University Press, 1994), p. 159.

From Gail Hamilton, *Gail Hamilton's Life in Letters*, edited by H. Augusta Dodge, vol. 1 (Boston: Lee and Shepard, 1901), pp. 594–595.

# [Stowe's Life after the Civil War]

### Florine Thayer McCray

Florine Thayer McCray (1851?–1899), a journalist and novelist, was a neighbor of the Stowe family in Hartford in the 1880s. She was a regular contributor to the *Hartford Sunday Globe*, edited the *City Mission Record*, and published articles and stories in New York newspapers and the *Lady's Home Journal*.[1] According to Forrest Wilson, McCray was a colorful character with a reputation as a "rather vulgar pushing person" who "was fond of driving, manwise, a smart turnout."[2] Nonetheless, McCray and Stowe were friendly, visiting one another and taking long walks together. In 1887, McCray asked Stowe if she might write a sketch of her life. Stowe consented, sending her a note that later appeared as the frontispiece of McCray's *The Life and Work of Harriet Beecher Stowe* (1889):

> Dear Friend:—You are quite welcome to write the sketch you propose. I believe that all the material for such an one is quite at hand and at your disposal. Yours very truly, H. B. Stowe.

In fact, McCray's 450 page biography was considerably more than a "sketch," and while she was at work on it Stowe evidently worried that she should not have given her permission. In the meantime, her son, Charles Edward Stowe, was preparing his biography, *The Life of Harriet Beecher Stowe* (1889), which appeared just before McCray's book and was the one that Stowe considered authorized and definitive. Stowe reportedly did not like McCray's biography and was furious about the inclusion of her note at the beginning of the book. However, McCray worked hard to get her facts right, and her book is an animated account of Stowe's life. In this chapter, McCray provides a detailed picture of Stowe's life in the years following the Civil War, describing her first visit to Florida, her new writing projects, and her growing interest in spiritualism.

In 1865, after the war was finished, Mrs. Stowe for the first time in her life went South. She spent some weeks in Florida at Jacksonville, at a plantation upon the St. John's river, and later, purchased an estate at Mandarin. Mrs. Stowe made this purchase with a view to the comfort and betterment of her oldest son Frederick, who had been from his youth afflicted with

Engraving of Harriet Beecher Stowe, ca. 1866, used as frontispiece for *Our Young Folks* (1866). Harriet Beecher Stowe Center, Hartford, Connecticut.

a delicate and nervous organization, and a weak will which could not restrain him from indulgence in stimulants, which accentuated his misery, and made his unhappy life a deeper sorrow to his friends.

Under the supervision of a practical planter, the land was cleared, orange trees were set and a house built upon the banks of the St. John's river, under the shade of some immense live oak trees. This place became the much loved winter home which George Eliot in one of her letters to Mrs. Stowe refers to as "your Western Sorrento." Thither were annually transported the *lares* and *penates*[3] of the family, animate as well as inanimate, for some pet dogs and cats made the trip several times, returning with the family, at the approach of warm weather, to their Hartford home.

Mrs. Stowe became deeply interested in the building of an Episcopal church at Mandarin, lending effective pecuniary assistance, as well as personal aid in collecting funds.

She humorously related to the writer how she once became an involuntary and successful speculator in real estate,—buying a small piece of land at $200, and selling it afterwards for $7,000, a fair profit she thought upon the investment. The money was put to good use in the purchase of a parsonage for her youngest son, when he became pastor at the Windsor Avenue Congregational church in Hartford.

Professor Stowe, who was now at liberty to employ his profound knowledge of ancient history, Eastern languages, ancient and modern, as well as his rich fund of Biblical lore, in giving to the world what had heretofore been locked in the ancient languages and specially studied by theological students, was deeply absorbed upon a work, which was published two years later by the Hartford Publishing Company—"The Origin and History of the Books of the New Testament."

Of a very special nature, Professor Stowe naturally talked of his work and his family were called upon to listen to his conclusions. Mrs. Stowe as usual offered many suggestions of value, receiving in return practical assistance from him in the literary work which pressed heavily upon her.

During the year 1867 Mrs. Stowe prepared a set of biographical sketches which was published early in 1868, being issued by the Hartford Publishing Company, "by subscription only." The collection made an octavo volume of some five hundred and seventy-five pages, with eighteen fine steel plate portraits. This house had made a success of Professor Stowe's book upon "The Origin and History of the Books of the New Testament," selling some sixty thousand copies. They sold about forty thousand of Mrs. Stowe's "Men of Our Times," paying her a handsome royalty, besides an extra thousand dollars for the sketch of her brother Henry Ward Beecher, which she rather reluctantly supplied.

The volume, "Men of Our Times; or Leading Patriots of the Day," comprised narratives of the lives and deeds of American statesmen, generals and orators, including biographical sketches and anecdotes of Lincoln, Grant, Garrison, Sumner, Chase, Wilson, Greeley, Farragut, Andrew,

Colfax, Stanton, Douglas, Buckingham, Sherman, Sheridan, Howard, Phillips and Beecher.

It was appropriately dedicated to the young men of America, and in the preface where the writer speaks of herself as the editor, thus acknowledging her indebtedness to various sources from which she collected her facts, she gives this terse and cheering paragraph:

> It will be found when the sum of all these biographies is added up, that the qualities which have won this great physical and moral victory have not been so much exceptional gifts of genius or culture, as those more attainable ones which belong to man's moral nature.

This line of literary work, which may perhaps without disparagement be called mechanical, as it certainly is not imaginative if the biographer be true to his high calling, is alas! frequently made to serve base uses, in which good will becomes the father to fair statement, or personal bias sees through a glass darkly the doubtful incidents of a career. But Mrs. Stowe demonstrated, to the surprise of her friends, the possession of a faculty which is supposed to be quite apart from that of a graceful essayist, or a successful novel writer, or the swift re-incarnation of painful realities into such a burning creation as that of *Uncle Tom's Cabin*.

Mrs. Stowe's able handling of the complex political questions, and the sifting of the essential factors from a mass of materials bearing upon events in the history of the war which had lately closed, was natural to her logical mind and clear judgment, and enhanced by the intense interest with which she had for years followed the succeeding events in our nation's history. Men were events, in those surcharged times, and Mrs. Stowe's sketches of reformers, politicians, generals and naval heroes are instinct with individual life and are rare memorials of men all of whom but one, Lincoln, were then living; more than two-thirds of whom have now preceded their illustrious biographer, into the "undiscovered country."

In the same year Mrs. Stowe published a small volume of Religious Poems. It comprised twenty-eight of her published contributions to *The Independent* and other periodicals. They are unassuming in style, but sweetly and tenderly religious in sentiment, with flavors of the woods and sky and youthful memories of music and poetry pervading them all, as they did her prose writings.

In Dec., 1868, Mrs. Stowe, in answer to the solicitations of the projector appeared as co-editor, with Donald G. Mitchell (Ik. Marvel), of a weekly illustrated journal called *Hearth and Home*. It was devoted to the interests of the "Farm, Garden and Fireside." Joseph B. Lyman and Mary M. Dodge, the present editor of *St. Nicholas*, were associate editors. Among the contributors were Oliver Wendell Holmes, William Cullen Bryant, J. T. Trowbridge, Grace Greenwood, Rose Terry and other well known writers of high literary merit. Mrs. Stowe, who followed Mr. Mitchell in the editorial columns in the first number, wrote a characteristic "Greeting," and furnished a long article descriptive of "How we kept Thanksgiving at Oldtown." The editor-in-chief appended a note announcing it was to appear the following season, and sure enough, here nearly all the personages, which later appeared in "Old Town Folks," made their first bow. It was a draft from the salient points of her book in preparation.

But Mrs. Stowe's precarious health forbade any engagement so exacting as that of editorship, and her connection with *Hearth and Home* continued but a few months.

As Mrs. Stowe became past middle life the fits of abstraction which were peculiar and natural to her, increased and deepened to so great a degree, that her personal appearance which had always been quite remarkable in various ways, became decidedly eccentric. A friend who was entertaining her in New York about this time, relates having invited a company of enthusiastic admirers, a number of whom were young ladies, to meet her at luncheon. As the time arrived, the hostess observed with considerable dismay that her distinguished guest was falling into a state of moodiness, which augered little for the entertainment of the expectant company.

When the ladies arrived and were presented, Mrs. Stowe greeted them with the far-away expression which was becoming habitual, and sat through the luncheon absorbed in thought, speaking only once of her own volition, when she requested some one to "Please pass the butter," and immediately relapsed into impenetrable mental solitude. It amusingly suggests those people so cleverly described in one of the essays of whimsical young Winthrop Macworth Praed, who in the midst of noisy crowds or the attacks of direct conversationalists, were still—alone. Mrs. Stowe afterwards declared that she was thinking out scenes for *Old Town Folks*, which story she then had in hand.

Early in 1869, Fields, Osgood & Co. published this book, which must be counted as the third of Mrs. Stowe's great works and, though it is open to criticism on several points, judging as we must from the effect of a work, rather than by its conformation to certain canons laid out by literary law makers, it must be pronounced one of her most powerful and characteristic works. Its popular success sufficiently attests to the intrinsic worth of its sentiments and the picturesque power of its delineations.

Next in numbers to the people who universally respond to a mention of *Uncle Tom's Cabin*, are the vast army of readers who know *Old Town Folks*, and instantly express their enjoyment of it. Though announced and sometimes spoken of as a novel, it cannot, strictly speaking, be characterized as such. It is rather, a series of vivid and natural pictures of New England life, near the close of the last century, loosely strung together upon the romance of four young persons, a tale so uneventful in its course, and mild in its denouements as to scarcely deserve the name of plot.

In *Uncle Tom's Cabin* the author's strength was in her burning earnestness of purpose in laying existing facts before the Christian world. In *Minister's Wooing* her power was in the practical grasp and forcible presentation of the results of certain theological doctrines. In *Old Town Folks* she excels most rarely in the admirable depictions of characters peculiar to the locality and time, in which the story is laid. The word characters is used advisedly, for Harriet Beecher Stowe looked at the world from the outside, believing that actions are materialized motives, and results, the accumulation of intentions. She had no taste for the analytical style which tends ever toward a dyspeptic anxiety for the workings of internal springs, often disappointing expectation in resultant effects.

The story is laid in the town of Natick, Massachusetts, at a period when New England was the seed-bed of American civilization. The author observed that New England had been to our republic what the Dorian Hive was to Greece; a capital place to emigrate from, whence were carried the ideas and principles which, disseminated over the vast area of our country, have grown into the tense and strong fibre of the American character. The author, who chose to write *Old Town Folks* under the pseudonym of "Horace Holyoke," acknowledges her studies for this object to have been pre-Raphaelite, drawn from real characters, real scenes and real incidents. Some of her material was gleaned from early colonial history, but many of the characters were drawn from conversations with Professor Stowe, who had rare descriptive and mimetical powers, and suggested weaving some of his personal recollections and experiences into the work.

The portion laid in "Cloudland" plainly indicates reminiscences of her youth in Litchfield. The whole was connected by the genius of the writer into the remarkable work so familiar to American readers, by whom it is fondly prized and believed in, as a rarely truthful and graphic description of the New England people, from whom sprung all the intellectual strength and firm principle which dwell in the American character.

The social history of Old Town, as it is known in these traditions, transpired during Professor Stowe's youth, and much of it is reproduced in this story, which is considered one of the most artistic of its gifted author. It appeared more easy, taking much of it from her husband's childish experiences, to write the book in the first person, and from a masculine standpoint. She must put herself into a boy's shoes to know Sam Lawson, who was an early friend of Professor Stowe, as she has made us know him, the typical Yankee do-nothing and universal genius. Glimpses of him we have seen embodied in various thriftless and intolerable men, who yet had a vast and fascinating range of homely lore, and that natural faculty to do interesting things which is such a delight to youth. As well try to describe Sam Lawson to the readers of this chapter, as to tell them of Uncle Tom. He is as well known as George Washington, and alas! perhaps dearer to the hearts of average republican humanity. He is perhaps the best instance of character drawing, ever done by the artist who made such portraiture her specialty.

Uncle "Fliakim," the dear Grandmother, Old Crab Smith, Miss Asphyxia, and Miss Mehitable Rossiter, are indisputably real people. They still exist, possibly modified in form by the friction of advancing civilization, which ever tends to wear away individual peculiarities and reduce outward demeanor to a dead level of cultivated repression, but we know them, or have known them at some time.

The stately Congregational minister in his white wig and impressive silk gown with ruffles at his throat and wrists, his awe-inspiring, brocaded "Lady," the colored retainers who felt but lightly the fetters which bound them to their Colonial owners, and the remnants of the tribes of Massachusetts Indians who are introduced as a sort of living scenic effect, we do not know. But we can easily believe in them, since all testimony goes to prove that they were features of the time.

They all live and speak and possess distinct personality, but the figures of Harry and Tina Percival do not strike us as real young people. Tina seems not half so charming as the author would have us feel, in fact is a repetition of similar failures who appear up to this time in Mrs. Stowe's writing, whenever she essays to depict a pretty, frivolous darling, who beneath all her fascinating lightness and brilliant scintillations (which the reader cannot see) is said to have a fund of moral strength and right feeling. Harry, who is the poetical counterpart of the hero, is, in spite of the author's intentions, something of a prig. Neither does Horace Holyoke take on the rounded personality which we expect and desire in the scholarly, nervous, high strung and conscientious boy which he should appear. The inference is forced upon one, that she has not personally known such personalities and is not able to construct symmetrical characters, from stray bits of disjointed skeletons.

The interest and value of the work, taken as a whole, would seem to raise it above criticism of these characters for it is no less art which employs models, when the portraiture is a perfect representation of life and the composition well balanced, and carefully managed as to tone and color, but they demonstrate the fact that imagination was not one of the special gifts of Harriet Beecher Stowe. She possessed rare descriptive power, a pure quality of humor, shrewdness, philosophy, and a certain happy selection of language which gave a graphic touch to the whole, but where purely creative genius was needed, she was not successful.

Indeed, her natural make-up almost of necessity precluded this faculty, which is the concomitant of pure fiction. Its resultant action was remarkably absent in her life and social intercourse, as she never seemed to find a necessity for the polite prevarications or quick inventions which are sometimes employed to anoint the wheels of social life. Her inherent and instinctive honesty, her habitual concern for the higher certitudes of existence and for historical facts, were not related to the genius of fiction. She had, rather, the talent for biography, having the memory for such work, and the perception of the logic of events, which has made her a historian, rather than a poet.

It is indeed a poverty of invention which necessitates or permits the chief characters in *Old Town Folks* to make their advent as waifs of foreign birth, and orphans who are thrown upon the charity of cross-grained relatives, who in various ways, short of absolute cruelty, make their young lives miserable; to re-incarnate her typical minister, Lyman Beecher, and schoolmaster, John P. Brace, under the thin disguise of new names; introducing again the woman of high education and deep feeling who suffers under the cruel logic of the theology of the period, who originated in Mrs. Fisher, lived in "Minister's Wooing" as Mrs. Marvyn, and again completes a short cycle and is born in "Old Town Folks" as Esther Avery; and showing forth the fascinations and villainies of a *cousin of Aaron Burr*, as the only possible conqueror of the well-read but inexperienced, country girls.

The reader loses faith in these persons who walk as cheerfully upon the stage as if they were a "new attraction," and wishes the artist could renew her selection of choice models. But these portraits taken from persons she had known, and the discussion of social and political questions always strongly flavored by theology, were Mrs. Stowe's natural, inherited stock in trade. This was her world, her line of thought, her idea of intellectual and physical existence. It was doubtless, taken all in all, the most remarkable literary endowment of the generation which rolled in a wave of talented American authors. In it we see reproduced her own spirit, tastes, preferences and beliefs. If for nothing else, *Old Town Folks* is valuable as a suggestion of her mental environment at mature life, for the conversations and tenor of life at Hartford rested upon such topics and questions as these which underlay the story of *Old Town Folks*, and formed a solid basis upon which to rest her opinions upon themes of recent occurrence, all over the world. It may be said that Mrs. Stowe had no literary life in its social sense—that while she met and talked with many of the gifted writers and thinkers of her day, she formed no intimacies, was not in the least diverted from her own individuality, or wrought upon by the gradual change which was coming over the methods and manners of literature.

She remained first and always a Beecher, living in her recollections of New England people, contented, more, proud to dwell upon her family, past and present, and to let the less pronounced thinking world go on its way, as she went on hers. In the second place, she was a Stowe, affectionately devoted to her husband, whom she fervently respected as a scholar of deep research, and acquirements which took hold upon the past, through ancient languages even to the word of God; who was furthermore possessed of versatile gifts, and some spiritual insights and perceptions, which were quite outside of common, human experience.

The fact that Mrs. Stowe wrote to George Eliot with whom she entered into an interesting correspondence at about this period, that Professor Stowe was the "visionary boy," whom she made the hero of *Old Town Folks*, and that the experiences which she related were phenomena of frequent occurrence with him, and had been so even from his earliest childhood, makes relevant a notice of some of the psychological conditions which were peculiar to the scholarly man, one who was by temperament and trend of mind as far as possible from the credulity or hallucination commonly attributed to believers in manifestations that appear to be supernatural. The descriptions of clairvoyant phenomena, which in themselves scarcely give adequate excuse for their frequent introduction in the experiences of Horace Holyoke, the hero of *Old Town Folks*, take on new significance and interest, when it appears that they are unexaggerated instances of the spiritual visitations, if one chooses to so call them, which were a life long, and recurring fact, with Professor Stowe.

Certain it is that Professor Stowe came into the world possessed of an uncommon attribute, which may be adversely considered, either as a sixth sense revealing hidden things, or as peculiar hallucinations. The latter conclusion, and the more natural one perhaps, is hardly compatible with his clear mentality and the sound judgment which he brought to bear upon this phenomenon itself, no less than upon all other topics. Neither is the theory held by Professor Park of Andover that his sight of things which were not apparent to other people was due to a disease of the optic nerve, altogether reasonable in consideration of the nervous ebullition which preceded and accompanied his visions, as has been described in *Old Town Folks*. The conclusion must be from the reader's point of view. Suffice to say that he was at times utterly unable to distinguish between tangible objects and the visions which passed before his mind's eye. In early childhood he was quite unaware that he held any power which was not common to humanity, supposing, naturally, that all people saw as he did, objects which were far out of reach of the eye.

As a near-sighted child sooner or later becomes aware that it is wanting in the far sight which is common, so Calvin E. Stowe early inferred that his friends could not see absent things and departed souls as he did, and he became as a young man somewhat in awe of his power, and loth to speak of it. When, however, in later years he recognized it as a peculiarity which he shared with a few other people, he came to regard it as an interesting fact, and conversed freely with intimate friends as to his sights and perceptions. In common with most other intelligent people, and especially so, because of his strange experiences, Professor and Mrs. Stowe became deeply interested in psychological manifestations. The matter was under frequent discussion and with friends they evoked surprising manifestations from "Planchette" and attended various so-called spiritualistic seances in New York. While in Rome, Mrs. Stowe in company with Elizabeth Barrett Browning and others received some surprising evidences of things occult and strange.

Upon this theme much of the correspondence with George Eliot dwelt, and Mrs. Stowe most feelingly interpreted the wave of spiritualism then rushing over America, as a sort of Rachel-cry of bereavement, towards the invisible existence of the loved ones; but her mature judgment, like that of her husband's, was against the value of mediumistic testimonies. So involved were they in trickeries and so defiled by low adventurers, that it was impossible to regard the movement in its imperfect development (which has not materially changed in twenty years), as otherwise than repulsive.

Though filled with the yearning which draws human hearts so strongly towards the hidden future, Mrs. Stowe could not be satisfied that the veil had ever been rent for human eyes. Professor Stowe never allied himself in any way with spiritualists, not deeming such revelations as had been given him, evidence which could be formulated into a creed, or depended upon as a religion. He joined his wife in the delightful correspondence with George Eliot and said, referring to the subject, "I have had no connection with any of the modern movements, except as father confessor."

He investigated his personal condition intelligently, and noted that the action of this sense depended greatly upon his physical condition, observing that when he was not in perfect health, his visions were of an unpleasant nature, though he did not perceive that an unhealthy state of the nerves or body at all increased the frequency or clearness of his visions. This fact, of course, will in the mind of most readers tend to relegate them to the realm of waking dreams, though it does not conclusively disprove the theory of the existence, either bodily or spiritually, of what he saw.

Those who desire to believe that Professor Stowe was a "medium" will receive as valuable testimony the fact that he not only saw, but believed he heard and conversed with these etherealized personalities. He was in the habit of conversing freely during the last ten years of his life with a dear friend, a young clergyman of Hartford, whom he found particularly vigorous in thought, and refreshing to his intellectual life. He often spoke to him of talking with his son Henry who had died years before, and one morning told him that the devil, taking advantage of his illness, had been grievously tempting him, night after night. Coming in the guise of a horseman, with terribly dark, hostile and violent manner yelling that his son Charles was dead, and questioning his faith in various aggravating ways.

"But," said he smiling with satisfaction, "I was ready for him last night. I had fortified myself with passages of Scripture. I found some things in Ephesians which were just what I wanted, and when he came last night, I *hurled* them at him. I tell you, it made him bark like a dog, and he took himself off. He won't trouble me again."

Professor Stowe also recounted to a friend an interview which he declared he had with Goethe, one day out under the trees. He intensely enjoyed the discussion with the great mind of the German Shakespeare and reported a most interesting explanation which the author of Faust gave of the celebrated closing lines of the second part of that great work—

> All of mortality is but a symbol shown,
> Here to reality longings have grown;
> How superhumanly wondrous, 'tis done.
> The eternal, the womanly Love leads us on.

These experiences, which seem to so singularly combine scholarship and speculation, positive knowledge of the highest order and beliefs which by a literal minded generation are generally deemed weakness, were not peculiar to his old age, but had continued with him all through his long, remarkably vigorous and logical, intellectual career.

While it must be allowed that Mrs. Stowe's representations of family life and its general trend of thought and conversation, are an inimitable reproduction of the thinking people of the old New England communities, and that this state of things was so general as to make families who were not so concerned and discursive, seem ignorant or set-apart as anomalies; dwelling so earnestly upon these themes in her books, not only proves her a true daughter and sister of her family, but by nature as naturally a minister of the gospel, a teacher of religion, a reformer and essayist, as Dr. Lyman Beecher himself, or the deepest thinker or most graceful speaker among his seven clerical sons. She had all of their impulse towards expression, all of their force and lucidity of thought, their grace, tenderness and humor, to which were added her feminine intuitions and sympathies.

George Eliot wrote to her—"I think your way of presenting the religious convictions, which are not your own, except by indirect fellowship, is a triumph of insight and true tolerance." It made Harriet Beecher Stowe what she was, the most remarkable and influential woman of her time.

*Old Town Folks* was published in Boston in May 1869, and by the first of August twenty-five thousand copies had been sold. It appeared simultaneously through Sampson and Low, in London. It ran through three large editions there in the same time. By the first of June, five forthcoming translations were announced in Germany, and it still remains constant in demand in several languages. The name of Sam Lawson became a household word all over the land, and Mrs. Stowe humored the public wish for more of him and his entertaining conversations, by issuing through Jas. R. Osgood & Co., a collection of fifteen tales called *Sam Lawson's Oldtown Fireside Stories.* It of course had a large sale and contains innocent amusement enough for many winter evenings.

### Notes

1. Details of McCray's life are taken from her obituary, "Mrs. Florine T. McCray," *Hartford Courant*, 13 March 1899, p. 3.

2. Forrest Wilson, *Crusader in Crinoline* (Philadelphia: J. B. Lippincott, 1941), pp. 629–630.

3. *Lares* is the Latin term for the gods and deities of the ancient Romans and *penates* is Latin for treasured household belongings.

From Florine Thayer McCray, *The Life-Work of the Author of "Uncle Tom's Cabin"* (New York: Funk and Wagnalls, 1889), pp. 367–383.

# From "International Copyright" (1867)

## JAMES PARTON

Born in England, James Parton (1822–1891) was a journalist and writer who became one of the most popular biographers of nineteenth-century America with his studies of Horace Greeley, Aaron Burr, Andrew Jackson, and Benjamin Franklin. Parton was also the third husband of Fanny Fern, whom he married in 1856. While his famous wife wrote weekly columns exclusively for the *New York Ledger*, Parton wrote for a number of influential periodicals, including the *Atlantic Monthly*. He was deeply absorbed in one of the most pressing issues of the day for writers—the lack of an international copyright. In the absence of such laws, writers had no control over foreign editions of their works, nor did they receive any share in the profits from international sales unless they went to a country and personally applied for a copyright, as Stowe did when she traveled to England to establish copyright for *Dred* (1856). Further, American writers had no control over dramatic performances of their works, since domestic copyright laws did not protect works of fiction from being adapted for the stage. Versions of *Uncle Tom's Cabin* were the most popular performances in the United States throughout most of the nineteenth century, but Stowe derived no profits from them. After Parton's "International Copyright" appeared in the *Atlantic Monthly* in 1867, Stowe wrote to thank him for his efforts on behalf of writers.[1] In so doing, she revived her friendship with Fern and enjoyed a lively correspondence with the couple for many years. In the following excerpt from his article, Parton uses Stowe as his major example of the ways in which the inadequate copyright laws harm American writers.

THERE IS AN American lady living at Hartford, in Connecticut, whom the United States has permitted to be robbed by foreigners of $200,000. Her name is Harriet Beecher Stowe. By no disloyal act has she or her family forfeited their right to the protection of the government of the United States. She pays her taxes, keeps the peace, and earns her livelihood by honest industry; she has reared children for the service of the Commonwealth; she

James Parton, 1869. Photographer/creator: Gurney and Son, Fifth Avenue, New York, copyright unknown. Fanny Fern and Ethel Parton Papers, Sophia Smith Collection, Smith College.

was warm and active for her country when many around her were cold or hostile;—in a word, she is a good citizen.

More than that: she is an illustrious citizen. The United States stands higher to-day in the regard of every civilized being in Christendom because she lives in the United States. She is the only woman yet produced on the continent of America to whom the world assigns equal rank in literature with the great authoresses of Europe. If, in addition to the admirable talents with which she is endowed, she had chanced to possess one more, namely, the excellent gift of plodding, she had been a consummate artist, and had produced immortal works. All else she has;—the seeing eye, the discriminating intelligence, the sympathetic mind, the fluent word, the sure and happy touch; and these gifts enabled her to render her country the precise service which it needed most. Others talked about slavery: she made us see it. She showed it to us in its fairest and in its foulest aspect; she revealed its average and ordinary working. There never was a fairer nor a kinder book than *Uncle Tom's Cabin*; for the entire odium of the revelation fell upon the Thing, not upon the unhappy mortals who were born and reared under its shadow. The reader felt that Legree was not less, but far more the victim of slavery than Uncle Tom, and the effect of the book was to concentrate wrath upon the system which tortured the slave's body and damned the master's soul. Wonderful magic of genius! The hovels and cottonfields which this authoress scarcely saw she made all the world see, and see more vividly and more truly than the busy world can ever see remote objects with its own unassisted eyes. We are very dull and stupid in what does not immediately concern us, until we are roused and enlightened by such as she. Those whom we call "the intelligent," or "the educated," are merely the one in ten of the human family who by some chance learned to read, and thus came under the influence of the class whom Mrs. Stowe represents.

It is not possible to state the amount of good which this book has done, is doing, and is to do. Mr. Eugene Schuyler, in the preface to the Russian novel which he has recently done the public the service to translate, informs us that the publication of a little book in Russia contributed powerfully to the emancipation of the Russian serfs. The book was merely a collection of sketches, entitled *The Memoirs of a Sportsman*; but it revealed serfdom to the men who had lived in the midst of it all their lives without ever seeing it. Nothing is ever seen in this world, till the searching eye of a sympathetic genius falls upon it. This Russian nobleman, Turgenef, noble in every sense, saw serfdom, and showed it to his countrymen. His volume was read by the present Emperor, and he saw serfdom; and he has since declared that the reading of that little book was "one of the first incitements to the decree which gave freedom to thirty millions of serfs." All the reading public of Russia read it, and *they* saw serfdom; and thus a public opinion was created, without the support of which not even the absolute Czar of all the Russias would have dared to issue a decree so sweeping and radical.

We cannot say as much for *Uncle Tom's Cabin*, because the public opinion of the United States which permitted the emancipation of the slaves was of a longer growth, and was the result of a thousand influences. But when we consider that the United States only just escaped dismemberment and dissolution in the late war, and that two great powers of Europe were only prevented from active interference on behalf of the Rebellion by that public opinion which *Uncle Tom's Cabin* had recently revived and intensified, we may at least believe, that, if the whole influence of that work could have been annihilated, the final triumph of the United States might have been deferred, and come only after a series of wars. That book, we may almost say, went into every household in the civilized world which contained one person capable of reading it. And it was not an essay; it was a vivid exhibition;—it was not read from a sense of duty, nor from a desire to get knowledge; it was read with passion; it was devoured; people sat up all night reading it; those who could read it to those who could not; and hundreds of thousands who would never have read it saw it played upon the stage. Who shall presume to say how many soldiers that book added to the Union army? Who shall estimate its influence in hastening emancipation in Brazil, and in preparing the amiable Cubans for a similar measure? Both in Cuba and Brazil the work has been read with the most passionate interest.

If it is possible to measure the political effect of this work, we may at least assert that it gave a thrilling pleasure to ten millions of human beings,—an innocent pleasure, too, and one of many hours' duration. We may also say, that, while enjoying that long delight, each of those ten millions was made to see, with more or less clearness, the great truth that man is not fit to be trusted with arbitrary power over his fellow. The person who afforded this great pleasure, and who brought home this fundamental truth to so many minds, was Harriet Beecher Stowe, of Hartford, in the State of Connecticut, where she keeps house, educates her children, has a book at the grocery, and invites her friends to tea. To that American woman every person on earth who read *Uncle Tom's Cabin* incurred a personal obligation. Every individual who became possessed of a copy of the book, and every one who saw the story played in a theatre, was bound, in natural justice, to pay money to her for service rendered, unless she expressly and formally relinquished her right,—which she has never done. What can be clearer than this? Mrs. Stowe, in the exercise of her vocation, the vocation by which she lives, performs a professional service to ten millions of people. The service is great and lasting. The work done is satisfactory to the customer. What can annul the obligation resting upon each to render his portion of an equivalent, except the consent of the authoress "first had and obtained"? If Mrs. Stowe, instead of creating for our delight and instruction a glorious work of fiction, had contracted her fine powers to the point of inventing a nutcracker or a match-safe, a rolling-pin or a needle-threader, every individual purchaser could have been compelled to pay money for the use of her ingenuity, and everybody would have thought it the most natural and proper thing in the world so to do. There are fifty American inventions now in use in Europe from which the inventors derive revenue. *Revenue!*— not a sum of money which, once spent, is gone forever, but that most solid and respectable of material blessings, a sum per annum! Thus we reward those who light our matches. It is otherwise that we compensate those who kindle our souls.

*Uncle Tom's Cabin*, like every other novelty in literature, was the late-maturing fruit of generations. Two centuries of wrong had to pass, before the Subject was complete for the Artist's hand, and the Artist herself was a flower of an ancient and gifted family. *The Autobiography of Lyman Beecher* has made known this remarkable family to the public. We can all see for ourselves how slowly and painfully this beautiful genius was nourished, —what a narrow escape it had from being crushed and extinguished amid the horrors of theology and the poverty of a Connecticut parsonage,—how it was saved, and even nurtured, by that extraordinary old father, that most strange and interesting character of New England, who could come home, after preaching a sermon that appalled the galleries, and play the fiddle and riot with his children till bedtime. A piano found its way into the house, and the old man, whose geniality was of such abounding force that forty years of theology could not lessen it, let his children read Ivanhoe and the other novels of Sir Walter Scott. Partly by chance, partly by stealth, chiefly by the force of her own cravings, this daughter of the Puritans obtained the scanty nutriment which kept her genius from starving. By and by, on the banks of the Ohio, within sight of a slave State, the Subject and the Artist met, and there, from the lips of sore and panting fugitives, she gained, in the course of years, the knowledge which she revealed to mankind in *Uncle Tom's Cabin*.

When she had done the work, the United States stood by and saw her deprived of three fourths of her just and legitimate wages, without stirring a finger for her protection. The book sold to the extent of two millions of copies, and the story was played in most of the theatres in which the English language is spoken, and in many French and German theatres. In one theatre in New York it was played eight times a week for twelve months. Considerable fortunes have been gained by its performance, and it is still a source of revenue to actors and managers. We believe that there are at least three persons in the United States, connected with theatres, who have gained more money from *Uncle Tom's Cabin* than Mrs. Stowe. Of all the immense sums which the exhibition of this story upon the stage has produced, the authoress has received nothing. When Dumas or Victor Hugo publishes a novel, the sale of the right to perform it as a play yields him from eighty thousand to one hundred and twenty thousand francs. These authors receive a share of the receipts of the theatre,—the only fair arrangement,—and this share, we believe, is usually one tenth; which is also the usual percentage paid to authors upon the sale of their books. If a French author had written *Uncle Tom's Cabin*, he would have enjoyed, —1. A part of the price of every copy sold in France; 2. A share of the receipts of every theatre in France in which he permitted it to be played; 3. A sum of money for the right of translation into English; 4. A sum of money for the right of translation into German. We believe we are far within the truth when we say, that a literary success achieved by a French author equal to that of *Uncle Tom's Cabin* would have yielded that author half a million dollars in gold; and that, too, in spite of the lamentable fact, that America would have stolen the product of his genius, instead of buying it.

Mrs. Stowe received for *Uncle Tom's Cabin* the usual percentage upon the sale of the American edition; which may have consisted of some three hundred thousand copies. This percentage, with some other trifling sums, may have amounted to forty thousand dollars. From the theatre she has received nothing; from foreign countries nothing, or next to nothing. This poor forty thousand dollars—about enough to build a comfortable house in the country, and lay out an acre or two of grounds—was the product of the supreme literary success of all times! A *corresponding* success in sugar, in stocks, in tobacco, in cotton, in invention, in real estate, would have yielded millions upon millions to the lucky operator. To say that Mrs. Stowe, through our cruel and shameful indifference with regard to the rights of authors, native and foreign, has been kept out of two hundred thousand dollars, honestly hers, is a most moderate and safe statement. This money was due to her as entirely as the sum named upon a bill of exchange is due to the rightful owner of the same. It was for "value received." A permanently attractive book, moreover, would naturally be more than a sum of money; it would be an estate; it would be an income. This wrong, therefore, continues to the present moment, and will go on longer than the life of the authoress. While we are writing this sentence, probably, some German, French, Spanish, Italian, Russian, or English bookseller is dropping into his "till" the price of a copy of *Uncle Tom's Cabin*, the whole of which he will keep, instead of sending ten per cent of it to Hartford on the 1st of January next. . . .

It was the intention of the founders of this Republic to give complete protection to intellectual property, and this intention is clearly expressed in the Constitution. Justified by the authority given in that instrument, Congress has passed patent laws which have called into exercise an amount of triumphant ingenuity that is one of the great wonders of the modern world; but under the copyright laws, enacted with the same good intentions, our infant literature pines and dwindles. The reason is plain. For a labor-saving invention, the United States, which abounds in everything but labor, is field enough, and the inventor is rewarded; while a great book cannot be remunerative unless it enjoys the market of the whole civilized world. The readers of excellent books are few in every country on earth. The readers of any one excellent book are usually very few indeed; and the purchasers are still fewer. In a world that is supposed to contain a thousand millions of people, it is spoke of as a marvel that two millions of them bought the most popular book ever published,—one purchaser to every five hundred inhabitants.

We say, then, to those members of Congress who go to Washington to do something besides make Presidents, that time has developed a new necessity, not indeed contemplated by the framers of the Constitution, yet covered by the Constitution; and it now devolves upon them to carry out the evident intention of their just and wise predecessors, which was, to secure to genius, learning, and talent the certain ownership of their productions. We want an international system which cannot be brought to market without exposing it to plunder,—property in a book being simply the right to multiply copies of it. We want this property secured, for a sufficient period, to the creator of the value, so that no property in a book can be acquired anywhere on earth unless by the gift or consent of the author thereof. There are men in Congress who feel all the magnitude and sacredness of the debt which they owe, and which their country owes, to the authors and artists of the time. We believe such members are more numerous now than they ever were before,—much more numerous. It is they who must take the leading part in bringing about this great measure of justice and good policy; and, as usual in such cases, some one man must adopt it as his special vocation, and never rest till he has conferred on mankind this immeasurable boon.

## Note

1. See Joyce Warren, *Fanny Fern: An Independent Woman* (New Brunswick: Rutgers University Press, 1992), pp. 275–276.

From James Parton, "International Copyright," *Atlantic Monthly* 20 (1867): 430–433; 451.

# "Petty Slanders" (1869)

## Catharine Beecher

After the publication of her *Treatise on Domestic Economy* (1841), Stowe's older sister Catharine Beecher (1800–1878) was among the most well-known women in the United States. A pioneer educator for women, she had established the Hartford Female Seminary in 1823 and wrote on a variety of religious and moral topics. Beecher was a major force in her sister's life. She remained single throughout her life and often lived with the Stowes, as she did during much of the time that Stowe was writing *Uncle Tom's Cabin*. In 1869, Beecher came to live in Stowe's home in Hartford and the two worked together on a revision of Beecher's *Treatise* under a new title, *The American Woman's Home.*[1] Stowe contributed several chapters on home decoration, and Beecher renewed her emphasis on the importance of the Christian home as the moral center of society. Although most of the reviews of the book were positive, Beecher was increasingly unhappy about the treatment the Beecher family was receiving in the press. She consequently sent a letter defending her family, and especially her sister, to several periodicals. While the *Saturday Evening Post* called it an "amusing" letter and regarded it as a clever way to advertise *The American Woman's Home*, the *New York Evangelist* agreed that the press was intrusive but told its readers: "The members of the Beecher family have done their full share to create the present morbid desire for gossip and personalities."[2] Indeed, the letter, one of Beecher's rare extended commentaries on her sister, also offers insights into the emerging culture of celebrity in the aftermath of the Civil War.

To the Honorable Conductors of the Public Press:

Gentlemen:—I have the greatest respect for your profession, and am pained by whatever tends to lessen its respectability and usefulness. I therefore beg leave to bring to your notice a matter which is both a private grievance and an injury to your calling.

I refer to the increasing circulation of falsehoods and slanders, especially as they bear on the private feelings and interests of my sex. To illustrate this, allow me to state some of my own experiences within a very short

[176]

Catharine Beecher, ca. 1870 to 1875. Harriet Beecher Stowe Center, Hartford, Connecticut.

time, premising the fact that slurs and falsehoods on honored and dear friends are often more painful than personal injuries.

Among many other false and discreditable stories circulated of my venerated father, I have again and again at different periods read in the newspapers that at an appointed meeting he wept through all the services, of reading psalms, the prayers and the preaching, when only one man was present, who was converted by this absurd performance. Again, and quite recently, I read a long account in various newspapers of the details of an abrupt courtship which were as false to his well known character for delicacy and discretion as they were to that of the lady thus implicated. Again, I read of one of my brothers, who at his son's ordination, charged him not to forget that he was the grandson of his grandfather, the son of his father, and the nephew of his uncle; which foolish speech, I believe was made, but by another person, and not by my brother.

Again, I read a version of an old Almanac story that amused our family circle in childhood, of a coarse and irreverent minister, who began his sermon with saying "it is damned hot!" and this stale anecdote was fastened on another brother, and discussed week after week, as to its probable truth, although publicly denied by him, while every attendant at his church will affirm its impossible occurrence.

Then, I read that my sister, owning a place in Florida, had lost it for want of a proper land title; and again, that all her orange crop was blasted, and again, that she had changed her opinion of the negro character and concluded them to be utterly worthless. These are but a small portion of the falsehoods freely circulated in the public press of only one family circle, and it is but one specimen of the manner in which very many other family friends are annoyed, and often wounded, by such violation of the rules of common courtesy and justice by a portion of the public press. At the same time, the effect of such things on the character of the press of our country is most unfortunate; so much so that it is fast becoming a proverb that, what is found in newspapers is as likely to prove false as true.

The most recent outrage of this kind toward my family friends is one for which legal redress is provided for men, but from which a sensitive woman is debarred. This is a falsehood current in connection with the criticism on a new work by my sister, Mrs. Stowe, and myself, *The American Woman's Home*, in which we appear as teachers of domestic duties and economy in all departments; and is a direct public attack upon what I may call the

[178]

professional reputation of my sister. In the very introduction of the book it is stated that the authors were trained in early life by mothers and an aunt, who united an extraordinary combination of domestic talents and experience. Add to this the fact that the sister whose domestic character has been assailed has not only the appropriate training, but has both talent and taste for domestic employments, and resorts to them as a pleasure and relief from literary labor, so that in no case is she necessarily a dependent on servile caprices. When resident in foreign lands, her interest and quick perceptions added to her home acquisitions, so that her easy and well appointed housekeeping is often a subject of admiring remark to her friends and visitors.

What, then, must be the feelings of her family and personal friends, who know her sensibility in regard to domestic reputation, and her desire to remove the common impression that literary tastes and domestic labor are incompatible or uncongenial, to find, as I have done, in respectable papers, some of them called "religious," such statements as that "Mrs. Stowe is just the poorest housekeeper in America, so that poor Mrs. Howe[3] is a model in comparison," (thus throwing, perhaps, quite as undeserved a slur upon another lady, with the added *quasi* concession worse than the original statement,) that "knowing how to do a thing does not imply ability to do it, and in this instance, what one sister cannot do the other can and does." This is applied to one of the authors of a work that aims to elevate domestic duties to the honor given to other sciences far less important; while the authors' profits are devoted to promote the domestic and industrial training of American women. Of course its influence is destructive both to the sale and the good influence of this work.

When a woman becomes an author, her writings are a proper subject for just criticism; but this gives no warrant to enter domestic privacy; and the American woman's home, whatever are her defects and weaknesses, should always be her safe castle of retreat and defence.

If a man finds his professional or business character assailed in the public prints, he can resort to a legal redress; but to a sensitive and delicate woman no such remedy is afforded. Her only chance for protection is the just and honorable feeling of the conductors of the public press, and to them I appeal for redressal of this wrong, by requesting an insertion of this in their columns. Very respectfully, Catharine Beecher.
New York, Aug. 14, 1869.

## Notes

1. See Kathryn Kish Sklar, *Catharine Beecher: A Study in American Domesticity* (New York: Norton, 1976), pp. 263–264.

2. "Amusing Letters," *Saturday Evening Post*, 4 September 1868, p. 2; "City Religious Press," *New York Evangelist*, 26 August 1869, p. 6.

3. Julia Ward Howe (1819–1910), most famous as the author of "The Battle Hymn of the Republic," became an outspoken advocate for women's suffrage after the Civil War.

Catharine Beecher, "Petty Slanders," *Hartford Daily Courant*, 18 August 1869, p. 1.

# [Stowe and the Lady Byron Controversy, 1869–1870]

### Rose Terry Cooke

The most controversial period in Stowe's later life followed the publication of her article "The True Story of Lady Byron's Life" in the *Atlantic Monthly* in September 1869 and her book, *Lady Byron Vindicated: A History of the Byron Controversy, from Its Beginnings in 1816 to the Present Time* (1870). During her first trip to England in 1853, Stowe met Lady Byron (born Anne Isabella Milbanke), who was legally separated from the famous English Romantic poet George Gordon, Lord Byron. Deeply impressed by Lady Byron, Stowe corresponded with her and learned the story of Byron's incestuous relationship with his half-sister, Augusta Leigh. Following Lady Byron's death in 1860, Countess Teresa Guiccioli, Byron's companion during the last years of his life, published *My Recollections of Lord Byron* (1869). Stowe was distressed by its negative portrayal of her friend Lady Byron and decided to write her own account. Although the incestuous relationship had long been the subject of rumor, her article "The True Story of Lady Byron's Life" was the first to print details. The public outcry over the publication of the story astounded Stowe and caused serious problems for the *Atlantic Monthly*, which began to lose subscribers. In the midst of the controversy, the editor, William Dean Howells, wrote his father:

> The world needed to know just how base, filthy and mean Byron was, in order that all glamour should be forever removed from his literature, and the taint of it should be communicated only to those who love sensual things, and no more pure young souls should suffer from him through their sympathy with the supposed generous and noble traits in his character. The need of this was so great that even if Mrs. Stowe had had no authority to tell the story I should almost be ready to applaud her for doing it. Generally I don't like her or her way of doing things—she did this particular thing wretchedly,—but I don't condemn her for having done it. I believe I'm only one of three or four in America who don't.[1]

In fact, most readers agreed with the writer of a letter to the *Independent* that Mrs. Stowe "had stooped to promulgate a foul and filthy scandal."[2] But she had her defenders, and many of them were fellow women writers such as Elizabeth Cady Stanton and Annie Fields.[3] Years later, Stowe's friend, the poet and fiction writer Rose Terry Cooke (1827–1892), wrote a biographical sketch of Stowe for *Our Famous Women: Comprising the Lives and Deeds of American Women* (1884). In the following selection from the sketch, Cooke offers a sympathetic account of what she described as "the second great sensation created by Mrs. Stowe in her literary career": her public vindication of Lady Byron.

WHILE MRS. STOWE was abroad she became very intimate with that unfortunate lady, who confided to her under the seal of absolute secrecy as long as Lady Byron herself lived the reasons for her separation from her husband. Mrs. Stowe, however, was requested by Lady Byron, if ever a necessity arose after her death, to make her secret known to the public.

When a *Life of Byron*, edited by the notorious Countess Guiccioli, was published in England, and aroused new interest in the poems and character of Byron, being written by a woman who had shared his licentious and indecent life, Mrs. Stowe felt that the time had come when Lady Byron's character as a wife needed to be vindicated from the implied or open assertions of Byron's mistress; and, accordingly, she gave to the public the painful and not by any means delicate story of Lady Byron's wrong and suffering.

In doing this, Mrs. Stowe was impelled, as all who knew her thoroughly understood, by a generous and brave affection for the dead woman who had been her lovely, living friend. It was an act of heroic justice, such as such a woman alone could have done.

Whether Lady Byron was deranged at the time her sorrows and her solitude began, or whether by long brooding over her loss in her worse than widowed loneliness, she created out of her suspicions what seemed to her grief an actual fact, or whether her story was indeed true to the letter, is still a matter of conjecture with most people; but it is certain that Mrs. Stowe believed her story implicitly, and was filled with the deepest pity and indignation when she heard it; and made its revelation in a conscientious desire to do good and not evil.

LORD BYRON

"Stowe It!" cartoon in *Fun Magazine* (September 1869), p. 17. University of Florida Digital Collections, Smathers Libraries, www.uflib.ufl.edu/ufdc.

But a tale like this, which in vindicating the character of one woman blasted in a peculiarly dreadful manner the reputation of another, and involved, collaterally, persons yet living, in the black shame and crime of near and dear relatives, could not fail to arouse a storm of indignation and disgust in England, and give rise to much low scoff and vulgar comment wherever it was read.

It is a melancholy reflection on human nature that it is never safe to trust its nobler instincts in a matter like this,—the story which Mrs. Stowe's best friends must regret that she ever published became a weapon in the hands of her enemies; and instead of vindicating her deceased friend from the attacks of post-mortem slander, she not only aroused them to fresh vigor, but drew upon herself a cloud of misrepresentation and scandalous sarcasm that pained all her myriad admirers, and must, no doubt, have wounded and discomfited her woman's delicate nature.

Still, with the rare, unflinching courage of her birthright, which has ever been one of her prominent characteristics, she says to-day, under her own hand, "I am never sorry for having written it,—spite of the devil and all his angels!"

### Notes

1. William Dean Howells to his father, 22 September 1869, *W. D. Howells: Selected Letters*, vol. 1: 1852–1872, edited by George Arms, et al. (Boston: Twayne, 1979), p. 340.

2. Justin McCarthy, "Mrs. Stowe's Last Romance," *Independent*, 16 August 1869, p. 1.

3. See Joan Hedrick, *Harriet Beecher Stowe: A Life* (Oxford: Oxford University Press, 1994), pp. 366–369.

From Rose Terry Cooke, "Harriet Beecher Stowe," in *Our Famous Women* (Hartford, CT: A. D. Worthington and Company, 1883), pp. 599–600.

# [Memories of a Neighbor at Nook Farm]

### MARK TWAIN

In 1871, the Stowes bought a house on Forest Street in an area of Hartford, Connecticut, called Nook Farm. Developed by John Hooker and Francis Gillette, the area became home to several famous people, including the actor and playwright William Gillette and the writer Charles Dudley Warner. Mark Twain, the pseudonym of Samuel Langhorne Clemens (1835–1910), first leased a home in Nook Farm in 1871 and then built an elaborate mansion next door to the Stowes, where he lived until 1891.[1] During his years there, Twain wrote some of his major works, including *The Adventures of Tom Sawyer* (1876), *The Prince and the Pauper* (1881), *Life on the Mississippi* (1883), and *Adventures of Huckleberry Finn* (1885). The Twains and Stowes were on good terms and frequently exchanged visits. Stowe enjoyed the gardens at both homes, painting or drawing images of their flowers and birds. Twain's maid, Katy Leary, recorded her memories in *A Lifetime with Mark Twain* (1925), in which she described the casual relationship between the families:

> [Stowe] loved flowers, and she loved roses the best of all; and she used to come over to our conservatory and help herself, pick the flowers herself—snap them right off, the roses, but Mrs. Clemens always said to let her do as she liked—let her pick all the roses she wanted herself and so she would always go away with a big bunch of them. She just loved flowers and couldn't see one without wanting to pick it. That was her way of doing things. She always wanted to help herself—never wanted anybody to give her anything.[2]

In an interview given near the end of his life and several years after Stowe's death, Twain recalled the following anecdote about one of his visits to Stowe, a story that was often repeated in both family histories.

MARK TWAIN WAS an editor in Buffalo about two years. He said he "couldn't live in Buffalo because of the frequency of fur overcoats." In 1871, his comfortable home in Hartford, Conn., was purchased. Here the family lived for more than fifteen years while Mr. Clemens wrote some of his most

Sketch of a hummingbird in ink by Harriet Beecher Stowe, ca. 1864.
Harriet Beecher Stowe Center, Hartford, Connecticut.

important books, became intertwined in a publishing business, lectured, and wandered in foreign lands.

The Hartford home is the one most closely identified with his name. So is a story of Mark Twain and Mrs. Harriet Beecher Stowe, one of his neighbors. Mr. Clemens' version of this anecdote exploded the popular conception of the yarn. It also gave an insight into a humorist's idea of humor.

"The version I've heard," said the reporter, "is that you called on Mrs. Stowe one day to find on your return that you had neither a collar nor a necktie on. Then, it is said, you wrapped a collar and a necktie in paper and sent it to Mrs. Stowe with the message that 'here is the rest of me.'"

"The incident was not like that," replied Mr. Clemens. "Mrs. Stowe and my family were neighbors and friends. We lived close to each other, and there were no fences between. I had a collar on when I made the call, but found when I got back that I had forgotten my necktie. I sent a servant to Mrs. Stowe with the necktie on a silver salver. The note I sent with it was ceremonious. It contained a formal apology for the necktie. I'm sorry now I didn't keep a copy of that letter. It had to be ceremonious. Anything flippant on such an occasion and between such close friends would have been merely silly."

[186]

## Notes

1. Details about Nook Farm are taken from Joseph S. Van Why, *Nook Farm*, edited by Earl A. French (Hartford, CT: The Stowe-Day Foundation, 1975), pp. 7–25; 52–60.

2. Mary Lawton, *A Lifetime with Mark Twain: The Memories of Katy Leary, for Thirty Years His Faithful and Devoted Servant* (New York: Harcourt, Brace and Co., 1925), p. 35.

From "Mark Twain's Wanderings at an End," *New York Times*, 31 March 1907, p. 3.

# [Stowe at Nook Farm]

## George Parsons Lathrop

George Parsons Lathrop (1851–1898) was a writer and critic who contributed to numerous periodicals in Boston and New York. He was friendly with many major writers and married Nathaniel Hawthorne's daughter Rose in 1871. Lathrop served for two years as an assistant editor of the *Atlantic Monthly* and published a book of poetry as well as a biography of Hawthorne. One of his most important accomplishments was founding the American Copyright League, an organization of over 175 writers working for the passage of international copyright laws, the absence of which cost writers like Stowe and her neighbor Mark Twain thousands of dollars in royalties from their works. In an article published in 1884 in the *New York Times*, Lathrop is quoted as saying:

> I consider it to be for the interest of the entire Nation that literature should have a fair chance. If it does not, it will in a few years become stunted in growth. As producers, authors form the only class that is denied the privilege of competition. If a man steals horses or houses or anything merchantable, and sells them for half their value, no one that does business in an honorable way can compete with him. It is the same way with authors; no writer can compete with matter that costs only the trouble of stealing it.[1]

The following excerpt from an article on Hartford, Connecticut, published in *Harper's Monthly Magazine* in 1885, provides Lathrop's account of visiting Stowe at her home at Nook Farm.

NEARBY, IN A slate-colored cottage of moderate size, lives the famous author of *Uncle Tom's Cabin*. The atmosphere within-doors is that of literary New England twenty-five years ago: the American Renascence has not yet invaded these rooms, so conspicuously neat and comfortable, yet with a kind of moral rectitude in their comfort. The library is also a sitting-room, where a glowing coal fire burned on the chilly autumn day when I was admitted there; and in the wall spaces between the windows were placed

Stowe house, Forest Street, Hartford, Connecticut, with Calvin Stowe sitting on the front porch, ca. 1880 to 1886. Harriet Beecher Stowe Center, Hartford, Connecticut.

tall panels painted with flowers, and terminating above in points that gave them a half-ecclesiastical air, as if they were tables of the law.

"Is this your study?" I asked.

"I have no particular study," said the authoress, "and I have not written much lately; but if I were to begin, I should be as likely to write here as anywhere."

Thus easily and informally she treats the genius that has given her a worldwide celebrity; indeed, there is nothing about her manner or in her surroundings to indicate a consciousness of the extraordinary power which endowed her first book with an influence that has never been paralleled. A very quiet little lady, plainly attired, and apt during conversation to become abstracted—a life-long habit of reverie which has enabled her to think out her designs and carry on composition in the midst of those interruptions to most writers unbearable—a lady quiet and undemonstrative, with an immense determination and character revealed in her face when seen at certain angles, but with an equally natural gentleness and benignity; this is what one sees to-day on meeting Mrs. Stowe. She gives the impression of one who wielded large weapons because Providence put them into her hands to right a great wrong, and not with any joy in the suffering and harm that must come with the good gained. She appears the wife, the mother, the grandmother, living in her domestic interests, rather than the woman distinguished in national history and literature. We talked on personal topics, and while this was going forward Professor Stowe came in from a walk, with a tall stick in his hand, which he grasped as a support in the middle. It was like a pilgrim's staff, and completed the suggestion of present and militant religion that somehow pervaded the whole spot. The conversation now passed easily to questions of faith, and Mrs. Stowe manifested a strong interest in the old Pilgrim and Puritan qualities of belief. To me it seems regrettable that the physiognomy of a person occupying so remarkable a position should not be carefully recorded in all its stages of development, since a distinctive face increased its sum of meaning with the years; but I learned that Mrs. Stowe had not submitted herself to the arts of the photographer for a long time, and Professor Stowe was firm in the conviction that the portrait painted by Richmond in 1852 was the only one worthy of perpetuation. "That," said he, referring to it, "is the way she will look at the resurrection." I confess that if the resurrection were to preserve the mild womanly maturity of her features as they are at the age of seventy, I should find no fault with its process.

The material aspect of Mrs. Stowe's abode, as perhaps I have hinted, gives little intimation of the part which its occupant has played; but in the small entrance hall stands a plain low cupboard, which, on being opened to the favored visitor, displayed two rows of massive volumes—a dozen on each shelf—containing a petition in favor of the abolition of slavery, signed by half a million women, and offered to Congress as a result of Mrs. Stowe's agitation. In a corner of the parlor, too, there is a closed beaufet[2] well stocked with editions of *Uncle Tom's Cabin*, and others of the authoress's works, in several foreign languages: an impressive collection, certainly, and one which has served a secondary purpose, for it has been duplicated in the British Museum, and is there used as the means of curious studies in comparative philology. Since her husband's withdrawal from his professorship at Andover, Mrs. Stowe has spent her time in these simple surroundings, leading a retired life, and going in winter to Florida, where she finds refuge among her orange groves, in a town which bears the fragrant name of Mandarin. She was drawn to Hartford partly by its general charm, and in part through associations which her sister had given the place by establishing there the Female Seminary. Speaking of the length of her residence here, she said, "I don't remember when I came; I do not live by years." This being repeated to Mark Twain, "I wish," he instantly observed, "the tax-collector would adopt that principle." One most agreeable memory will long remain with me, of an evening spent in Mrs. Stowe's company at the house of Mr. and Mrs. Clemens. Among other things there was after-dinner talk of the days preceding the war, and of the "under-ground railroad" for escaping slaves, and the strange adventures therewith connected. Mrs. Stowe gave her reminiscences of exciting incidents in her life on the Ohio border at that time, and told of the frightful letters she received from the South after publishing her great novel. These anonymous screeds voiced, no doubt, the worst element there, and teemed with threats and abuse that now, happily, would not be offered by even the most wanton survivor of the fire-eaters. To give an idea of the extremes to which these missives proceeded, Mrs. Stowe mentioned that one of them, duly forwarded to her by United States mail, enclosed a negro's ear! It was inevitable that we who listened should meditate upon the marvelous change that had been effected in the condition of our Union within twenty years, and one gentleman who was present said to another, aside, as emphasizing the extent of that change, "To think that I, who can remember when a Boston mob tried to hang William Lloyd Garrison, should have lived to see twenty respectable free negroes asleep at this funeral!" It was a frivolous remark, no doubt, but it was only the light mask of a sincere respect for the prodigious feat so largely prompted by the pen of the demure lady who had just been speaking with us. Extremely interesting, also, was the eager force with which Mrs. Stowe related one or two stories of later date on other themes that had presented themselves to her as deserving literary treatment. It showed that the narrative instinct was deeply ingrained in her, and had not lost its vigor even after so long an exertion as she has given it. Yet her presence, temperament, and conversation confirmed the theory one is likely to form in reading her books, that her imagination acts inseparably with the moral sense.

It is a convenient thing to have the antipodes anchored just around the corner. A few steps only from Mrs. Stowe's brings you to Mr. Clemens's house, and still fewer, if you take the short-cut through the lawns and shrubbery, by which briefly you pass from old New England to modern America—from the plain quarters of ethical fiction to the luxurious abode of the most Western of humorists.

## Notes

1. "American Copyright League," *New York Times*, 20 January 1884, p. 7.
2. An early spelling of "buffet," a cabinet for displaying valuables.

From George Parsons Lathrop, "A Model State Capital," *Harper's New Monthly Magazine* 71 (1885): 728–731.

# "The Birthday Garden Party
to Harriet Beecher Stowe" (1882)

ANONYMOUS

On 14 June 1882, the publishers of the *Atlantic Monthly*, Houghton, Mifflin and Company, hosted a party to honor Stowe on her seventy-first birthday. Held at the home of the former governor of Massachusetts, William Claflin, and his wife, Mary, the party was a lavish event. As the *New York Times* reported, it was the third of the "literary events given by the publishing house in honor of distinguished American authors attaining the ripe old age of threescore years and ten, with their lifework before the public which has made them famous."[1] Stowe was the first woman to be so honored, following events for John Greenleaf Whittier and Oliver Wendell Holmes, and this occasion was the first to include women.[2] The *Atlantic*, then under the editorship of Thomas Bailey Aldrich, was in a period of transition, with the generation of writers who had helped found the magazine either elderly or dead. In many ways, the party must have seemed a farewell to a bygone era of American literature, as the *Atlantic* struggled to maintain its place as an elite literary journal in a periodical marketplace filled with illustrated magazines of all varieties. The guest list included most of the eminent writers in the United States, ranging from Bronson Alcott to Julia Ward Howe. The descendants of famous writers were also there, including Ethel Parton, the granddaughter of Fanny Fern, and William Lloyd Garrison, Jr. In August 1882, the *Atlantic* published a supplement devoted to the event, printed here in its entirety. The supplement includes speeches, poems, and letters from Stowe's friends, family members, and fellow writers, all of whom attended the party or sent tributes to honor her long career.

IN CONTINUATION OF the festivals to authors, begun by the Dinner to Mr. Whittier, followed by the Breakfast to Dr. Holmes, Messrs. Houghton, Mifflin and Company offered a similar tribute to Mrs. Harriet Beecher Stowe on her birthday, June 14, 1882. Mrs. Stowe assented to their proposal, and as Hon. and Mrs. William Claflin generously tendered their spacious

### THE BIRTHDAY GARDEN PARTY TO HARRIET BEECHER STOWE.

IN continuation of the festivals to authors, begun by the Dinner to Mr. Whittier, followed by the Breakfast to Dr. Holmes, Messrs. Houghton, Mifflin and Company offered a similar tribute to Mrs. Harriet Beecher Stowe on her birthday, June 14, 1882. Mrs. Stowe assented to their proposal, and as Hon. and Mrs. William Claflin generously tendered their spacious and beautiful country home and grounds at Newtonville, near Boston, for the occasion, the season and the place suggested that the festival take the form of a Garden Party. The following invitation was sent to many persons in all parts of this country, and to several in Great Britain, eminent in letters, art, science, statesmanship, and philanthropy: —

> *Messrs. Houghton, Mifflin and Company request the pleasure of your presence at a Garden Party in Honor of the Birthday of*
>
> HARRIET BEECHER STOWE,
>
> *at "The Old Elms" (the residence of Hon. William Claflin), Newtonville, Mass., on Wednesday, June Fourteenth, 1882, from 3 to 7 P. M.*
>
> 4 PARK STREET, BOSTON,
> *June 1st, 1882.*

About two hundred guests gathered in response to this invitation, including —

Rev. Lyman Abbott, New York.
Mr. A. Bronson Alcott, Concord, Mass.
Mr. Thomas Bailey Aldrich, Boston.
Rev. and Mrs. Henry F. Allen, Boston.
Master Freeman Allen, Boston.
Mr. Howard Payson Arnold, Boston.
Mr. and Mrs. Edward Atkinson, Brookline, Mass.
Rev. and Mrs. S. J. Barrows, Boston.

Mr. Arlo Bates, Boston.
Miss Charlotte F. Bates, Cambridge.
Mr. Sylvester Baxter, Boston.
Rev. Charles Beecher, Bridgeport, Conn.
Rev. and Mrs. Edward Beecher, Brooklyn.
Rev. and Mrs. Henry Ward Beecher, Brooklyn.
Dr. Thomas W. Bicknell, Boston.
Miss Alice Stone Blackwell, Boston.
Mr. Henry B. Blackwell, Boston.
Dr. J. G. Blake, Boston.
Prof. and Mrs. Borden P. Bowne, Boston.
Mr. R. L. Bridgman, Boston.
Mr. James M. Bugbee, Boston.
Mrs. Frances Hodgson Burnett, Washington, D. C.
Hon. and Mrs. William Claflin, Newtonville, Mass.
Mr. Arthur Claflin, Newtonville, Mass.
Mr. E. H. Clement, Boston.
Mr. Samuel T. Cobb, Boston.
Mrs. Rose Terry Cooke, Winsted, Conn.
Miss A. J. Cooper, Birmingham, England.
Mr. and Mrs. George G. Crocker, Boston.
Mr. and Mrs. U. H. Crocker, Boston.
Mr. and Mrs. Prentiss Cummings, Boston.
Dr. and Miss Davidson, Boston.
Mr. Charles Deane, Cambridge.
Mr. P. Deming, Albany.
Mr. J. C. Derby, New York.
Mrs. Abby Morton Diaz, Boston.
Mr. Nathan H. Dole, Philadelphia.
Mrs. Julia C. R. Dorr, Rutland, Vt.
Mr. Francis S. Drake, Boston.
Mr. and Mrs. Geo. B. Farnsworth, Boston.
Miss Florence Finch, Boston.
Miss Alice E. Freeman, President Wellesley College.
Mrs. J. C. Gallup, Clinton, N. Y.
Mr. Francis J. Garrison, Boston.
Mr. William Lloyd Garrison, Jr., Boston.
Mr. Arthur Gilman, Cambridge.
Prof. and Mrs. Asa Gray, Cambridge.
Rev. and Mrs. G. Z. Gray, Cambridge.
Mayor Samuel A. Green, Boston.
Mr. and Mrs. Curtis Guild, Boston.

In a supplement appended to the August 1882 issue, the *Atlantic Monthly* published a detailed account of Stowe's birthday celebration of 14 June 1882, including the guest list as well as tributes and poems presented at the festivities. Love Library, University of Nebraska, Lincoln.

and beautiful country home and grounds at Newtonville, near Boston, for the occasion, the season and the place suggested that the festival take the form of a Garden Party. The following invitation was sent to many persons in all parts of this country, and to several in Great Britain, eminent in letters, art, science, statesmanship, and philanthropy:—

Messrs. Houghton, Mifflin and Company request the pleasure
of your presence at a Garden Party in Honor of the Birthday of
**HARRIET BEECHER STOWE,**
at "The Old Elms" (the residence of Hon. William Claflin), Newtonville,
Mass., on Wednesday, June Fourteenth, 1882, from 3 to 7 P.M.
4 PARK STREET, BOSTON,
June 1st, 1882.

About two hundred guests gathered in response to this invitation, including—

Rev. Lyman Abbott, New York.
Mr. A. Bronson Alcott, Concord, Mass.
Mr. Thomas Bailey Aldrich, Boston.
Rev. and Mrs. Henry F. Allen, Boston.
Master Freeman Allen, Boston.
Mr. Howard Payson Arnold, Boston.
Mr. and Mrs. Edward Atkinson, Brookline, Mass.
Rev. and Mrs. S. J. Barrows, Boston.
Mr. Arlo Bates, Boston.
Miss Charlotte F. Bates, Cambridge.
Mr. Sylvester Baxter, Boston.
Rev. Charles Beecher, Bridgeport, Conn.
Rev. and Mrs. Edward Beecher, Brooklyn.
Rev. and Mrs. Henry Ward Beecher, Brooklyn.
Dr. Thomas W. Bicknell, Boston.
Miss Alice Stone Blackwell, Boston.
Mr. Henry B. Blackwell, Boston.
Dr. J. G. Blake, Boston.

Prof. and Mrs. Borden P. Bowne, Boston.
Mr. R. L. Bridgman, Boston.
Mr. James M. Bugbee, Boston.
Mrs. Frances Hodgson Burnett, Washington, D. C.
Hon. and Mrs. William Claflin, Newtonville, Mass.
Mr. E. H. Clement, Boston.
Mr. Samuel T. Cobb, Boston.
Mrs. Rose Terry Cooke, Winsted, Conn.
Miss A. J. Cooper, Birmingham, England.
Mr. and Mrs. U. H. Crocker, Boston.
Mr. and Mrs. Prentiss Cummings, Boston.
Dr. and Miss Davidson, Boston.
Mr. Charles Deane, Cambridge.
Mr. P. Deming, Albany.
Mr. J. C. Derby, New York.
Mrs. Abby Morton Diaz, Boston.
Mr. Nathan H. Dole, Philadelphia.

Mrs. Julia C. R. Dorr, Rutland, Vt.

Mr. Francis S. Drake, Boston.

Mr. and Mrs. Geo. B. Farnsworth, Boston.

Miss Florence Finch, Boston.

Miss Alice E. Freeman, President Wellesley College.

Mrs. J. C. Gallup, Clinton, N. Y.

Mr. Francis J. Garrison, Boston.

Mr. William Lloyd Garrison, Jr., Boston.

Mr. Arthur Gilman, Cambridge.

Prof. and Mrs. Asa Gray, Cambridge.

Rev. and Mrs. G. Z. Gray, Cambridge.

Mayor Samuel A. Green, Boston.

Mr. and Mrs. Curtis Guild, Boston.

Mr. and Mrs. James Guild, Boston.

Mrs. E. E. Hale, Boston.

Miss Lucretia P. Hale, Boston.

Mr. William T. Harris, Concord, Mass.

Rev. J. B. Harrison, Franklin Falls, N. H.

Mr. E. B. Haskell, Auburndale, Mass.

Dr. Henry Cecil Haven, Boston.

Mrs. J. R. Hawley, Hartford, Conn.

Dr. Oliver Wendell Holmes, Boston.

Mr. and Mrs. John Hooker, Hartford, Conn.

Mr. Augustus Hoppin, Providence, R. I.

Prof. and Mrs. E. N. Horsford, Cambridge.

Mr. George Houghton, New York.

Mr. and Mrs. H. O. Houghton, Cambridge.

Mr. William A. Hovey, Boston.

Mr. and Mrs. John T. Howard, Brooklyn.

Mr. J. R. Howard, New York.

Rev. and Mrs. Frank E. Howe, Newton, Mass.

Mr. W. D. Howells, Belmont, Mass.

Miss Edith M. Howes, Boston.

Mr. and Mrs. J. F. Hunnewell, Charlestown, Mass.

Mr. and Mrs. J. D. Hurd, Newtonville, Mass.

Mr. Melancthon M. Hurd, New York.

Mr. and Mrs. Samuel Johnson, Boston.

Hon. John S. Keyes, Concord, Mass.

Mrs. Julia B. Kimball, Boston.

Mr. and Mrs. Horatio King, Washington, D. C.

Dr. Edward H. Knight, Washington, D. C.

Miss Lucy Larcom, Beverly, Mass.

Mr. and Mrs. George P. Lathrop, Concord, Mass.

Mr. and Mrs. John Lathrop, Boston.

Dr. J. Laurence Laughlin, Cambridge.

Prof. T. R. Lounsbury, New Haven, Conn.

Rev. A. L. Love, Southborough, Mass.

Mr. S. W. Marvin, New York.

Mr. and Mrs. George H. Mifflin, Boston.

Mr. J. B. Millet, Boston.

Mrs. Louise Chandler Moulton, Boston.

Rev. William Mountford, Boston.

Rev. and Mrs. Elisha Mulford, Cambridge, Mass.

Mr. A. J. Mundy, Newtonville, Mass.

Mr. and Mrs. Charles W. Munroe, Cambridge.

Miss Munroe, Newtonville, Mass.

Miss Lucretia G. Noble, Spencer, Mass.

Mr. and Mrs. S. B. Noyes, Canton, Mass.

Dr. and Mrs. J. P. Oliver, Boston.

Rev. J. W. Olmstead, Boston.

Mr. Henry O'Meara, Boston.

Mr. and Mrs. Peter Parker, Washington, D. C.

Mr. and Mrs. James Parton, Newburyport, Mass.

Miss Ethel Parton, Newburyport, Mass.

Rev. B. K. Peirce, Newton, Mass.

Miss Peirce, Newton, Mass.

Mr. Charles C. Perkins, Boston.

Mrs. Mary B. Perkins, Hartford, Ct.

Miss Nora Perry, Boston.

Miss Elizabeth Stuart Phelps, Andover, Mass.

Mr. and Mrs. Edward L. Pierce, Milton, Mass.

Mr. and Mrs. N. T. Pulsifer, North Manchester, Conn.

Mr. J. Pickering Putnam, Boston.

Miss Sallie Putnam, Boston.

Mr. Samuel M. Quincy, Boston.

Mrs. Abby Sage Richardson, New York.

Mr. William H. Rideing, Boston.

Hon. William A. Russell and Miss Russell, Lawrence, Mass.

Mr. and Mrs. Frank B. Sanborn, Concord, Mass.

Mrs. J. T. Sargent, Cambridge.

Mrs. Samuel Scoville, Norwich, N. Y.

Mr. and Mrs. Horace E. Scudder, Cambridge.

Mr. and Mrs. Samuel E. Sewall, Melrose, Mass.

Mrs. M. E. W. Sherwood, New York.

Mr. and Mrs. Charles W. Slack, Boston.

Miss Annie P. Slocum, Newtonville, Mass.

Mr. Winfield S. Slocum, Newtonville, Mass.

Mr. and Mrs. Azariah Smith, Boston.

Prof. Edward P. Smith, Worcester, Mass.

Rev. George B. Spalding, Dover, N. H.

Miss Spalding, Dover, N. H.

Mr. Edward Stanwood, Boston.

Mrs. Lucy Stone, Boston.

Prof. Calvin E. Stowe, Hartford, Conn.

Rev. and Mrs. Charles E. Stowe, Saco, Me.

Mrs. Bayard Taylor, New York.

Miss Lilian Taylor, New York.

Mr. and Mrs. L. R. Thayer, Newtonville, Mass.

Mrs. Thorp, Cambridge.

Mrs. E. P. Tileston, Milton, Mass.

Mr. John G. Tompson, Newtonville, Mass.

Judge and Mrs. Albion W. Tourgee, Philadelphia.

Prof. and Mrs. John Trowbridge, Cambridge.

Mr. J. T. Trowbridge, Arlington, Mass.

Rev. Kinsley Twining, New York.

Mr. D. Berkeley Updike, Boston.

Mrs. Lawson Valentine, New York.

Miss Mary Valentine, New York.

Mr. J. H. Walker, Worcester.

Rev. Julius H. Ward, Boston.

Mrs. Kate Gannett Wells, Boston.

Mr. and Mrs. E. P. Whipple, Boston.

Mr. and Mrs. S. B. White, Boston.

Miss Lilian Whiting, Boston.

Mrs. A. D. T. Whitney, Milton, Mass.

Miss Anne Whitney, Boston.

Mr. John G. Whittier, Danvers, Mass.

Mr. Justin Winsor and Miss Winsor,
    Cambridge.

Mrs. Abba Goold Woolson, Concord,
    N. H.

Mr. and Mrs. J. A. Woolson,
    Cambridge.

Mr. and Mrs. John C. Wyman, Valley
    Falls, R. I.

The day was perfect for such a festival. June never brings a day more exactly tempered and perfumed for a high holiday than was this at Newtonville.

From three o'clock until five was spent socially. As guests arrived they were presented to Mrs. Stowe by Mr. H. O. Houghton, and then they gathered in groups in the parlors, on the verandas, on the lawn, and in the refreshment rooms.

At five o'clock they assembled in a large tent on the lawn, and after a song by Mrs. Humphrey Allen, Mr. Houghton spoke as follows:—

### MR. HOUGHTON'S ADDRESS.

We have met two or three times within the last few years to set up, as it were, milestones in the lives of some of those who are justly esteemed the creators of American literature. On this occasion one thought oppresses us all: Two of the most eminent, whose grace and benignity cheered and exalted our former gatherings, are with us in bodily presence no more. The voice of our beloved Longfellow is hushed, but the cadences of his sweet songs will vibrate in our memories while life lasts. We shall never look again upon the benign countenance of our revered Emerson, but his precepts are written as with the point of a diamond, upon our hearts.

We come together again to celebrate a birthday, but what is the number of the birthday we will not inquire. If we estimate the age of our beloved guest by the amount of work she has accomplished, the number of her years would rank with those of the antediluvians. But if we judge by the vigor and freshness of her writings, and by her universal sympathy with young and old, we must say that she has discovered the fountain of perpetual youth, somewhere else, if not among the everglades of Florida, where Ponce de Leon sought it in vain. You have all doubtless heard the apocryphal stories of the difficulties encountered by the author of *Uncle Tom's Cabin* in getting a publisher, and of the marvelous sales of the first editions; but few here probably realize how great is its circulation to-day. This book began by being a prophecy, and is now history, and it is the rare felicity of its author to realize this fact in her own life-time.

The wanderings of Ulysses, the exploits of the heroes of the Iliad, and the trials of Æneas, because so intensely human, are the bonds which unite us to the civilizations that existed centuries ago; but the great epic of our age is the narrative of the wanderings and sorrows of Uncle Tom; and his trials and the victories which he wrought for this epoch are to be our Iliad and Æneid for centuries to come.

Providence selects its own instruments, and rules in the affairs of individuals as of nations. Behold the training which was necessary, and the fruits of which are seen in the author of *Uncle Tom's Cabin*! Descended from Puritan stock, of the straitest sect; educated in the severe school of New England Calvinism; living in her early married life in the great West, on the borders of a slave State, where, as a young housekeeper, she had to struggle with the whimsicalities and impracticabilities of Topsy, and where the real tragedies as well as comedies of slavery were acted daily before her eyes; where the very atmosphere favored a broad charity (not so congenial to New England), which pitied and sympathized alike with the slave and the slave-holder, while intensely hating the system of slavery itself; again removing to a quiet New England village, where her time was divided between exacting household cares, the instruction of pupils, and the contemplation of the great problems of sin, retribution, foreknowledge, and free will,—with such a training and such experiences, who can wonder that while sitting at the communion table, and meditating upon the infinite sorrows and ignominy of Him who gave himself for the redemption of humanity, she should have been inspired with the vision of another life of suffering and sacrifice, by which a race should be redeemed, and that while she mused the fire burned, and from the white heat came forth the vivid picture of the death of that other man of sorrows, so like its great prototype,—as like as a human copy can be to a divine original?

I need go no further. What followed the issue of this truly wonderful book you all know, and in the struggle many of you took an active part. From that day when her two children, ten and twelve years of age, convulsively wept over the sorrows of Uncle Tom, and one of them exclaimed, "Oh, mamma, slavery is the most cursed thing in the world!" the story has been repeated under every sky, in every land, and translated into nearly every tongue. Crowned heads, statesmen, scholars, and the people have alike read, wept over, and applauded the simple story. And to-day our own beloved country is redeemed. Slavery, with all its attendant evils, has disappeared forever, and no one, either North or South, desires it back again.

But the production of *Uncle Tom's Cabin* is not the only service done to literature by our honored guest. Her other writings are inimitable in their way, as illustrating New England life, and teaching the homely virtues of truth and duty: as, for instance, *The Minister's Wooing, Oldtown Folks*, Sam Lawson's *Fireside Stories*, and the other books which we all know so well. But as the sun in his meridian splendor eclipses the orbs of night, so Uncle Tom, by its universal human interest, eclipses these other books, which would make the reputation of any author.

And now, honored madam, as

> "When to them who sail
> Beyond the Cape of Hope, and now are past
> Mozambic, off at sea northeast winds blow
> Sabean odors from the spicy shore
> Of Arabic the blest,"

so the benedictions of the lowly and the blessings of all conditions of men are brought to you to-day on the wings of the wind, from every quarter of the globe; but there will be no fresher laurels to crown this day of your rejoicing than are brought by those now before you, who have been your co-workers in the strife; who have wrestled and suffered, fought and conquered, with you; who rank you with the Miriams, the Deborahs, and the Judiths of old; and who now shout back the refrain, when you utter the inspired song:—

> "Sing ye to the Lord, for he hath triumphed gloriously."
> ... "The Almighty Lord hath disappointed them by
> the hand of a woman."

Mr. Houghton then presented Rev. Henry Ward Beecher, intimating that Mrs. Stowe might say something later.

### MR. BEECHER'S REMARKS.

I don't know whether it is in good taste for any other member of my father's family to join in the laudation of Mrs. Stowe, but if it is, I am a very proper one to do it. I know that for a long time after the publication of *Uncle Tom's Cabin* there were a great many very wise people who said they knew that she never wrote it herself, but that I did it. The matter at last became so scandalous that I determined to put an end to it, and therefore I wrote "Norwood." That killed the thing dead.

I will admit that I had something to do with *Uncle Tom's Cabin*. I recollect that Mrs. Stowe asked me one day whether I took *The National Era*. I said No; but I would, if necessary. What was going to happen? She said that Dr. Bailey had sent her some money to write a story for that paper, as far as that money would go; that it would run through three or four numbers, for when she first planned Uncle Tom she thought it would probably extend through three or four issues of the paper. When, in the progress of the publication, people became very much excited, and it was resolved to publish the story in a volume, she was still writing it, and John P. Jewett, who was to be the publisher, said that the book must be limited to one octavo volume. Such was the low estate of antislavery literature that it was not believed an antislavery book of more than one volume would find readers. I thought so and wrote a most persuasive letter to her to kill off Uncle Tom quickly, and to give the world the book in one volume, if she expected it to be read. What became of that letter I don't know, and perhaps she cannot recollect; but, with a peculiarity which belongs to no other member of my father's family, she had her own way about it.

Now, I think we might have a good experience meeting here this afternoon, if every one would tell under what circumstances he read the book, and how he acted. I can still remember plainly the circumstances under which I finished it. I had got well into the second volume. It was Thursday. Sunday was looming up before me, and at the rate at which I was going there would not be time to finish it before Sunday, and I could never preach till I had finished it. So I set myself to it and determined to finish it at once. I had got a considerable way into the second volume, and I recommended my wife to go to bed. I didn't want anybody down there. I soon began to cry. Then I went and shut all the doors, for I did not want any one to see me. Then I sat down to it and finished it that night, for I knew that only in that way should I be able to preach on Sunday. I know that many of you must have read it something as I did at that time.

I am in sympathy with you in your rejoicing this afternoon, and thank you for your courtesy shown to my sister and your sister, for she has won that place in the hearts of many. I leave the gratulations to you.

Professor Guyot, of Princeton, says that progress in the world is like the development of plant life. It has three periods of growth. The first is that in the soil,—growth by the root. The second is more accelerated,—growth by the stem. The third is the most rapid of all,—growth by the blossom and fruit. The world has been growing by the root, obscurely, lingeringly, slowly. It is growing by the stem now, very much faster. It is beginning to break into the blossom and fruit, when progress will be wonderful compared with our past experience in all other periods. Other years have seen great changes, but men in this generation have seen changes begin and have seen their ripening fruit. We are now living in that period of the world in which you have a long time of former life compressed, and men may see the beginning and end of a great movement. I have always been glad that that noble man, Mr. Garrison, lived to see the chains broken and the slaves go free. It took only the golden middle part of his life to see the beginning and the end. Mrs. Stowe, when a wife and mother, established in life, began her part of this great work. She yet numbers her years here, and their blossom is on her head. It lingers long, and long may it linger before it falls. She saw slavery intrenched in all the power of politics, in all the power of government, in all the power of commerce, and with the benediction of a sham religion, at the time in which she entered upon this career. And, behold, where is it today? It is in history only. Upon that black cloud which rested over all the land has risen the Sun of righteousness. In a short period have occurred these great changes, in ways that no man would have brought about. It is God who has done it.

Of course you all sympathize with me to-day, but, standing in this place, I do not see your faces more clearly than I see those of my father and my mother. Her I only knew as a mere babe-child. He was my teacher and my companion. A more guileless soul than he, a more honest one, more free from envy, from jealousy, and from selfishness, I never knew. Though he thought he was great by his theology, everybody else knew he was great by his religion. My mother is to me what the Virgin Mary is to a devout Catholic. She was a woman of great nature, profound as a philosophical thinker, great in argument, with a kind of intellectual imagination, diffident, not talkative,—in that respect I take after her,—a woman who gave birth to Mrs. Stowe, whose graces and excellencies she probably more than any other of her children—we number but thirteen—has possessed. I suppose that in bodily resemblance, perhaps, she is not like my mother, but in mind I presume she is most like her.

I thank you for my father's sake and for my mother's sake for the courtesy, the friendliness, and the kindness which you give to Mrs. Stowe.

### MR. WHITTIER'S POEM.

Mr. Whittier was present, to the great satisfaction of all the company, but he excused himself from reading the poem he had written, which was read by Mr. Frank B. Sanborn:—

John Greenleaf Whittier, ca. 1885. Prints
and Photographs Division, Library of
Congress.

Thrice welcome from the Land of Flowers
And golden-fruited orange bowers
To this sweet, green-turfed June of ours!
To her who, in our evil time,
Dragged into light the nation's crime
With strength beyond the strength of men,
And, mightier than their sword, her pen;
To her who world-wide entrance gave
To the log-cabin of the slave,
Made all his wrongs and sorrows known,
And all earth's languages his own,—
North, South, and East and West, made all

The common air electrical,
Until the o'ercharged bolts of heaven
Blazed down, and every chain was riven!

Welcome from each and all to her
Whose Wooing of the Minister
Revealed the warm heart of the man
Beneath the creed-bound Puritan,
And taught the kinship of the love
Of man below and God above;
To her who keeps, through change of place
And time, her native strength and grace,
Alike where warm Sorrento smiles,
Or where, by birchen-shaded isles,
Whose summer winds have shivered o'er
The icy drift of Labrador,
She lifts to light the priceless Pearl
Of Harpswell's angel-beckoned girl.
To her at threescore years and ten
Be tributes of the tongue and pen,
Be honor, praise, and heart-thanks given,
The loves of earth, the hopes of heaven!

Ah, dearer than the praise that stirs
The air to-day, our love is hers!
She needs no guaranty of fame
Whose own is linked with Freedom's name.
Long ages after ours shall keep
Her memory living while we sleep;
The waves that wash our gray coast lines,
The winds that rock the Southern pines,
Shall sing of her; the unending years
Shall tell her tale in unborn ears.
And when, with sins and follies past,
Are numbered color-hate and caste,
White, black, and red shall own as one
The noblest work by woman done.

### DR. HOLMES'S POEM.

Dr. Holmes, on being presented, described the circumstances in which he first read *Uncle Tom's Cabin*, and the deepening of his interest in it, so that he soon laid aside the novel of Dickens which he had been reading, and gave himself up wholly to *Uncle Tom's Cabin* until he had reached the end. He then read this poem:—

> If every tongue that speaks her praise
> For whom I shape my tinkling phrase
>   Were summoned to the table,
> The vocal chorus that would meet
> Of mingling accents harsh or sweet,
> From every land and tribe, would beat
>   The polyglots of Babel.
>
> Briton and Frenchman, Swede and Dane,
> Turk, Spaniard, Tartar of Ukraine,
>   Hidalgo, Cossack, Cadi,
> High Dutchman and Low Dutchman, too,
> The Russian serf, the Polish Jew,
> Arab, Armenian, and Mantchoo
>   Would shout, "We know the lady!"
>
> Know her! Who knows not Uncle Tom
> And her he learned his gospel from,
>   Has never heard of Moses;
> Fall well the brave black hand we know
> That gave to freedom's grasp the hoe
> That killed the weed that used to grow
>   Among the Southern roses.
>
> When Archimedes, long ago,
> Spoke out so grandly, "*Dos pou sto,*—
>   Give me a place to stand on,
> I'll move your planet for you, now,"—
> He little dreamed or fancied how
> The sto at last should find its pou
>   For woman's faith to land on.

Her lever was the wand of art,
Her fulcrum was the human heart,
    Whence all unfailing aid is;
She moved the earth! Its thunders pealed,
Its mountains shook, its temples reeled,
The blood-red fountains were unsealed,
    And Moloch sunk to Hades.

All through the conflict, up and down
Marched Uncle Tom and Old John Brown,
    One ghost, one form ideal;
And which was false and which was true,
And which was mightier of the two,
The wisest sibyl never knew,
    For both alike were real.

Sister, the holy maid does well
Who counts her beads in convent cell,
    Where pale devotion lingers;
But she who serves the sufferer's needs,
Whose prayers are spelt in loving deeds,
May trust the Lord will count her beads
    As well as human fingers.

When Truth herself was Slavery's slave,
Thy hand the prisoned suppliant gave
    The rainbow wings of fiction.
And Truth who soared descends to-day
Bearing an angel's wreath away,
Its lilies at thy feet to lay
    With Heaven's own benediction.

**MRS. A. D. T. WHITNEY'S POEM.**

Queen of the months of the year!
    Hour of her crowning and prime!
Everything royal and dear
    Comes in this bountiful time.

Everything noble and high,
   Everything lowly and sweet;
Tree-tops are grand in the sky,
   Daisies in bloom at our feet;

Roses aglow in the sun,
   Grass growing rich for the blade:
Summer's sweet marvel begun
   Now, as it never were made.

Sunshine, and blossom, and song,
   Glory, and beauty, and praise;
Blessing and gladness belong
   To souls that are born on such days.

Came she but these to inherit,
   Signs of her nature's attune,—
Joyous and affluent spirit
   Born in that far-away June?

Gladdest is tenderest, too,
   Joy is diviner of trouble;
Power hath a service to do,
   Sight that is true seeth double.

"We and our neighbors." That word
   Grew in the heart of her heart;
Haunted the life-feast, and stirred
   Plea for a people apart.

"Seest Thou, hearest Thou not?
   *It faileth*," was all she said.
Leaving her prayer with the Thought
   That cares for the children's bread.

She minded the marriage board ,—
   The wine that had not sufficed;
And one who looked to the Lord,—
   Mary, the mother of Christ.

"It faileth!" was all she said.
    She knew that He knew the rest;
That his ear interpreted
    The longing of her request.

Unto such pitiful asking
    Strange that the answer should be,—
Swift and keen with its tasking,—
    *"What have I to do with thee?*

*"My time yet cometh."* "Ah, Lord,"—
    That cry for a people's pain
Went up afresh with a word
    That would not beseech in vain,—

"Behold the death of their living!
    The anguish of thy long years!
The thirst for wine of thanksgiving,
    The drink of their bitter tears!"

Thirsted and suffered they still;
    Strange was the waiting and loss;
None to deliver his will,—
    None to bear forward his cross!

"Waiteth it ever for me,
    Message and process divine?
*Woman, what do I do with thee?"*
    Was it denial, or sign?

Was it rebuke, or a mission,
    For her who turned in a breath,
Commanding with holy prevision,
    "Do ye whatever He saith!

"Yes, though ye hear the sentence,
    *Go, fill ye up to the brim*
*The measure of your repentance,*
    Fill up, and bear unto him!"

Into the hearts of the human
  Purification of tears,—
That was the work of the woman;
  God gave the wine of the years!

Mary, elect of the Lord,
  Yield we thy praise to another?
She who hath wrought for his word
  Is daughter and sister and mother!

### MISS ELIZABETH STUART PHELPS'S POEM.

was read for her by Dr. Holmes, as follows:—

Arise, and call her blessed,—seventy years!
Each one a tongue to speak for her, who needs
No poor device of ours to tell to-day
The story of her glory in our hearts,
Precede us all, ye quiet lips of love,
Ye honors high of home, nobilities
Of mother and of wife, the heraldy
Of happiness; dearer to her than were
The homage of the world. We yield unto
The royal rights of tenderness. Speak, then,
Before all voices, ripened human life!

Arise, and call her blessed, dark-browed men,
Who put the silver lyre aside for you,
Who could not stroll across the silken strings
Of fancy, while you wept uncomforted,
But rang upon the fetters of a race
Enchained the awful chord which pealed along
And echoed in the cannon-shot which broke
The manacle, and bade the bound go free.
She brought a nation on its knees for shame;
She brought a world into a black slave's heart.
Where are our lighter laurels, O my friends,
Brothers and sisters of the busy pen?

Five million freemen crown her birthday feast,
Before whose feet our little leaf we lay.

Arise and call her blessed, fainting souls,
For whom she sang the strains of holy hope!
Within the gentle twilight of her days,
Like angels hid, her own hymns visit her.
Her life no ivy-tangled door but wide
And welcome to his solemn feet, who need
Not knock for entrance, nor one ever ask,
"Who cometh there?" So still and sure the step,
So well we know God doth "abide in her."
Oh, wait to make her blessed, happy world,
To which she looketh onward ardently!
Lie distant, distant far, ye streets of gold,
Where up and down light-hearted spirits walk,
And wonder that they stayed so long away!
Be patient for her coming, for our sakes,
Who will love heaven better, keeping her.
This only ask we: When from prayer to praise
She moves, and when from peace to joy, be hers
To know she hath the life eternal, since
Her own heart's dearest wish did meet her there.

### MR. TROWBRIDGE'S POEM.

Mr. J. T. Trowbridge read a poem, which was afterwards printed in the Youth's Companion; and by the kind courtesy of the proprietors of that paper it is reprinted here:—

### THE CABIN.

Genius, 't is said, knows not itself,
  But works unconscious wholly.
Even so she wrought, who built in thought
  The Cabin of the Lowly.

A wife with common wifely cares,
  What mighty dreams enwrapt her!

What fancies burned, until she turned
  To write some flaming chapter!

Over the humblest household task
  The vision came, it may be;
While one hand held the flying pen,
  The other hushed her baby.

Her life was like some quiet bridge,
  Impetuous tides sweep under.
So week by week the story grew,
  From wonder on to wonder.

Wisdom could not conceive the plot,
  Nor wit and fancy spin it;
The woman's part, the wife's deep heart,
  All mother's love, were in it.

Hatred of tyranny and wrong,
  Compassion sweet and holy,
Sorrow and Guilt and Terror built
  That Cabin of the Lowly.

And in the morning light, behold,
  By some divine mutation,
Its roof became a sky of flame,
  A portent to the nation!

The Slave went forth through all the earth,
  He preached to priest and rabbin;
He spoke all tongues: in every land
  Opened that lowly Cabin.

Anon a school for kinder rule,
  For freer thoughts and manners;
Then from its door what armies pour
  With bayonets and banners!

More potent still than fires that kill,
  Or logic that convinces,

The tale she told to high and low,
   To peasants and to princes.

That tale belongs with Freedom's songs,
   The hero's high endeavor,
And all brave deeds that serve the needs
   Of Liberty forever!

I greet her now, when South and North
   Have ceased their deadly quarrels;
And say, or sing, while here I fling
   This leaf upon her laurels:

She loosed the rivets of the slave;
   She likewise lifted woman,
And proved her right to share with man
   All labors pure and human.

Women, they say, must yield, obey,
   Rear children, dance cotillions;
While this one wrote, she cast the vote
   Of unenfranchised millions!

### MRS. ALLEN'S POEM.

Mrs. Allen, daughter of Mrs. Stowe, contributed the following poem, which was read by her husband, Rev. Henry F. Allen:—

A child came down to earth
   Just seventy years ago,
And round its form the angels trod,
   Whispering low,
     " 'T is an instrument
To be played by the hand of God."

Time sped its steadfast way;
   The child grew rosy and strong;
Unconscious she sweetly played,
   With music right
   And discord wrong,
The song that God had made.

The notes of the instrument rose
 Sweeter and better each day,
Till it sung in clearest trumpet-tones,
 "Cast off the bond,
 Release the slave;
'T is thy brother who bleeds and groans!"

"Oh, hear the cry of the wronged,
 The hapless children of God!
With folded hands and tearful eyes,
 Hopeless they stand;
 Patient and meek,
They bow and kiss the rod."

O'er sea and mountain and shore,
 The music thundered and rolled,
Till the angels in heaven reëchoed its strain,
 And the love of man,
 With the mercy of God,
Revived in our hearts again.

Though the instrument's feebler grown,
 'T will sound loud and full until death,
Like a harp with its strings Æolian blown,
 Rising and falling,
 Whispering and calling,
With the strength of God's own breath.

### MRS. ANNIE FIELDS'S POEM.

Mrs. Fields was in Europe, but she wrote the following poem in honor of the occasion:—

Birds were singing in the trees;
 Summer was abroad as now,
With her troop of murmuring bees,
 And blossoms' round her brow,

When, seventy years ago, there came
 A little child to view the land,

Who found a torch with lighted flame
    Made ready to her hand.

Fearless she held the fiery tongue
    Close to her white and tender breast;
When lo! The pain became a song
    And prayers for the oppressed.

Mother of a new-born race,
    Daughter of a race to be,
Regent through the boundless space
    Of sad humanity!

Is there realm to vie with thine,
    Whither mortals may aspire?
Torch of love, the flame divine,
    Hath called thee ever higher.

Who has taught the seer to know
    Sorrow that was not her own!
Who has made her face to glow
    Glad for another's crown!

But by home fires, when day is done,
    Charming young and soothing old,
Dearest laurels you have won,
    While hearth-stones have grown cold.

Friend, how calm your sunset days!
    Your peaceful eyes are set on heaven,
For peace upon the promise stays,—
    Who loves much is forgiven.

### MISS CHARLOTTE F. BATES'S POEM.

England has Eliot, France has Sand, to show;
America, her Harriet Beecher Stowe!
Thy fame, like his whose greeting fails us now,
Leaving the light on his remembered brow,
Has spanned the earth, till both to all belong:
One through the might of story; one, of song.

What language where thy Uncle Tom is not?
It speaks in every tongue,—a polyglot.
While tears and laughter rolled from it apace,
Its soul helped gain the freedom of a race;
That freedom gained, for ages yet to come
The world will laugh and weep o'er Uncle Tom.
From sea to sea hath histrionic art
Made its creations into being start,
And lonely readers, seeing all they read,
Have ached with mirth, or with oppression bled.
Would that thy genius with a kindred stroke
The chains of mental slavery also broke!
Now against that we fain would have thee deal
The massive blow that all the world shall feel;
And while they laugh and weep at truth's own face,
Seek to burst off the shackles that disgrace!
However much already we may owe,
Make our debt larger to the name of Stowe!

### SEVERAL SPEECHES

were made, but cannot be given here in full, as no complete report was taken of them.

Judge Albion W. Tourgee told in detail the story of his first reading of *Uncle Tom's Cabin*,—of neglecting his hoeing to do it, of fleeing from an irate father, and of finishing the book in the woods. Mrs. Stowe had come into his life so that he looked back to her as his Jeanne d'Arc. He closed by saying, "I followed her thought. I followed her lead, gloriously, gladly, though humbly, through that struggle; and now I come gladly, earnestly, and feelingly to give my thanks to my mother."

Rev. Edward Beecher spoke at some length of the bearing of the works of Mrs. Stowe upon the woman-suffrage question. He told of her work with the late Miss Catharine Beecher at Hartford to extend the education of women, and affirmed that the course of God's events is upward and onward to a perfect coördination of the sexes in the work of the race.

Mr. Edward Atkinson described an interview between Professor Lieber and Senator Preston, of South Carolina, who was of the extreme type of

Southern men before the war. *Uncle Tom's Cabin* had just appeared, and conversation turned upon it. The senator was strongly excited, and in reply to a question he said, "We have read *Uncle Tom's Cabin*, and I know it is true. I can match every incident in it out of my own experience."

Mr. Houghton stated that Mrs. Stowe would say a few words, and as she came to the front of the platform the company rose by a simultaneous impulse of affectionate respect, and listened with eager interest while she spoke as follows:—

### MRS. STOWE'S RESPONSE.

I wish to say that I thank all of my friends from my heart,—that is all. And one thing more,—and that is, if any of you have doubt, or sorrow, or pain, if you doubt about this world, just remember what God has done; just remember that this great sorrow of slavery has gone, gone by forever. I see it every day at the South. I walk about there and see the lowly cabins. I see these people growing richer and richer. I see men very happy in their lowly lot; but, to be sure, you must have patience with them. They are not perfect, but have their faults, and they are serious faults in the view of white people. But they are very happy, that is evident, and they do know how to enjoy themselves,—a great deal more than you do. An old negro friend in our neighborhood has got a new, nice two-story house, and an orange grove, and a sugar-mill. He has got a lot of money, besides. Mr. Stowe met him one day, and he said, "I have got twenty head of cattle, four head of 'hoss,' forty head of hen, and I have got ten children, all mine, every one mine." Well, now, that is a thing that a black man could not say once, and this man was sixty years old before he could say it. With all the faults of the colored people, take a man and put him down with nothing but his hands, and how many could say as much as that? I think they have done well.

A little while ago they had at his house an evening festival for their church, and raised fifty dollars. We white folks took our carriages, and when we reached the house we found it fixed nicely. Every one of his daughters knew how to cook. They had a good place for the festival. Their suppers were spread on little white tables, with nice clean cloths on them. People paid fifty cents for supper. They got between fifty and sixty dollars, and had one of the best frolics you could imagine. They had also for supper ice-cream, which they made themselves.

That is the sort of thing I see going on around me. Let us never doubt. Everything that ought to happen is going to happen.

[216]

Music by the Germania Band and the Beethoven Club, and songs by Mrs. Humphrey Allen at intervals during the speeches and poems, lent variety and enjoyment. After Mrs. Stowe's remarks, Mr. Houghton felicitously expressed the gratitude of the company to Mr. and Mrs. Claflin for the kind courtesy which had, with rare generosity, given their house and grounds for the festival. The company then dispersed slowly, many gathering about Mrs. Stowe for congratulation and farewell.

### LETTERS.

Many letters of regret were received, but only four of them were read at the Garden Party. All of them were placed in Mrs. Stowe's hands, and some are printed below:—

FREMONT, OHIO, *May* 31, 1882.

I think I told you of our fondness for the books of Mrs. Stowe, and especially for Oldtown Folks. Since it first appeared, Mrs. Hayes has been in the habit of reading parts of it aloud in the family circle. Our children know the characters as old familiar acquaintances from childhood. Gloomy days have been made cheerful and sunny by reading it. We have often thought of writing Mrs. Stowe, and thanking her for the happiness she has given us. Her seventieth birthday! Surely the author of Oldtown Folks can never grow old. Present to her our warm good wishes and congratulations and thanks. Your invitation is very welcome, and we regret that it cannot be accepted.

Sincerely,      R. B. HAYES.

LEGATION OF THE UNITED STATES,
LONDON, *May* 29, 1882.

Nothing would give me greater pleasure than to join in any manifestation of esteem for my old friend Mrs. Stowe, but it will be impossible for me to join the Garden Party, and almost as much so for me to write anything for the occasion, occupied as I continually am with matters so alien from poetry and sentiment.

I hope your Garden Party may have the success it deserves, and that Mrs. Stowe may survive many years to enjoy the honors she has so fully won.

Faithfully yours,      J. R. LOWELL.

WEST NEW BRIGHTON,
STATEN ISLAND, N. Y., *June* 10, 1882.

I am sincerely obliged by your kind invitation, and I regret exceedingly that it is impossible for me to accept it. It is the great happiness of Mrs. Stowe not only to have written many delightful books, but to have written one book which will be always famous, not only as the most vivid picture of an extinct evil system, but as one of the most powerful influences in overthrowing it. The light of her genius flashed the monster into hideous distinctness, and the country arose to destroy him. No book was ever more a historical event than *Uncle Tom's Cabin*. In all times and countries women have nobly served justice and liberty, but it is doubtful if any single service to the good cause in this country is greater than that of Mrs. Stowe. You could have no guest more worthy of honor, and none to whom honor would be more gladly and universally paid. If all whom she has charmed and quickened should unite to sing her praises, the birds of summer would be outdone.     Very truly yours, GEORGE WILLIAM CURTIS.

ELMIRA, N. Y., *June* 10, 1882.

I regret that distance and occupation (in search of health) will not permit me to attend the Garden Party which you give in honor of Mrs. Harriet Beecher Stowe. With due respect to other able and charming writers, I put Mrs. Stowe at the head of all living American novelists, especially in the characteristics of power and sincerity, both of feeling and style. No intelligent contemporary can ignore, and the centuries to come will not soon forget, the immense influence which she has exercised over the history of our country. She has had, and will keep, a fortune of fame, and, by her talents and the nobility of her motives, has deserved it. I beg that you will present her an expression of the profound respect which I owe her as an author, as an American citizen, and as a man.     Very respectfully yours, J. W. DE FOREST

OFFICE OF THE OBSERVER
NEW YORK, *June* 7, 1882.

No lady has done more by her pen to make a distinctively American literature than Mrs. Stowe, and every true American is proud to know that among women there is no name in letters more widely known to fame than hers. With many thanks for your invitation, I am very truly yours,

S. IRENÆUS PRIME.

BOSTON, *June* 7, 1882.

Thanks for your invitation to the gathering in honor of Mrs. H. B. Stowe.

No tribute could be too great to her. I wish I could join in it, but the state of my family prevents.

Yours respectfully, WENDELL PHILLIPS.

NEW HAVEN, CONN., *June* 7, 1882.

No one has a higher admiration than myself of what this noble lady has done by her pen for humanity. It is a great deprivation not to be present. Most truly yours, J. M. HOPPIN.

BOSTON, *June* 6, 1882.

I much regret that a previous engagement on the 14th instant must prevent my acceptance of your kind invitation for that day; the more that it would give me special pleasure to honor the birthday of one for whom I have so high and long-standing a regard as for Mrs. Harriet Beecher Stowe. Faithfully yours,

HENRY M. DEXTER.

NEWPORT, R. I., *June* 7, 1882.

I exceedingly regret that I cannot join the "troops of friends" who will, by your kind invitation, unite in celebrating the birthday of one whom I have never had the pleasure of seeing, but shall always have the pleasure of reading, re-membering, and admiring. With sincere regard, CHARLES T. BROOKS.

NEW YORK, *June* 8, 1882.

I thank you for the invitation to the Garden Party to be given in honor of the most renowned of our countrywomen, and I regret that I can find no way of escaping from arrangements already made, so as to give myself the pleasure of being present on that occasion. Mrs. Stowe's well-deserved literary fame has had but one dangerous rival, namely, the world-wide celebrity of her brilliant and never-to-be-forgotten services opportunity rendered to humanity. It seems a trifle to add, but it marks a nature generous in small things as well as great that the author of *Uncle Tom* and of *The Minister's Wooing* has always known how to show the most graceful and grateful kindness to younger and less famous writers.

Thanking you again for your kind invitation, I am, gentlemen, yours very sincerely, EDW. EGGLESTON.

LEXINGTON, VA., *June* 8, 1882.

It would give me very great pleasure to attend the Garden Party given in honor of the birthday of Harriet Beecher Stowe, did my college engagements permit. Mrs. Stowe's brilliant genius deserves all possible recognition, not only from the North, but from the South, now "the institution" has passed away, and I should be one of the first to acknowledge its far-reaching power. I have the honor to be very truly yours, JAMES A. HARRISON.

797 GREENE AVENUE, BROOKLYN,
*June* 9, 1882.

The loss of two children recently has unfitted me for participation in any social pleasure, else I should eagerly embrace the opportunity to do honor to a gentlewoman who has done more, perhaps, than any other one person to influence the character and destinies of our land.

May she continue for many years to enjoy the serene consciousness of work well done, and of the abiding respect and affection of her countrymen.

Sincerely yours,     GEORGE CARY EGGLESTON.

NEW ORLEANS, *June* 9, 1882.

I thank you most gratefully for the kindness that remembers me at such a distance, and regret extremely my inability to respond in person. To be in New England would be enough for me. I was there once,—a year ago,—and it seemed as though I never had been home till then. To be there again, to join friends in rejoicing over the continuance on earth of one who has earned the gratitude of two races of humanity, is greater than the measure of my cup. I can only send you, Blessings on the day when Harriet Beecher Stowe was born. Yours truly,

G. W. CABLE.

230 SOUTH TWENTY-FIRST STREET,
PHILADELPHIA, *June* 12, 1882.

Mr. Davis being absent from home, it is left to me to say how sorry we are that we cannot be with you on Wednesday, to offer our friendliest greeting to your guest at this pleasant halting-place on her journey. She reminds me of that noble lady in the Arabian Nights, who sent before her to the king seventy slaves, each bearing a golden casket full of jewels. As at seventy, however, you men and women of New England only begin to understand your full vigor, there will be many birthdays yet to come, on which we may hope to take her by the hand, and tell her how thoroughly we honor her and her work.     Yours sincerely,

REBECCA HARDING DAVIS.

WASHINGTON, D. C., *June* 5, 1882.

I am very much obliged by your kind and thoughtful invitation to be present at a party in honor of the birthday of Mrs. Harriet Beecher Stowe. I should be delighted to be present on such an occasion, for to no one person has it been given to move so many minds and hearts in behalf of the lately enslaved as to Mrs. Stowe. Hers was the word for the hour, and it was given with skill, force, and effect. Let us honor her birthday, and hold up her example of great talents devoted to a great cause to the appreciation and edification of present and future generations.     Respectfully,     FREDERICK DOUGLASS.

ATLANTA, GA., *June* 20, 1882.

I owe a great deal, in one way and another, to the author of *Uncle Tom's Cabin*. In 1862, when quite a youngster, I chanced to get hold of a copy of the book, and it made a more vivid impression upon my mind than anything I have ever read since. It may interest you to know that I read it on the plantation where Uncle Remus held forth, and within a stone's throw of where ex-Secretary Seward taught school when he was a young man. Yours truly,

JOEL CHANDLER HARRIS.

MADISON, WIS., *June* 9, 1882.

It would afford me the greatest pleasure to accept your kind invitation to be present at the Garden Party in honor of the birthday of Harriet Beecher Stowe. I am a great admirer of Mrs. Stowe, and am proud of her reputation for her own sake, and not less for the sake of our country.

Yours faithfully,     R. B. ANDERSON.

STAR OFFICE, NEW YORK,
*June* 9, 1882.

Please accept my hearty thanks for your invitation to the Garden Party in honor of Mrs. Stowe. The press of previous engagements renders it quite impossible for me to join you and her other friends in celebrating the "threescore and ten" of the woman whose one work did more to educate the North and make emancipation possible than anything else which was done. It is fitting that she should be greeted anew by the generation that read her story and recognized it as a battle, as well as the generation that has grown up since it became a classic. Mrs. Stowe has the good fortune of combining the genius of a remarkably gifted family with the strength and tenderness of New England womanhood. She has anteceded immortality by all the years since her worth was recognized and her fame was assured. It is her happiness to live in the atmosphere of friendship and admiration she herself has made, as the sun moves in the splendor his own shining creates. Sincerely yours,     W. T. CLARKE.

104 MADISON AVENUE, NEW YORK,
*June* 9, 1882.

Alike as a woman, an author, and a philanthropist, Mrs. Stowe has honored the country of her birth, and Americans will honor themselves in recognizing her exalted worth and the great value of her labors. As an abolitionist I am deeply grateful to her. It was in 1852, just after the last desperate effort of the slave power, by the aid of its Northern supporters, to overwhelm and crush the antislavery movement, when humanity was shuddering in view of the atrocities of the fugitive slave law, and the fires of persecution were raging furiously around the champions of freedom, that *Uncle Tom's Cabin* came from the press to kindle fresh sympathy for the bondman throughout the civilized world, and fill the hearts of its enemies with despair. For twenty years the abolitionists had struggled against all the prejudices of caste, the hostility of political parties, and the combined opposition of the great ecclesiastical bodies of the land to create a public sentiment that would destroy slavery; and at the very moment when the prospect of success was eclipsed, and the hearts of multitudes were filled with fear and dread, Mrs. Stowe's great work turned the tide of battle; and from that day forth the hosts of freedom, with constantly augmenting strength, marched with unfaltering step toward their great victory. All honor, then, I say, to Mrs. Stowe, and may her old age be crowned with light and peace.

Yours respectfully,     OLIVER JOHNSON.

BROOKLINE, MASS., *June* 10, 1882.

Mrs. Stowe commands my most affectionate admiration and reverence. I suppose she will be instantly recognized as the greatest of all American humorists, not only that she, like Cervantes and Molière, has elicited and delineated the fine lights and shades of character, but used her humor for the purpose of putting great social wrongs and vices out of countenance. Her tender and pathetic pictures of old New England life and character will, I believe, give to her in future years a place in your literature; historical, like our English Fielding and Smollett, but with a purity and piety to which they have no claim. It would have been a great pleasure to me to tell Mrs. Stowe how often I have announced in my church in England some of her sweet verses, and heard them sung with hearty enjoyment by great congregations.

If your meeting of next Wednesday were in England, I think I could not forbear from calling, in our old English fashion, for three cheers for Old Tiff and Topsy. Please accept my grateful acknowledgments and regrets, and believe me, in hearty sincerity,     EDWIN PAXTON HOOD.

BROOKLYN, *June* 9, 1882.

It would afford me great pleasure to be present on that occasion, as I hold Mrs. Stowe's contributions to the world of letters in high estimation. Who has not suffered with that hero, Uncle Tom? Who has not wished to take part in the *Minister's Wooing*? Who would not learn the genesis of that delicate creation, the "Quaker settlement," and buy a corner lot there? Who has not felt that the pen which outlined the life and death of little Eva was guided by an angel hand?

Respectively yours,     J. NEILSON.

ELMIRA, N. Y., *June* 9, 1882.

The original Uncle Tom (the only one known as such by the children of her who has given the name a world-wide reputation) regrets his inability to share in the festivities of the 14th instant, to which you invite him.

He will not be, however, unmindful of his sister's birthday when it shall come, and is grateful to you and to other distinguished friends for the honors with which you are planning its decoration, and he remains, gentlemen, with sincere regard,     Yours Truly,     THOMAS K. BEECHER.

CINCINNATI, *June* 9, 1882.

Nothing could afford me greater pleasure than an opportunity to unite in honoring a woman who has done so much for the cause of humanity. Mrs. Stowe's pen did more to strike the chains from four million slaves than the sword. She is justly appreciated in her own day, and her name will occupy in history one of its brightest pages. Do me the favor to convey to Mrs. Stowe my regards, and the wish that her useful life may be long continued and enjoyed.

Truly yours,     RICHARD SMITH.

BROOKLYN, N. Y., *June* 12, 1882.

It gives us great pleasure to learn that you propose to celebrate, by appropriate honors, the birthday of one of the most gifted of American authors. The writings of Mrs. Stowe have been our familiar reading, from her earliest sketches in the *Mayflower.* We have followed her brilliant career as an author through all the varied productions of her pen, which have won for her a world-wide reputation, wherever English literature is known. She ranks, by universal consent, among the foremost of female writers; surpassed by none, and approached by few. What is still higher and nobler than mere literary merit, the tendency of her writings is uniformly healthful, and their moral and religious influences are always elevating and inspiring. We have long enjoyed the personal friendship of Mrs. Stowe and her honored husband, and we would gladly share in the festivities in honor of her birthday, were it in our power to leave our home at this time.

Very respectfully,     T. J. and E. C. CONANT.

UNION THEOLOGICAL SEMINARY,
30 CLINTON PLACE, NEW YORK,
*June* 12, 1882.

In common with the many thousands who have been delighted and thrilled by the words her pen has written,—thousands in this, and thousands in many another land,—I wish for her yet long and faithful years on earth, and the joy that may come as she understands how her name will be cherished in the years still beyond.

Thanking you for the honor of your remembrance, I am, with great respect,

Yours sincerely,      FRANCIS BROWN.

INTER-OCEAN OFFICE, CHICAGO,

*June* 9, 1882.

I know of no one whom it would delight me more to honor than Mrs. Stowe. She has indelibly impressed the most important era of our country, and made us a grander and nobler people. Hundreds of thousands of young people like myself were brought to a higher appreciation of humanity through *Uncle Tom's Cabin* than they ever could have had without that wonderful book. Please give to your honored guest the congratulations of one who from his boyhood has been an ardent admirer.      Yours truly,      WM. PENN NIXON.

HARPER AND BROTHERS' EDITORIAL ROOMS,

FRANKLIN SQUARE, NEW YORK,

*June* 10, 1882.

My remembrance of Mrs. Stowe is always associated with delightful June days at the old Stowe Cottage in Andover. I am glad that her birthday is to be celebrated by a Garden Party, and not by a great dinner. She always, I remember, preferred a picnic to an evening party. She loved nature, and for her there was a charm in the natural and characteristic expression of men and women (of even the lowliest) that she could not feel in the elaborate utterances of the most brilliant orator. She almost demanded of poetry that it should be an improvisation, and this love of the natural is the key to the understanding of her own work, and has been the secret of her power, which has not been a literary power only; it has been illustrated by events within her own life-time.

It was my good fortune to receive through Mrs. Stowe my first introduction to the world of letters,—that is, as a writer,—and I cordially unite with her friends in their tribute to her genius, and in that which is more precious to her, the tribute of affectionate remembrance.

Regretting that I cannot be one of your Garden Party, and thanking you for your courteous invitation, I am sincerely yours,      H. M. ALDEN.

NEW YORK, *June* 13, 1882.

It would be a great pleasure to me if I could unite with you and your guests, on the 14th, in doing honor to Mrs. Stowe. But as I am unable to be present at the Garden Party, I must content myself with being one of the vast body of absent friends and well-wishers who rejoice in everything that adds to Mrs. Stowe's honor and happiness.

Yours very truly,      MARY MAPES DODGE.

OTTAWA, ILL., *June* 12, 1882.

Did the circumstances permit, nothing could give me more pleasure than to join you in doing honor to one who has so largely contributed to American literature, and done so much to elevate its tone and extend its fame. May she live to witness many returns of the happy day which gave to the world a light whose radiance has illuminated all lands where letters are cultivated and refinement appreciated. But circumstances forbid my personal attendance, though in thought I shall be with you.

Most respectfully yours,     J. D. CATON.

SUB-TREASURY, U. S.,
BOSTON, MASS., *June* 15, 1882.

I beg to congratulate you upon your privilege of thus honoring this so much esteemed and distinguished lady, and upon the remarkable success and historical character of the occasion. It was an event of which your house may well be proud.

Thanking you for the compliment, which the Fates seem to have miscarried, believe me yours very truly,     M. P. KENNARD.

CHICAGO TRIBUNE EDITORIAL ROOMS,
*June* 14, 1882.

Mrs. Stowe's noble work in the cause of the freedom of man makes her birthday one of the anniversaries of humanity, and I should be glad to testify my deep respect by my presence.

Very kindly yours,     HENRY D. LLOYD.

JOURNAL OFFICE,
CHICAGO, *June* 12, 1882.

It would be to me a special privilege and pleasure to participate, if it were possible, in the event that is intended to be a tribute of respect to the author of *Uncle Tom's Cabin*, which ushered in the dawn of the new and glorious day that gave liberty to the slave, and made human freedom in America an actual verity, rather than an empty boast.

I bow with the profoundest respect and veneration to the noble woman who has done so much for our country and for humanity.

Respectfully yours,     ANDREW SHUMAN.

GENEVA, OHIO, *June* 7, 1882.

Your kind invitation, which makes me guest-elect at the Garden Party of June 14th, gives me very great pleasure, exceeded only by the regret I feel at my inability to attend. To meet the lady whose birthday is honored has been a long-cherished wish, and I scarcely permit myself—for aggravation of disappointment—to think of the many others among the dii majores of our literature who will doubtless be present, and whom I must forego seeing. Believe me, with grateful appreciation of your courtesy, very sincerely yours,

EDITH M. THOMAS.

Letters of regret were also received from Rev. William H. Beecher, Gov. John D. Long, Judge E. H. Bennett, Rev. Phillips Brooks, President Eliot, Dr. Samuel Eliot, Prof. Alexander Agassiz, Mr. John T. Morse, Jr., Mr. Henry Cabot Lodge, Prof. Moses Coit Tyler, Hon. Carl Schurz, Mr. E. L. Godkin, Mr. John Burroughs, Mr. Whitelaw Reid, Col. John Hay, Mr. Henry James, Rev. Samuel Longfellow, Mr. Ernest Longfellow and the Misses Longfellow, Dr. E. W. Emerson and Miss Ellen Emerson, Mr. and Mrs. William H. Forbes, Mr. J. Elliot Cabot, Gen. A. C. McClurg, Mr. Robert Clarke, Mr. J. W. Harper, Jr., Mr. Alexander Williams, Mr. E. P. Dutton, Rev. J. M. Buckley, Rev. H. L. Wayland, Mr. Murat Halstead, Judge Nathaniel Holmes, Gen. F. A. Walker, Judge Charles A. Ray, Rev. Dr. C. A. Bartol, Prof. J. W. Churchill, Prof. Charles Eliot Norton, Miss L. M. Alcott, Mrs. Julia Ward Howe, Col. T. W. Higginson, Mr. S. L. Clemens, Mr. John S. Dwight, Mr. Francis Parkman, Mr. Josiah Quincy, Mrs. Owen Wister, Rev. Dr. F. H. Hedge, Rev. Edward Abbott, Mr. Wendell P. Garrison, Miss Anna E. Ticknor, Rev. T. T. Munger, and many others.

## Notes

1. "Mrs. Stowe's Birthday Party," *New York Times*, 15 June 1882, p. 5.

2. Joan Hedrick, *Harriet Beecher Stowe: A Life* (Oxford: Oxford University Press, 1994), pp. 393–394.

"The Birthday Garden Party to Harriet Beecher Stowe," *Atlantic Monthly Supplement* 50 (August 1882): A001–A016.

# "Mrs. Harriet Beecher Stowe
# in Hartford" (1886)

## Joseph H. Twichell

> One of Mark Twain's closest friends, Joseph Hopkins Twichell (1838–1918),
> was the minister of a Congregationalist church in Hartford, Connecticut. In-
> troduced to Twain in 1868, Twichell presided at the marriage of Twain and
> Olivia Langdon in 1870 and was the model for Mr. Harris in Twain's humor-
> ous travel book *A Tramp Abroad* (1880). He was a frequent visitor to the Twain
> home in Hartford, where he met Stowe. Twichell wrote the following account
> of Stowe for a series, "Authors at Home," published in the *Critic*, a literary
> magazine edited by Jeanette L. Gilder and her brother, Joseph B. Gilder. A
> number of American authors were featured in the series, including John
> Greenleaf Whittier, Thomas Wentworth Higginson, Walt Whitman, James
> Russell Lowell, and Harriet Prescott Spofford. The purpose of the series was
> to introduce the public to American authors by what the *Critic* called "literary
> interviewers," who visited writers in their homes. When the popular series
> was published as a book, *Authors at Home* (1889), a reviewer commented:
> "Turning a corner, we are brought face to face with the venerable Mrs. Stowe,
> and learn how beautifully that lost grace of our grandmothers—the art of
> growing old—is rediscovered in her and wrought into a fine art."[1]

CONSIDERING THAT SHE is seventy-five years of age, Mrs. Stowe is in a condition of excellent health. This, it may be assumed, is due in part to the
Beecher constitution; but it is also a result of her settled habits of physical
exercise. Twice a day regularly she walks abroad for an hour or more, and
between times she is apt to be more or less out of doors. The weather must
be unmistakably prohibitory to keep her housed from morning till night.
Not infrequently her forenoon stroll takes her to the house of her son, the
Rev. Charles E. Stowe, two miles away, in the north part of the city. So
long as the season admits of it, she inclines to get off the pavement into the

Harriet Beecher Stowe in front of her home in 1886. Harriet Beecher Stowe Center, Hartford, Connecticut.

fields; and she is not afraid to climb over or under a fence. As one would infer from her writings, she is extremely fond of wild flowers, and from early spring to late autumn invariably comes in with her hands full of them. To a friend who met her lately on one of her outings, she exhibited a spray of leaves, and passed on with the single disconsolate remark, "Not one flower can I find;" as if she had failed of her object. As a general thing she prefers to be unaccompanied on her walks. She moves along at a good pace, but—so to speak—quietly, with her head bent somewhat forward, and at times so wrapped in thought as to pass without recognition people whom she knows, even when saluted by them. Yet she will often pause to talk with children whom she sees at their sports, and amuse both herself and them with kindly inquiries about their affairs—the game they are playing, or what not. A few days since she stopped a little girl of the writer's acquaintance who was performing the rather unfeminine feat of riding a bicycle, and had her show how she managed the mount and the dismount, etc., while she looked on laughing and applauding. It is very much her way in making her pedestrian rounds to linger and watch workingmen employed in their various crafts, and to enter into conversation with them—always in a manner to give them pleasure. She said recently: "I keep track of all the new houses going up in town, and I have talked with the men who are building most of them." Three or four years ago her brother, Henry Ward Beecher, sent her a letter which he had received from a friend in Germany, condoling with him on the supposed event of her decease, a rumor of which had somehow got itself started in Europe; and this letter afforded her no little entertainment, especially its closing with the expression "Peace to her ashes." "I guess," she observed with a humorous smile, and using her native dialect, "the gentleman would think my ashes pretty lively, if he was here." It seems now as though this might be said of Mrs. Stowe for quite a while yet. Heaven grant it! To what multitudes is her continued presence in the world she has a blessed a grateful circumstance!

Mrs. Stowe has resided in Hartford since 1864, the family having removed thither from Andover, Mass., upon the termination of Prof. Stowe's active professional career. Her attachment to the city dates back to her youth, when she passed some years there. It was also the home of several of her kindred and near friends. She first lived in a house built for her and of her own design—a delightful house, therefore. But its location proved, by and by, for various reasons, so unsatisfactory that it was given up; and after an interval, spent chiefly at her summer place in Florida, the present house was purchased. It is an entirely modest dwelling, of the cottage style, and stands about a mile west of the Capitol, in Forest Street, facing the east. The plot which it occupies—only a few square rods in extent—is well planted with shrubbery (there is scarcely space for trees) and is, of course, bright with flowers in their season. On its rear it joins the grounds of Mark Twain, and is but two minutes' walk distant from the home of Charles Dudley Warner. The interior of the house is plain, and of an ordinary plan. On the right as you enter, the hall opens into a good sized parlor, which in turn opens into another back of it. On the left is the dining-room. In furnishing it is altogether simple, as suits with its character, and with the moderate circumstances of its occupants. Yet it is a thoroughly attractive and charming home; for it bears throughout, in every detail of arrangement, the signature of that refined taste which has the art and secret of giving an air of grace to whatever it touches. The pictures, which are obviously heart selections, are skillfully placed, and seem to extend to the caller a friendly greeting. Among them are a number of flower-pieces (chiefly wild) by Mrs. Stowe's own hand.

While there are abundant indications of literary culture visible, there is little to denote the abode of one of the most famous authors of the age. Still, by one and another token, an observant stranger would soon discover whose house he was in, and be reminded of the world-wide distinction her genius has won, and of that great service of humanity with which her name is forever identified. He would, for instance, remark on its pedestal in the box-window a beautiful bronze statuette, by Cumberworth, called "The African Woman of the Fountain;" and on an easel in the back parlor a lovely engraving of the late Duchess of Sutherland and her daughter—a gift from her son, the present Duke of that name—subscribed: "Mrs. Stowe, with the Duke of Sutherland's kind regards, 1869." Should he look into a low oaken case standing in the hall, he would find there the twenty-six folio volumes of the "Affectionate and Christian Address of Many Thousands of Women in Great Britain and Ireland to their sisters of the United States of America," pleading the cause of the slave, and signed with over half-a-million names, which was delivered to Mrs. Stowe in person at a notable gathering at Stafford House in England in 1853; and with it similar Addresses from the citizens of Leeds, Glasgow and Edinburgh, presented at about the same time. The house, indeed is a treasury of such relics, testimonials of reverence and gratitude, trophies of renown from many lands— enough to furnish a museum—all of the highest historic interest and value; but for the most part they are out of sight. Hid away in closets and seldom-opened bookcases is a priceless library of "Uncle Tom" literature, including copies of most of its thirty-seven translations. Somewhere is Mrs. Stowe's copy of the first American edition, with the first sheet of the original manuscript (which, however, was not written first) pasted on the flyleaf, showing that three several beginnings were made before the setting of the introductory scene was fixed upon. Many of these things it is Mrs. Stowe's intention ultimately to bequeath in some fashion to the public.

There are relics, also, of a more private sort. For example, a smooth stone of two or three pounds weight, and a sketch or study of it by Ruskin, made at a hotel on Lake Neufchâtel, where he and Mrs. Stowe chanced to meet; he having fetched it in from the lakeshore one evening and painted it in her presence to illustrate his meaning in something he had said. One of her most prized possessions is a gold chain of ten links, which on occasion of the gathering at Stafford House that has been referred to, the Duchess of Sutherland took from her own arm and clasped upon Mrs. Stowe's, saying:—"This is the memorial of a chain which we trust will soon be broken." On several of the ten links were engraved the great dates in the annals of Emancipation in England; and the hope was expressed that she would live to add to them other dates of like import in the progress of liberty this side of the Atlantic. That was in 1853. Twelve years later every link had its inscription, and the record was complete.

It is difficult to realize, as one is shown memorials of this kind, that the fragile, gentle-voiced little lady, who stands by explaining them, is herself the heroine in chief of the sublime conflict they recall. For a more unpretending person every way, or one seeming to be more unconscious of gifts and works of genius, or of a great part acted in life, it is not possible to imagine. In her quiet home, attended by her daughters, surrounded by respect and affection, filled with the divine calm of the Christian faith, in perfect charity with all mankind, the most celebrated of American women is passing the tranquil evening of her days. She will often be found seated at the piano, her hand straying over its keys—that hand that has been clothed with such mighty power—singing softly to herself those hymns of Gospel hope which have been dear to her heart through all her early pilgrimage, alike in cloud and in sunshine. Of late she has almost wholly laid her pen aside; though just now she is engaged, with her son's assistance, in preparing for publication a brief memoir of her honored husband, who passed away a few months since.

There continue to come to her in retirement, often from distant and exalted sources, messages of honor and remembrance, which she welcomes with equal pleasure and humility. Not very long ago she received a letter from Mr. Gladstone, inspired by his reading *The Minister's Wooing* for the first time, and written in the midst of his public cares. What satisfaction it gave her may be judged by an extract from it. After telling her that, though he had long meant to read the book he had not found an opportunity to do so till a month or two before, he says:—"It was only then that I acquired a personal acquaintance with the beautiful and noble picture of puritan life which in that work you have exhibited, upon a pattern felicitous beyond example, so far as my knowledge goes. I really know not among four or five of the characters (though I suppose Mary ought to be preferred as nearest to the image of our Saviour), to which to give the crown. But under all circumstances and apart from the greatest claims, I must reserve a little corner of admiration for Cerinthy Ann."

## Note

1. "Authors at Home," *Critic*, 4 May 1889, p. 217.

Joseph H. Twichell, "Mrs. Harriet Beecher Stowe in Hartford," *Critic*, 18 December 1886, pp. 301–302.

# "Harriet Beecher Stowe" (1888)

### Alexandra Gripenberg

The member of a prominent Swedish-Finnish family and a well-known fiction writer, journalist, and women's rights activist in Finland, Alexandra Gripenberg (1857–1913) traveled the United States in 1888. She came to the United States as a delegate to the international women's congress in Washington, D.C., and subsequently spent six months traveling from New York to San Francisco. She was especially interested in studying the temperance and women's rights movements during her visit and became friendly with Elizabeth Cady Stanton and Susan B. Anthony.[1] She was also very interested in American literature and visited Mark Twain as well as Stowe at Nook Farm. When she returned to Helsinki, Gripenberg wrote *A Half Year in the New World* in Swedish, and it was later translated into Finnish and Danish. Gripenberg's account of her efforts to meet Stowe reveals much about Stowe's declining years. While Gripenberg did not have all of the facts exactly right about the circumstances of the publication of *Uncle Tom's Cabin*, she provides a European perspective on the importance of the novel and Stowe's enduring reputation.

NOT FAR FROM Mark Twain's splendid villa is a small, light-gray wooden house, also a villa like all the rest of the homes along Forest Street.

The house is embedded in vegetation. On both sides of a narrow walk paved with slate, which leads from the street to the house, stand gently sighing birch trees. The lawn is smooth and mowed level and adorned by rows of bright gillyflowers, asters, and blue lobelia, a small espalier with sweet peas, and azalea shrubs with their pink and white flowers. A wild grape vine climbs up the pillars of the veranda.

Everything is quiet and still. It seems as though all voices have been hushed to the point of silence. The stillness brings to mind the silence of a sick room. This attractive, silent house is indeed a sick room. Here Harriett Beecher Stowe is spending her last days far away from the world's commotion.

Alexandra Gripenberg, ca. 1890. Prints and Photographs Division, Library of Congress.

With a sister of Harriet Beecher Stowe I stepped into this house early
one spring morning. Harriet Beecher Stowe has been a widow for a few
years and lives with her unmarried twin daughters; her son is the minister
of a Congregationalist church in the same city.

The sister left me alone in the reception hall while she went to inquire
if I could be received. Although the dwelling gave the impression of a sick
room from the outside, inside it was just like an art gallery in miniature. In
furnishing the room, blue and white colors had been used, and the wood-
work was light. Even the piano was of light wood and the needlework on
the piano stool was in blue and white. The rugs, couch covers, pillows, has-
socks, chairs, and wall hangings were of the same color. In the lovely morning sunlight the room with its colors looked sweet and childishly peaceful.

In two corner cupboards decorated with beautiful carvings were all of
Mrs. Stowe's works; in one were the fine and national editions; in the other,
all the rest of the editions from the first little, inconspicuous *Uncle Tom's*

*Cabin* to the most recent editions with a vignette at the beginning of each chapter. Above the fireplace hung a full-length painting of the author's deceased brother, the famous minister, Henry Ward Beecher, with a face revealing his joy in life and with a thinker's forehead and eyes. Just opposite hung another picture: Professor Stowe. A fine, sharp, almost sly-looking face gazed from the picture; around the mouth and eyes were furrows indicative of melancholy and suspicion. Photographs of the son appeared to be in many places; here he was as a small baby in a fluttering muslin dress; there as a school boy, and from over there he looked forth as a newly ordained minister. Then came the grandchildren, alone or in groups, smiling, dimpled, mischievously glancing little faces, chubby hands.

In many places hung photographs, oil paintings, and crayon drawings of the same woman's face. It was Lady Byron for whose sake Mrs. Stowe won herself so many enemies in Europe. Many other high-born ladies' pictures graced the walls, and there were even some among them of royal blood. They were gifts to Mrs. Stowe from the various persons respectively and all of them were from the time when the author was at the peak of her fame, i.e. from the period of the abolitionist movement. In addition to them, there were on the walls oil paintings of greater or lesser value, gifts from the artists themselves. On the tables were gold and silver trinkets, and small articles made of ivory, genuine china, tortoise shell, and mother of pearl, from different quarters of the world. Letters of greeting from abolitionist societies, letters from and photographs of the leaders; elegantly bound presentation copies of authors' works; egg, mineral, and shell collections; travel souvenirs from different parts of Europe and America—all this filled two or three rooms completely. Many full bookcases added to the amount of material. Everything was old and from former times, and Europe was comparatively better represented than America.

Harriet Beecher Stowe began her literary career with *Uncle Tom's Cabin*. Until that time she was comparatively little known, even in America. The publisher to whom she took her work shrugged his shoulders and glanced through the manuscript indifferently. Negroes? That was a barren subject and distasteful to the people. And the manuscript was thick. The book would cost a great deal. But she was the sister of the famous Henry Ward Beecher? At least that was something. But even so the experiment was risky. He decided to send the manuscript back, but happened to talk about the matter to his wife, who asked to see the novel. After reading it, she said to her husband, "Do you know that there is money in this book?" The man thought about the matter, followed his wife's advice, and *Uncle Tom's Cabin* was published serially in the literary section of his weekly newspaper. Immediately after that it appeared in book form and attracted such violent attention that Thackeray's *Vanity Fair*, which emerged from the press at the same time, was almost left behind. When a friend of his deplored this matter, the famous English novelist replied, "Well, it was stupid of me to forget to put a Negro into my book."

Mrs. Stowe, then, from the very beginning tied in her literary activities with abolitionism, which was a very unpopular movement. Many ministers preached against her and against the emancipation of the slaves, since it supposedly "attempted to overthrow God's universal order." Newspapers and critics said that her book was a shameful lie and its characters the productions of the author's maudlin imagination. Hatred, malice, and slander finally became so overwhelming that her friends advised her to write the *Key to Uncle Tom's Cabin*, in which she published all the true events, newspaper stories about slave markets, and the torture of slaves as witnessed by known persons, which had been the basis for *Uncle Tom's Cabin*.

Of course, it was not sufficient to calm down tempers. The agitation had already become too violent and it ended in the war between the northern and southern states; a woman's voice was not able to check it. But the book and its authors remained as the center of the movement. Mrs. Stowe earned a great deal of money and her publisher even more. Her name was on everyone's lips, even though it was not always pronounced sympathetically. So far as her earnings as an author are concerned, at that time a New England wife did not have the right to control her earnings herself. Mrs. Stowe's royalties went into the large, rapidly increasing family's household expenses. Her husband was, as Americans say, "very clever," but he lacked worthier qualities. When his wife wanted to make a testament in favor of the children, he forbade it. When this prohibition became known, it aroused general indignation in the state of Massachusetts, where the couple then lived. Soon after that the state legislature gave the married woman the right to her inherited and earned wealth, and the incident in the Stowe family was considered an important influence on this legal decision.

Everyone who knew Harriet Beecher Stowe personally and saw her in her family circle became fond of her. She was sweet, cheerful, patient with her husband and children, energetic and active in her housekeeping. It was known in America as an open secret that her husband was unusually tyrannical and narrow-minded and ruled his family with an iron hand. In spite of that, his wife was such a loving mate that she said she had been rewarded for the rest of her life when her husband, on his death-bed, admitted having wronged her and said that during his last illness he had begun to love his wife tenderly.

Even after Mrs. Stowe began to lend her pen to causes other than anti-slavery work, she remained comparatively unpopular. The visitor is puzzled by the fact that of all American authors just those two, Bret Harte and Harriet Beecher Stowe, who perhaps have done most to make their country known in Europe, are so little understood in their own land. America is still too young; it dislikes to find itself portrayed as a wilderness and a haunt of gold prospectors. But so truly and faithfully, depending on real facts, although at the same time poetically, has Bret Harte depicted California that at every step there one seems to recognize familiar places. Likewise the stranger notices that he is familiar with New England through Mrs. Stowe's descriptions. Reflecting the puritanical life of old, New England's regular, churchgoing, homespun, practical, active, solemn life has found in Mrs. Stowe an ingenious and faithful portrayer. One has only to visit in a home there for a short time to recognize it all: an early breakfast of freshly baked corn bread and hot dishes, a daily routine proceeding like the wheel of a clock, men and women with outdoor and indoor practicality who can just as well "nail a rug to the floor with an iron ladle" (Harriet B. Stowe) as draw up a petition to Congress, a complete interest in corner politics, zealots for religious sects, the fever to increase one's income . . . all of these one will find here in actuality after having read about them first in *Oldtown Folks* or in *Sam Lawson's Oldtown Fireside Stories*. But New England does not see them itself; these portrayals still come too close to it. Perhaps it will see sometime when *The Minister's Wooing* and many other works of Mrs. Stowe have become rich and valuable accounts of civilization; perhaps it will then learn to appreciate its warm-hearted, talented daughter's worth. It has been said that the mentioned work has already begun to attain its rightful place. Gladstone, the poet Lowell, Tennyson and others are its enthusiastic admirers. Lowell is reported to have said to his wife, "My dear, I wonder what we Americans were thinking about when we first read this book? This is the best psychological description of Puritanism's struggle against the newer religious point of view that has been written in America or will be written."

Quietly I moved about among the relics of Harriet Beecher Stowe's period of greatness until her sister returned. She looked sad, and with tears in her eyes she told me that I could not meet her sister just then because she had had one of her attacks of illness during the night and did not even recognize any of those around her.

"But," she added comfortingly, "tomorrow is Sunday and no matter how sick she is, she never neglects or forgets to go to church to hear Charlie preach. We will meet her there."

With heavy hearts we left the author's sunny but nevertheless melancholy home.

The next morning when we arrived at church, it was already full to overflowing, for even though the Reverend Charles Stowe is young, he has a great reputation. In addition, the Congregationalists had a so-called "children's day," when small children are baptized and the church is decorated with flowers.

We came early but in the pew ahead of us Harriet Beecher Stowe already sat. She had her two daughters with her, one on each side, and an older unmarried sister and her daughter-in-law with her children. The daughters were beautiful, stern-looking women; black eyes flashed from beneath their white hats.

I had come with another of the author's sisters, who now leaned forward and in a soft voice informed Mrs. Stowe and her companions of our arrival. These turned and greeted us politely, but Mrs. Stowe herself did not stir at all. She sat as though hewn out of stone, hands crossed, staring at the altar. As soon as her son took his place, the mother began to look at him. In singing the morning hymn, she was the first one to stand up and at the same moment she turned toward me so that I could see her face clearly.

So pale and withered! She did not look aged, hardly older than fifty, but her facial features were flabby and the lines about the corners of her mouth indicated dullness. Her look was blank and aimless; its gleam had been snuffed by long sickness; the disease had taken away the color from her skin. Although she was sickly herself, Mrs. Stowe took care of her husband so faithfully and eagerly, when he was suffering his lengthy last illness, that she neglected regular eating hours, sleep, and moving about in the open air. This irregularity and also the severe emotional strain after her husband's death resulted in a dangerous brain disease which caused dullness of the reasoning faculties and disturbance of the memory.

Hymn singing appeared to have a soothing effect on her. She stood up and kneeled according the demands of the service; she found the prayers and hymns in her book herself, and appeared to be very devout. But as soon as the sermon began she became restless. Absent-mindedly, sometimes with painful bewilderment, she looked around, she turned and moved, opened her Bible, closed it again, whispered to her daughters, who frequently gave her warning glances, and finally began to play with her oldest grandson, a small, black-haired five-year-old boy. She played with him quietly and secretly, not as an older person with a child but as two of the same age play together. In the middle of her play she once turned toward me, appeared surprised to find a total stranger near her and looked at me sharply. Gradually her searching glance chanced into an expression of affectionate kindness. She extended her hand over the back of the pew and pressed my hand, smiling in a friendly way with the look in her eyes of a person in her right mind.

Then she again turned away and her former restiveness began anew. A number of times she rose up impatiently, frightened-looking, and wanted to leave the church, but her relatives stopped her.

Her son did not look at all like her. He had the same kind of fine face, dark hair and eyes as his sisters did, but he looked more ingenuous. He spoke simply and enthusiastically and performed the baptismal ceremony in a charming and beautiful manner. According to the custom of the Congregationalists, he took each of the five little children dressed in white who was to be baptized—some of them could already walk—in his arms and baptized him then with the water from a baptismal font. Fatherly concern shone from his face as he gave the infants the names which they were to carry in fighting life's battles.

Mrs. Stowe looked earnestly at every movement of her son, but immediately after the baptismal service ended, her restlessness returned. It was agonizing to watch that mind, once so clear and sharp, now dull—to look at that forehead under which so many great and humane thoughts originated now darkened by pain and suffering. With a sigh of sorrow and sadness but also of relief, I watched the tired cross-bearer climb into her carriage after the church service.

The rest of the day I spent in the minister's pleasant, cheerful home, where the young wife and attractive children added delight to home life. My host himself was pleasant and gentle; he was well acquainted with the literature of his own land and of Europe and talked feelingly and respectfully about his mother. He related many interesting small episodes from her life. But everything seemed to be only pale reflections of the author's true, warm, sacrificing life. Her existence already seemed to be in the past; only its shadow remained.

### Note

1. Details of Gripenberg's life are taken from Ernest J. Moyne, "Translator's Preface," *A Half Year in the New World: Miscellaneous Sketches of Travel in the United States* (1888) by Alexandra Gripenberg (Newark: University of Delaware Press, 1954), pp. v–x.

From Alexandra Gripenberg, *A Half Year in the New World: Miscellaneous Sketches of Travel in the United States* (1888), translated by Ernest J. Moyne (Newark: University of Delaware Press, 1954), pp. 73–80.

# [An Exchange between Harriet Beecher Stowe and Oliver Wendell Holmes in 1893]

Stowe and Oliver Wendell Holmes (1809–1894) were among the writers who founded the *Atlantic Monthly*, and the two maintained a long, enduring friendship. A physician by training as well as a professor of anatomy first at Dartmouth College and then at Harvard University, Holmes began writing poetry as a student and published his first book of poems in 1836, the same year that he earned his M.D. He soon earned a reputation as a poet and as a writer of witty essays, first published in the *New-England Magazine* and then as *The Autocrat of the Breakfast Table* (1858). Like Stowe, the reform-minded Holmes had been raised in a strongly Calvinist tradition, which he repudiated as an adult. Holmes was a popular guest, in demand in Boston social circles and renowned for his conversation. In 1868, Annie Fields, the wife of the publisher James T. Fields, recorded an evening at her home with Stowe and Holmes:

> Wednesday morning, January 19, 1868.—Last night Professor Holmes, Mrs. Stowe, her daughter Georgie, and the Howellses, took tea here. The Professor came early and was in good talking trim—presently in came Mrs. Stowe, and they fell shortly into talk upon Homeopathy and Allopathy. He grew very warm, declared that cases cited of cures proved nothing, and we were all "incompetent" to judge! We could not but be amused at this heat, for we were more or less believers in Homeopathy against his one argument for Allopathy. In vain Mrs. Stowe and I tried to turn and stem the fiery tide: Georgie or Mrs. Howells would be sure to sweep us back into it again. However, there were many brilliant things said, and sweet and good and interesting things too. . . . [Holmes] had a long quiet chat with Mrs. Stowe before the evening ended. They compared their early Calvinistic education and the effect produced upon their characters by such training.[1]

By 1893, Stowe and Holmes were among the last of their generation of writers still living. In the following exchange of letters, written in 1893, the year before Holmes's death, he and Stowe write each other as old friends nearing the end of their lives. Their frank discussion of their health, losses, and occupations poignantly reveal their mutual regard and their shared outlook on life.

Oliver Wendell Holmes, ca. 1894. Prints and Photographs Division, Library of Congress.

Boston Jan. 31st 1893

My dear Mrs. Stowe

This comes from your old friend, Oliver Wendell Holmes. I was thinking that you might like to know how I was getting along with my burden of
eighty three years, and that I would write and tell you. While I was thinking about it I got a letter from another old friend of yours, whom you call
"Susie Howard," of Brooklyn N.Y.[2] She seemed to think that you would
like to get a letter from me, and I thought that if you would not feel obliged
to answer it, you might like to see my handwriting again. For though I keep
a Secretary I write my own autographs and certain letters—and certainly in
writing to you I will not employ the hand of another. You may like to know
what I am about—if, indeed I am about anything.

I go to meeting Sunday, and I must own I get two or three good naps, generally speaking, during the sermon.

I go to my Club on the last Saturday of every month. I am the President of this same "Saturday Club" where we used to meet Emerson, Longfellow, Lowell, Agassiz, Motley, Sumner, Andrew—sometimes Hawthorne and others of name and repute. This is my principal dissipation. Much of my working time is taken up in answering letters from everybody and everywhere. You know all about *that*—I believe your correspondence would have loaded a haycart in the time of your largest interchange of letters.—I do a little walking and a good deal of driving. I dine out once in a while and go to luncheon occasionally. I read a good many hours in the day—but I am a very slow reader,—and I sleep more than in my younger days, a good deal, falling asleep in my chair now and then but never getting into bed until between eleven and twelve.

There! I have accounted for myself physically, and the upshot of it all is that my habits are regular and I keep very well for the most part. About the end of November I had an attack of erysipelas of the face which kept me sick for a fortnight almost, but has left me none the worse—perhaps rather better for it.

I am ashamed of having told you all this about myself, but somehow we oldish people like to know how other oldish people bear the burden of years.

My sight is pretty dim; my hearing dull, but pretty serviceable, my wits—well they may seem dull to other folks but they don't to me. They may be, though, for all I cannot see it.

My views of life are cheerful, as they always have been,—my theology is quite as unorthodox as it ever was, but I do not quarrel with anybody about his or her belief. I go to a Unitarian church in winter and to a baptist church in summer and to tell the truth I like a sermon with a *piece de resistance* in it—something I can dispute and haggle over (internally) and so keep awake.

I hope you are happy, dear Mrs. Stowe. The beautiful record of your life ought to give you a tranquil and sweet old age. I trust that it does. "Blessed among women" you have certainly been and welcome among angels you must certainly be when you are called to that higher company.

Now, if my handwriting bothers you please get somebody to read my slight and hasty letter to you, and remember that pleasant as a reply from you would be, if it should be a labor to write it and I should find it out, it would be a source of regret to me that I had disturbed your peace and comfort.

Always affectionately yours
OWHolmes

Hartford Feby 5th
1893
My Dear Friend Dr. Holmes,

Your more than kind—your most charming really lovely letter of Jany 31 was, to me, the profoundest surprise and the greatest pleasure I have had in many a day—I might say year. That you should remember & think of me & write me so at length with your own hand too, is a kind courtesy, and an honor that I sincerely appreciate.

I must tell you, my dear friend, if you do not know it yourself—and I say it not to flatter, but because it is true. Your lamp burns as brightly as ever. The oil in it, has not run low leaving but a feeble gleam, as mine has done. Your noble and beautiful lines to our friend Whittier, show no diminution of mental power, but only the sweetness and richness of many summers.[3]

I am glad to know, how you pass your time, & that you have such a peaceful cheerful happy life. That you make others happy, I know—for your presence always was like the sunshine.

As to myself, there is not so much to tell, as of you. I am passing the last days of my life in the city where I passed my schoolgirl life. My physical health, since I recovered from the alarming illness, I had four years ago has been excellent, and I am almost always cheerful & happy. My mental condition might be called nomadic—I have no fixed thoughts or objects. I wander at will from one subject to another. In pleasant summer weather, I am out of doors most of my time rambling about the neighborhood & calling upon my friends. I do not *read* much. Now & then I dip into a book, much as a hummingbird poised in the air on whirring away. Pictures delight me, and afford me infinite diversions & interests. I pass many pleasant hours in looking over books of pictures.

Of music also I am very fond—I could not have too much of it and I never do have as much as I should like. The street bands even organs, give me great pleasure but especially the singing and playing of my kind friends, who are willing to gratify me in this respect.

I make no mental effort of any sort my brain is tired out. It was a womans [*sic*] brain & not a mans [*sic*] & finally from sheer fatigue & exhaustion in the march & strife of life, gave out before the end was reached. And now I rest me, like a moored boat, rising & falling on the water with loosened cordage & flapping sail. I thank you much, for your kind words, regarding myself. Blessed I have been, in many ways, in seeing many of the desires of my heart fulfilled & in having the love of many people as has been made manifest to me in these my declining years.

Sorrows also, I have had, which have left their mark on heart & brain.

But they are all passed now. I have come to the land of Bulah [*sic*] which is Heaven's border land, from whence we can see into the gates of the celestial city, and even *now* all tears are wiped from my eyes. Thanking you again & again for your great kindness in writing me and letting me know of your friendship & regard for me.

I am Most sincerely your friend,

Harriet Beecher Stowe

## Notes

1. M. S. DeWolfe Howe, *Memories of a Hostess: A Chronicle of Eminent Friendships, Drawn Chiefly from the Diaries of Mrs. James T. Fields* (Boston: Atlantic Monthly Press, 1922), pp. 38–39.

2. Beverly Peterson identifies Susie Howard as Mrs. John T. (Susan) Howard, a member of Henry Ward Beecher's church and a friend since 1852 ("Hitherto Unpublished Letters from Oliver Wendell Holmes to Harriet Beecher Stowe," *Resources for American Literary Study* 23.1 [1997], p. 79).

3. "In Memory of John Greenleaf Whittier," a poem written on the occasion of Whittier's death on 7 September 1892 (Peterson, p. 82). Holmes's poem was published in the *Atlantic Monthly* in November 1892.

From Beverly Peterson, "Hitherto Unpublished Letters from Oliver Wendell Holmes to Harriet Beecher Stowe," *Resources for American Literary Study* 23.1 (1997): 78–79; 80–81.

# [Eulogies and Remembrances of Stowe at Her Death in 1896]

After a few years of declining health, Stowe died at her home on 1 July 1896, attended by her son, Charles Edward Stowe, and her daughters Eliza and Harriet Stowe. The writer of the extensive obituary in the *New York Times* on 2 July called Stowe's death "one of the closing leaves in an era of our century."[1] Similarly, the *Hartford Courant* observed: "The death of Mrs. Stowe removes from this world one of the most interesting and conspicuous figures of this generation, one of the women whose names make up the comparatively short roll of her sex that illustrated its highest achievements."[2] The Episcopalian funeral service was a simple one held at Stowe's home in Hartford, and she was buried at the cemetery in Andover, Massachusetts, next to the grave of her husband, Calvin. Newspaper accounts report that a large number of friends and family members attended, including Annie Fields and Sarah Orne Jewett. In a letter to Fields written on 5 July 1889, Jewett expressed her admiration of Stowe and her recollections of that day:

> I have been reading the beginning of "The Pearl of Orr's Island" and finding it just as clear and perfectly original and strong as it seemed to me in my thirteenth or fourteenth year, when I read it first. I never shall forget the exquisite flavor and reality of delight that it gave me. I do so long to read it with you. It is classical—historical—anything you like to say, if you can give it high praise enough. I haven't read it for ten years at least, but there it is! Alas, that she couldn't finish it in the same noble key of simplicity and harmony; but a poor writer is at the mercy of much unconscious opposition. You must throw everything and everybody aside at times, but a woman made like Mrs. Stowe cannot bring herself to that cold selfishness of the moment for one's work's sake, and the recompense for her loss is a divine touch here and there in an incomplete piece of work. I felt at the funeral that none of us could really know and feel the greatness of the moment, but it has seemed to grow more great to me ever since. I love to think of the purple flowers you laid on the coffin.[3]

The first selection in this chapter is an article from the *Hartford Times* describing the funeral and burial. The second selection contains an excerpt from a eulogy given by the Reverend Dr. James M. King during a memorial service held at the Union Methodist Episcopal Church in New York City on 5 July 1896. The third selection is the text of a sermon on Stowe's life preached by Reverend C. T. Weitzel at the Plymouth Church in Brooklyn, New York, on 13 July 1896.

## "Burial of Mrs. Stowe"

Burial of Mrs. Stowe. At Rest in Andover Cemetery. Simple Services. Episcopal Commitment Ritual Conducted by Prof. Smyth. Prof. Stowe's Grave Strewn With Flowers.

The funeral services at the home of Mrs. Stowe Thursday afternoon were of a simple character. Selected passages of scripture were read by Rev. Jos. H. Twichell of Asylum Hill Congregational Church. He was followed by Rev. Chas T. Weitzel, assistant pastor of Plymouth Church of Brooklyn, NY who read selected passages of scripture.

A male quartette F. M. Green, Theo. Hannum, Frank Ahearn, H. S. Bullard, under direction of John M. Gallup sang "Nearer My God To Thee."

Rev. Francis Goodwin read the prayers from the Episcopal funeral services. Quartette sang five verses Mrs. Stowe's poem "The Other World."

Services closed with benediction by Rev. Francis Goodwin. Those present took last look at Mrs. Stowe. Beside immediate relatives in this city and the family of Rev. Chas. E. Stowe, Simsbury, Conn. there were present as mourners with the family—Mrs. Henry Ward Beecher of Brooklyn, accompanied. Major Jas. B. Pond of New York. Rev. Chas. T. Weitzel, Plymouth Church Brooklyn, representing Plymouth Church. Rev. Samuel Scofield, Stamford, son-in-law of Henry Ward Beecher. Freeman Allen, Boston, grandson of Mrs. Stowe. Mrs. Howard Knight, Bridgeport, grand niece of Mrs. Stowe. Mrs. Mary Foote Perkins, aged sister of Mrs. Stowe was too feeble to attend.

On Friday July 3, her remains were taken to Andover, Mass. for burial.

The funeral cortege passed up School Street to Chapel Avenue to the cemetery. There were simple decorations at the grave, bouquets on the cross over Professor Stowe's grave, some roses entwined the stone which

The grave at Andover, *New England Magazine* 21 (September 1896), p. 16. Love
Library, University of Nebraska, Lincoln.

marks Henry's grave. They were placed by wives of seminary professors,
headed by Mrs. John W. Churchill.

The Episcopal commitment form was used. There was no music. When
Professor Smyth pronounced the words "Dust to Dust," handfuls of earth
were dropped on the box containing the remains.

The old Stowe house on Chapel Avenue which the cortege passed was
draped with an American flag over the portico, festooned with black. The
house with its stone front is practically the same as when Mrs. Stowe lived
there. Between her husband and son Mrs. Stowe will rest.

Accompanying the remains were Mrs. Stowe's son, Rev. Charles Edward
Stowe, Mrs. Stowe's daughters, Eliza and Harriet, Mrs. Isabella Beecher
Hooker, her husband Hon. John Hooker, and Dr. Edward Beecher Hooker,
nephew of Mrs. Stowe.

Professor John W. Churchill, Dr. C. P. F. Bancroft, Professor George F. Moore and Dr. Selah Merril, former United States consul to Jerusalem, acted as pall-bearers. Professor Egbert C. Smyth conducted simple services at the grave. Her final resting place is behind the chapel of Andover Theological Seminary on Andover Hill. The narrow strip encloses hardly 100 graves of those who have [brought] fame to Andover's institutions.

The grave of the author of "Uncle Tom's Cabin" is set in a beautiful landscape. In a corner is a sunken slab of granite, a cross sets on it. At the foot is the inscription—Calvin Ellis Stowe, born April 26, 1802, died August 22, 1887. The text "The common people heard him gladly"—Mark XII, 37.

In opposite corner is a plain marble cross on a granite base with this inscription—Henry E. Stowe, drowned in the Connecticut River while a student at Dartmouth College, July 19, 1857, aged 19 years.

While at Andover in this house Mrs. Stowe lived from 1853 to 1864, while her husband was a professor at the seminary. During her residence here "Uncle Tom's Cabin" was published by John P. Jewett and Co. of Boston. First 6 months 50,000 copies sold. Mrs. Stowe received $10,000 in royalties later. In 4 years 313,000 copies sold in United States.

In this house Mrs. Stowe received many Americans and foreigners noted in literature, after her fame as an authoress had become assured.

### "Mrs. Stowe Eulogized"

The Union Methodist Episcopal church in West Forty-eight Street, near Broadway, was fairly well filled last evening to hear a sermon on the life work of Mrs. Harriet Beecher Stowe, delivered by her pastor, the Rev. Dr. James M. King. Dr. King took for his subject, "The Declaration of Independence" and "Uncle Tom's Cabin," and his remarks were eulogistic of the deceased authoress. In the course of his sermon Dr. King said:

> The Declaration of Independence read that all men were created free and equal, but it was not for eighty-eight years that the free and liberty-loving American people saw the great hypocrisy of this statement. It was Mrs. Stowe's grand work, conceived in the Lord that drove this great lie out of our Declaration of Independence. No permanent victory crowned the Union forces until the proclamation abolishing slavery was issued. It was the story of "Uncle Tom's Cabin" that quickened the spirit of the North, and many a mother gave up her son to her country with tears in her eyes but with the story of Uncle Tom's wrongs in her heart.

The secret of the success of Mrs. Stowe's work was simple. It came from the heart. Mrs. Stowe religiously believed that her book was divinely inspired. Once in her later married life, in Connecticut, a traveler came to see her and said that it was with great pleasure and with a high appreciation of the honor that he grasped the hand of the author of "Uncle Tom's Cabin." Mrs. Stowe solemnly said: "God wrote the book."

The book was conceived and born in the sacrament of the Lord's Supper. It was during the solemn service that the inspiration came to her. I believed that Mrs. Stowe was called, as Lincoln was, by God to come forward in the great crisis in our Nation's history. The story of "Uncle Tom's Cabin" served admirably to quicken the National conscience until the great blot of slavery was removed from our escutcheon.

## "A Tribute to Mrs. Stowe"

The Rev. C. T. Weitzel, one of the assistant pastors of Plymouth Church, Brooklyn, preached an eloquent sermon on the life of Harriet Beecher Stowe yesterday morning, taking his text from I. John iv., 7–8: "Beloved, let us love one another: for love is of God. He that loveth not knoweth not God; for God is love."

Dr. Weitzel said:

If there is one church in the land more than another where the memory of Harriet Beecher Stowe should be honored at this time, it is this church.

Here, in this pulpit, made forever sacred by her brother's magnificent championship of the wronged and oppressed, she was known and loved.

Through all those years of our Nation's fiery trial, Plymouth Church and freedom were synonymous terms, wherever the name of Henry Ward Beecher was known.

Whoever has been charmed by her humor or touched by her pathos knew her to love her. She took all the world to her heart, and we have taken her to ours.

Harriet Beecher Stowe was the most influential woman of our country, and was worthy to be named with Abraham Lincoln, Gen. Grant, Henry Ward Beecher, and others whom the Nation revered.

Love was the favorite theme of her brother when speaking from the pulpit. In that one word lay Mrs. Stowe's extraordinary power, and in her remarkable humor she set out the wrongs which she sought to right.

But what she did or what she wrote was always inspired by love. "Uncle Tom's Cabin" or "The Minister's Wooing" could never have been written except by one to whom love was the "life blood of existence, the all in all of mind."

There are degrees of love, as there are degrees of heat or light. There may be a love that is blind, but hers was not of that kind.

She had studied the various aspects of negro slavery, from a residence of seventeen years on the borders of a slave State, and the actual occurrences which appear in her book came under her personal knowledge.

Those who knew her say that she did not appear to take particular notice of things about her, but when they read her book they at once recognized the different scenes and situations. Hers were farseeing eyes, and she spake whereof she knew. Her words were true to life.

Again, the character of Harriet Beecher Stowe was broad. It is no wonder that there was praise for her book, even in the South, for throughout the work there is not one word of condemnation for the South as such. Her great love was forever leading her to set herself in other's places.

In regard to slavery, she early felt an irrepressible desire to do something. When war loomed up, she knew that the North would suffer with the South.

In a preface to a European edition of "Uncle Tom's Cabin," she utters this agonized cry: "Would that this work were indeed a fiction, and not a mosaic of facts." The book was, indeed, an inspiration.

With perfect truth she might answer the old sea Captain of Sag Harbor: "I didn't write the book. God wrote it. I merely did His dictation."

But it is doubtful if she would have been a fit amanuensis for God's dictation if she had not been very different from those who see not, neither do they understand.

She recognized the faults and absurdities of men of noble hearts, whom oppression had made mad, but she refused to be swept away by their vagaries.

In the divine madness which seized her when she cried, "I will write something; I will, if I live"; in the solemn hour of that sacramental day when the death scene of Uncle Tom took shape in her mind, she was sane, true to facts, to life.

In her person, she was willing to suffer, and did suffer. In the "Key to Uncle Tom" she says: "I wrote it in the anguish of my soul, with tears and prayers, with sleepless nights and weary days."

No wonder she touched the human heart. No wonder she roused a Nation's conscience. Is there anything too hard for a love that is willing to suffer? It is an all-conquering love.

We may not have her gifts of nature and education. We may not have her genius, but we can all have that which was the greatest of all in her—a love that sees and plans, a love that reaches out to every living soul, a love that counts not its life dear unto itself, but like His, who could not save Himself because He must save others, a love that gladly lays down life for those it loves.

## Notes

1. "Harriet Beecher Stowe: Death of the Authoress of 'Uncle Tom's Cabin,'" *New York Times*, 2 July 1896, p. 5.

2. "Harriet Beecher Stowe," *Hartford Courant*, 2 July 1896, p. 8.

3. Annie Fields, ed., *Letters of Sarah Orne Jewett* (Boston: Houghton Mifflin Co., 1911), pp. 46–47.

"Burial of Mrs. Stowe," *Hartford Times*, 3 July 1896, handwritten transcription, Harriet Beecher Stowe Center, Hartford, CT; "Mrs. Stowe Eulogized," *New York Times*, 6 July 1896, p. 8; "A Tribute to Mrs. Stowe," *New York Times*, 13 July 1896, p. 9.

# A Brief Sketch of the Life of
# Harriet Beecher Stowe (1896)

ISABELLA BEECHER HOOKER

Isabella Beecher Hooker (1822–1907) was Stowe's much younger half-sister, the daughter of Lyman Beecher and his second wife, Harriet Porter Beecher. Hooker attended Catharine Beecher's Hartford Female Seminary and married John Hooker, a prosperous Hartford lawyer. The couple owned a home in the Nook Farm area of Hartford, where their neighbors included the Stowes. Hooker became deeply involved in the women's rights movement and worked with Elizabeth Cady Stanton and Susan B. Anthony in planning women's rights conventions. Although Stowe's views were more conservative than her sister's, the two remained close. When their brother Henry Ward Beecher was accused of adultery in 1872 and Hooker sided with his accusers, she and Stowe were estranged for a time. But in later life, they shared a mutual interest in spiritualism and enjoyed a warm relationship.[1] Hooker was with Stowe when she died on 1 July 1896. Shortly afterwards, Hooker prepared a brief biography of her famous sister. The William Rogers Manufacturing Company sponsored the publication of the biography as a pamphlet advertising a commemorative "Souvenir Spoon," a memento of the author of *Uncle Tom's Cabin*.[2]

IN THE LATTER YEARS of her life Mrs. Stowe was unable to aid the benevolent objects which had greatly interested her, by reason of the failure of receipts from "Uncle Tom's Cabin," the copyright having expired.

I have designed this Souvenir Spoon as a memento of my sister, and, should the sale of it bring some return to me, I shall delight to spend it largely in ways which she would have approved and for objects that always had her sympathy.

ISABELLA BEECHER HOOKER.

HARTFORD, Nov. 1, 1896

Harriet Beecher Stowe, the author of "Uncle Tom's Cabin," was born in Litchfield, Conn., June 14, 1811. Her father, Lyman Beecher, was a

Isabella Beecher Hooker, ca. 1873. Harriet Beecher Stowe Center, Hartford, Connecticut.

Congregational minister of remarkable ability, both as an orator and a profound thinker, and it is said that his six sermons on intemperance, though the first ever printed in this country, have never been surpassed for effectiveness in the cause of temperance. They were reprinted abroad, and read nearly everywhere that the English language was spoken.

Harriet attended the village school with her brother, Henry Ward Beecher, who was two years younger than herself, and later the school taught by John P. Brace, and was so interested in his talks on composition, given to the older classes while she was supposed to be studying her primary books, that she offered, when only nine years old; to write a composition *every week*, the first subject being "The difference between the Natural and the Moral Sublime."

When twelve years old she wrote a composition of such merit that it was selected to be read with two others at the annual exhibition—the subject: "Can the immortality of the soul be proved by the light of nature?"—and her father, being one of the judges, after listening with deep interest, turned to Mr. Brace, and said, "Who wrote that?" "Your daughter, sir," was the reply, and she was so overjoyed that in after years she declared it was the proudest moment of her life.

It was from her father also that in these young days she learned the true nature of slavery and the slave trade. This is her own story as written to a friend in 1851: "I was a child in 1820 when the Missouri Compromise was agitated, and one of the strongest and deepest impressions on my mind was that made by my father's sermons and prayers and the anguish of his soul for the poor slave at that time. I remember his preaching drawing tears down the hardest faces of the old farmers in his congregation. I well remember his prayers, morning and evening, in the family, for 'poor, oppressed, bleeding Africa,' that the time of her deliverance might come; prayers offered with strong crying and tears, and which indelibly impressed my heart and made me what I am from my very soul, the enemy of all slavery."

Story books were rare in those days, but ransacking barrels in the garret she found a few odd pages of *Don Quixote*, which she devoured with eager relish, and at last a full copy of *The Arabian Nights*. This she fairly committed to memory, and it is one of the family traditions, that when sleeping in the same room with her two young brothers she made bedtime a joy to them by rehearsing those wonderful stories, and when these were exhausted, at their earnest request, she originated new ones of the same order. Finally

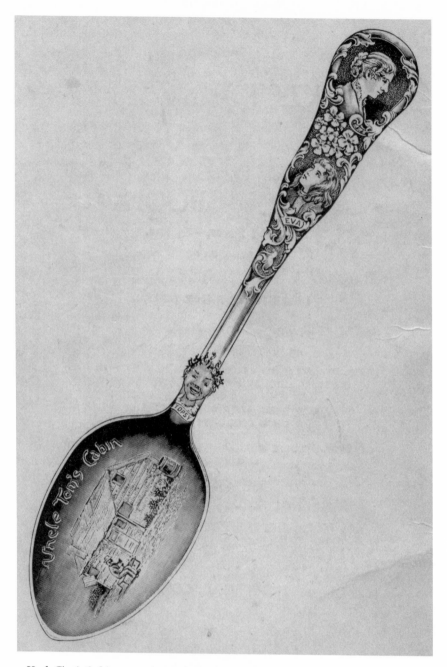

*Uncle Tom's Cabin* souvenir tea spoon, back cover illustration for *A Brief Sketch of the Life of Harriet Beecher Stowe* (1896). Harriet Beecher Stowe Center, Hartford, Connecticut.

her father, overcome by the genius of Sir Walter Scott, said to his children, "You may read Scott's novels; I have always disapproved of novels as trash, but in these are real genius and real culture and you may read them," and, she adds, "we did read them, for in one summer George and I went through *Ivanhoe* seven times, and were both of us able to recite many of its scenes from beginning to end, verbatim."

When about thirteen she was sent to her sister Catharine's seminary, just being established in Hartford, Conn., and soon became teacher as well as scholar, being set to teach a class of girls as old as herself in Butler's Analogy, and thus compelled to master each chapter just ahead of her class.

She remained in Hartford till 1832, when her father, being called to Cincinnati as President of Lane Theological Seminary, took nearly the whole of his family with him, and made for them a home on Walnut Hills, three miles out of the city, and in a most lovely grove of native forest trees. For several years the sisters conducted a seminary like the one in Hartford. On January 6, 1836, she was married to Prof. Calvin E. Stowe, who was sent to Europe immediately after as a Commissioner appointed by the State of Ohio to investigate the public school systems of Europe, especially Prussia, and report to the Legislature. During his absence Mrs. Stowe lived with her father, and wrote short stories for a literary society called "The Semi-Colon," which were read aloud at its meetings and excited much admiration, the reader being sometimes moved to tears, and unable to proceed; and occasionally she wrote for the *Western Monthly Magazine* and the *New York Evangelist*. Most of these stories will be republished in the Houghton & Mifflin edition of her complete works now being issued, under the title of *Household Papers and Stories*.

She also assisted her brother Henry on the *Journal*, a small daily paper, of which he was the temporary editor. The Anti-Slavery movement in Cincinnati began at this time. Mr. J. G. Birney, of Huntsville, Alabama, having liberated his slaves, came to Cincinnati, and, in connection with Dr. Gamaliel Bailey, founded an anti-slavery paper called the *Philanthropist*. This paper was mobbed by Kentucky slaveholders and their allies, and finally suppressed, and Mrs. Stowe says of this time, "All the papers in the city, except *Hammond's Gazette* and brother Henry's *Journal*, were either silent or openly mobocratic."

On September 29, 1836, her twin daughters were born, and named Harriet Beecher Stowe and Eliza Tyler Stowe, and on January 14, 1838, her son Henry was born. Thus her domestic life began, and from this date she struggled with ill health and poverty for fourteen years, giving birth to six children, until, in 1850, Mr. Stowe became a Professor in Bowdoin College, Brunswick, Maine, and, in 1852, *Uncle Tom's Cabin* was published, and brought her $10,000 at once and a yearly income which made her comfortable for life.

It was during this life in Ohio, however, that she became familiar with the cruelties of slavery, through the fugitives from Kentucky who were continually crossing the Ohio river and being protected and helped on their way by what was known as the "Underground Railroad," their house and barn being one of the first stations. Talking with these poor runaways nearly broke her heart, and thus it was she was able, in after years, to draw tears of sympathy from thousands all over the world, and thus was aroused that irresistible force of public opinion which finally put an end to the whole system.

While living in Brunswick her seventh child was born, and *Uncle Tom's Cabin* was written from the nursery, and amid serious cares and distractions, the days of poverty not yet being over.

Early in 1853 the family moved to Andover, Mass., and, in April, Mrs. Stowe visited England with her husband and brother Charles, and was royally entertained by some of the most distinguished families on account of her "wonderful book," and her after correspondence with statesmen and authors on subjects of vital importance gives evidence of rare ability in other fields than mere story writing.

Twice again she traveled in Europe, writing *Sunny Memories of Foreign Lands* and *Agnes of Sorrento*, and, on her return, she wrote several stories of New England life, all of which are now being republished.

In 1863 Professor Stowe's failing health caused him to resign his work in Andover, and the family moved to Hartford, the home of Mrs. Stowe's early days, where she resided until her death, which occurred July 1, 1896. During the last ten years of her life failing health prevented her writing or taking any serious interest in affairs. She spent most of her time in long walks with a faithful attendant, gathering wild flowers, of which she was passionately fond in summer, and breathing the crisp air of winter as a physical luxury, tenderly cared for by her twin daughters, who still reside in her house, and by her son, Rev. Charles E. Stowe, who is settled over a Congregational church in Simsbury, Conn.

Mr. Stowe died in 1886, and four of her children were waiting with him to welcome her on the other shore, besides her parents, her sister Catharine and five brothers. She has left only three children and three grandchildren.

She was buried in the village church-yard at Andover, by the side of her husband and her son Henry.

In the retrospect, it seems to me that her genius was well matched by her gentleness and patience under great trials, her indomitable courage and power of execution, her hatred of all wrong doing, yet tender pity toward the transgressor, and her heavenly mindedness in the midst of earthly cares and sorrows. She lived as seeing the invisible.

The following hymn, written by her, many years ago, and which was sung at her funeral, gives the clue to her whole life.

### THE OTHER WORLD.

IT lies around us like a cloud.
    A world we do not see;
Yet the sweet closing of an eye
    May bring us there to be.

Its gentle breezes fan our cheek;
    Amid our worldly cares,
Its gentle voices whisper love,
    And mingle with our prayers.

Sweet hearts around us throb and beat,
    Sweet helping hands are stirred,
And palpitates the veil between
    With breathings almost heard.

The silence, awful, sweet, and calm,
    They have no power to break;
For mortal words are not for them
    To utter or partake.

So thin, so soft, so sweet, they glide
    So near to press they seem.
They lull us gently to our rest,
    They melt into our dream.

[259]

And in the hush of rest they bring
    'Tis easy now to see
How lovely and how sweet a pass
    The hour of death may be:—

To close the eye, and close the ear,
    Wrapped in a trance of bliss,
And, gently drawn in loving arms,
    To swoon to that—from this

Scarce knowing if we wake or sleep,
    Scarce asking where we are,
To feel all evil sink away,
    All sorrow and all care.

Sweet souls around us! watch us still;
    Press nearer to our side;
Into our thoughts, into our prayers,
    With gentle helpings glide.

Let death between us be as naught,
    A dried and vanished stream;
Your job be the reality,
    Our suffering life the dream.

## Notes

1. For details of the life of Isabella Beecher Hooker, see Barbara A. White, *The Beecher Sisters* (New Haven: Yale University Press, 2003).

2. See "'Brief Sketch of the Life of Harriet Beecher Stowe' and 'Suggestions for the Holidays,'" *Hartford Courant*, 10 December 1896, p. 3.

Isabella Beecher Hooker, *A Brief Sketch of the Life of Harriet Beecher Stowe, By Her Sister, Isabella Beecher Hooker* (Hartford, CT: Plimpton Mfg. Co. Press, 1896), pp. 1–16.

# "Harriet Beecher Stowe" (1898)

## PAUL LAURENCE DUNBAR

By 1896, the year of Stowe's death, the African American poet Paul Laurence Dunbar (1872–1906) had gained a considerable reputation, befriended by Frederick Douglass and praised by one of the most influential white critics, William Dean Howells. In a lengthy review of Dunbar's second book of poetry, *Majors and Minors* (1895), Howells described him as a poet of "fresh and direct authority."[1] Dunbar's versatility included writing poems in dialect as well as what Howells called "American English." Some African Americans felt that Dunbar's dialect poetry perpetuated the plantation myth, a pervasive idea that life in the antebellum South had been better for both masters and slaves. Recent scholars, however, have suggested that Dunbar's poems subverted this plantation myth at a time when repression of blacks was omnipresent, reminding readers of a major reason for the Civil War: the horrific realities of the slavery system. As historian David Blight has noted, "By 1900 the flame of emancipationist memory still burned, but it lit isolated enclaves in a darkening age of racial antagonism."[2] In many poems, Dunbar celebrated abolitionist leaders for their efforts, implicitly calling for full emancipation for African Americans in the aftermath of the failure of Reconstruction. Dunbar's sonnet to Stowe, which affirms the central role that *Uncle Tom's Cabin* played in the struggle for freedom and justice, was first published in the *Century Magazine* on 6 November 1898.

### HARRIET BEECHER STOWE

She told the story, and the whole world wept
  At wrongs and cruelties it had not known
  But for this fearless woman's voice alone.
  She spoke to consciences that long had slept:

Her message, Freedom's clear reveille, swept
  From heedless hovel to complacent throne.
  Command and prophecy were in the tone,
  And from its sheath the sword of justice leapt.

Paul Laurence Dunbar, ca. 1900. Dayton Metro Library.

Around two peoples swelled a fiery wave,
    But both came forth transfigured from the flame.
    Blest be the hand that dared be strong to save,

And blest be she who in our weakness came—
    Prophet and priestess! At one stroke she gave
    A race to freedom, and herself to fame.

## Notes

1. William Dean Howells, "Life and Letters," *Harper's Weekly*, 27 June 1896, p. 630.

2. David Blight, *Race and Reunion: The Civil War in American Memory* (Cambridge: Harvard University Press, 2003), p. 345.

Paul Laurence Dunbar, "Harriet Beecher Stowe," *Century Illustrated Monthly Magazine* 57 (1898): 61.

# "The Creator of 'Uncle Tom'" (1911)

ANONYMOUS

The centennial of Stowe's birthday in 1911 was marked by several celebrations across the United States, including one at Fisk University, where Stowe's son Charles Edward Stowe gave the commencement address.[1] A number of newspapers and magazines published articles about her life and career, including the *New York Observer and Chronicle* and the *Independent*, in which Stowe had published many articles and stories. In one of several articles in the *New York Times*, the author rather flatly observed that Stowe was "not a great or original thinker" but called *Uncle Tom's Cabin* "a good story, a novel of exceptional spirit and force."[2] An article mostly devoted to Stowe's writing in the *Washington Post* termed *Uncle Tom's Cabin* "an epoch maker in an epoch-making day."[3] In an admiring article in the *New England Magazine*, the writer and playwright Constance D'Arcy Mackay recounted the familiar details of Stowe's life and stressed her achievements as a writer despite the demands of her family. The major event of that centennial year was the appearance of a new family biography, *Harriet Beecher Stowe: The Story of Her Life*, by Stowe's son and grandson, Charles Edward Stowe and Lyman Beecher Stowe. As Charles Edward Stowe had done in his earlier biography, they drew on letters, family papers, and other biographies such as Annie Fields's *Life and Letters of Harriet Beecher Stowe* (1897) and *The Autobiography and Correspondence of Lyman Beecher* (1865). The following review of the new biography in the *New York Times* suggests the extent to which the Beecher family continued to work in the twentieth century to shape the image of Harriet Beecher Stowe as a writer who was first and foremost a wife and a mother.

THIS PRESENT YEAR is remarkably full of anniversary days whose recognition quickens the emotions of those whose memories reach back a half-century, and for the younger generations clothes historical events with fresher colors. Since Harriet Beecher Stowe's *Uncle Tom's Cabin* had so much to do with the making of those events, it is very fitting that the centenary of her birthday (June 14th) should be recognized in this semi-centennial of the beginning of the Civil War.

"The Evening of a Fruitful Life—Mrs. Harriet Beecher Stowe and Her Dream Children." *Frank Leslie's Illustrated Newspaper*, 6 April 1889, p. 140. Harriet Beecher Stowe Center, Hartford, Connecticut.

A new book[4] concerning her life and character is the joint work of her youngest son, Charles Edward Stowe, and her grandson, Lyman Beecher Stowe, and, while a good deal of its material has been drawn from previous volumes about her and her father, her son has been able to add, out of his own recollections, many fresh facts and intimate views. The authors characterize their book very truly when they say that they have not attempted to write an ordinary biography, but rather "the story of a real character; tell, not so much what she did as what she was, and how she became what she was."

As a chronicle of Mrs. Stowe's seventy-five years of varied, incessant and untiring labors the book is not at all complete, and the impress it leaves upon the mind is rather scrappy and unsatisfactory, but it does make a remarkably real and vivid picture of the woman herself, of the environment which helped to mould her character and of the conditions which compelled her to do nearly all of her literary work at a tremendous disadvantage. By copious quotations from her letters the authors have allowed her to reveal much of her own heart and soul; and, for the rest, their intimate knowledge has made it possible for them to interpret actions and facts into the language of character and temperament.

Equally successful they have been, also, in which would seem nowadays to be a task of much difficulty—the sympathetic description of a New England Calvinistic household of a century ago. They devote considerable space to the surroundings and influences of Harriet Beecher's childhood under the strictly orthodox teachings of her father, and they do not make the picture a repellant one. On the contrary, they contrive to put into it so much cheer, good nature and general joyousness that the reader does not once feel that sympathetic pity for the youngsters of the Beecher family to which he has been accustomed by accounts of other orthodox New England families of those days. On the whole, these opening chapters, which deal with Harriet Beecher's childhood and youth, up to the time, in her twenty-first year of the family's migration to Cincinnati, are the most interesting part of the book. They interpret so vividly and with so much insight the effects of the Calvinistic theology upon the minds of Dr. Beecher's children, and the consequent spiritual wrestlings and conflicts, that they make their pages significant of the general religious conditions and movements of that time.

Very appropriately, the authors treat of *Uncle Tom's Cabin* as the centre of interest in their subject's career and they endeavor to show how all the influences of her life shaped her character and her capacities toward the writing of that book. They would have added to the worth and interest of this chapter, however, had they dwelt at greater length upon the physical conditions under which the work was done. And they hurry much too rapidly over the effect which the story produced and the results which flowed from it. One does not get from their pages an adequate idea of the whirlwind of success and emotional and literary interest that followed the book's publication. It is well-nigh impossible for anyone born since the Civil War to read *Uncle Tom's Cabin* and realize the reception it had. And it is quite impossible for him to understand the high encomiums passed upon it by European critics who had little interest in the conditions out of which it was born. Whoever attempts in these days to set down the story of the book has need to make lavish use of the figures of publishers and the words of the literary great.

The sum of the impressions the reader gets from this story of Harriet Beecher Stowe's life is pre-eminently that of a woman who felt herself to be above all else wife and mother, who held herself ready to respond at any moment to any call from her household, who constantly drained herself of strength and energy in its service and found happiness in so doing.

## Notes

1. "Harriet Beecher Stowe's Centennial," *Independent*, 22 June 1911, p. 1384.
2. "Harriet Beecher Stowe," *New York Times*, 14 June 1911, p. 8.
3. "The Stowe Centenary," *Washington Post*, 15 June 1911, p. 6.
4. *Harriet Beecher Stowe: The Story of Her Life*. By her son, Charles Edward Stowe, and her grandson, Lyman Beecher Stowe. Illustrated. Houghton Mifflin Co. $1.50. [*New York Times* note.]

"The Creator of 'Uncle Tom,'" *New York Times*, 11 June 1911, p. LS363.

# Permissions

"Letter to Gamaliel Bailey," by Harriet Beecher Stowe, 9 March 1861 (ms. A.1.2.v.20p.9). Reprinted by permission of the Department of Rare Books and Manuscripts, Boston Public Library.

Fanny Fern, [Mrs. Stowe and *Uncle Tom's Cabin*,] *Olive Branch*, 28 May 1853, p. 3. Courtesy American Antiquarian Society.

Charles Beecher, *Harriet Beecher Stowe in Europe: The Journal of Charles Beecher*, eds. Joseph S. Van Why and Earl French. Hartford, CT: The Stowe-Day Foundation, 1986, pp. 30–33. Reprinted by permission of the Harriet Beecher Stowe Center, Hartford, CT.

Harriet Jacobs to Amy Post, (undated [1852?]); 14 February [1853]; 4 April [1853]; and 9 October [1853]. Post Family Papers. By permission of the Department of Rare Books & Special Collections, University of Rochester Library.

Harriet Beecher Stowe to Eliza Cabot Follen, 16 December 1852, Dr. Williams's Library, London, Estlin Papers, MS 24.123.1. Reproduced by permission of the Trustees.

Harriet Beecher Stowe to Frederick Douglass, 9 July 1851. Quoted by permission of the E. Bruce Kirkham Collection, Harriet Beecher Stowe Center, Hartford, CT.

"Mrs. Stowe Wrote 'Uncle Tom's Cabin' Under Trying Circumstances," *Hartford Times*, December 1869. Typescript. Quoted by permission of the Harriet Beecher Stowe Center, Hartford, CT.

"Jenny Lind's letter to Harriet Beecher Stowe May 23, 1852," *Hartford Times*, 6 June 1914. Typescript. Quoted by permission of the Harriet Beecher Stowe Center, Hartford, CT.

"Mrs. Stowe's Reading," *Hartford Courant*, 24 September 1871. Typescript. Quoted by permission of the Harriet Beecher Stowe Center, Hartford, CT.

"Thackeray and Mrs. Stowe, London, Friday, 3 June 1863." Copy of an undated article from an unknown newspaper. Quoted by permission of the Harriet Beecher Stowe Center, Hartford, CT.

Harriet Beecher Stowe to Sarah Josepha (Buell) (Mrs. David) Hale, 10 November 1851. Quoted by permission of the E. Bruce Kirkham Collection, Harriet Beecher Stowe Center, Hartford, CT.

Lydia Maria Child to [Sarah Blake (Sturgis) Shaw], 21 July 1861, bM S Am 1417 (78). By permission of the Houghton Library, Harvard University.

Alexandra Gripenberg, "Harriet Beecher Stowe," in *A Half Year in the New World: Miscellaneous Sketches of Travel in the United States* (1888), translated by Ernest J. Moyne (Newark: University of Delaware Press, 1954), pp. 73–80. Reprinted by permission of the University of Delaware Press and Elizabeth Moyne Homsey.

Beverly Peterson, "Hitherto Unpublished Letters from Oliver Wendell Holmes to Harriet Beecher Stowe." *Resources for American Literary Study* 23.1 (1997): 78–79; 80–81. Reprinted by permission of the editors, *Resources for American Literary Study*, Pennsylvania State University Press, and Beverly Peterson.

"Burial of Mrs. Stowe." *Hartford Times*, 3 July 1896. Handwritten transcription, reproduced by permission of the Harriet Beecher Stowe Center, Hartford, CT.

Isabella Beecher Hooker, *A Brief Sketch of the Life of Harriet Beecher Stowe, By Her Sister, Isabella Beecher Hooker* (Hartford, CT: Plimpton Mfg. Co. Press, 1896), pp. 1–16. Reprinted by permission of the Harriet Beecher Stowe Center, Hartford, CT.

# Bibliography

Addison, Daniel Dulany, ed. *Lucy Larcom: Life, Letters, and Diary*. Boston: Houghton, Mifflin, 1894.

"American Copyright League." *New York Times*, 20 January 1884, 7.

Ammons, Elizabeth, and Susan Belasco, ed. *Approaches to Teaching* Uncle Tom's Cabin. New York: MLA, 2000.

"Amusing Letters." *Saturday Evening Post*, 4 September 1868, 2.

Arms, George, et al., ed. *W. D. Howells: Selected Letters*. 2 vols. Boston: Twayne, 1979.

"Authors at Home." *Critic*, 4 May 1889, 217.

Baldwin, James. "Everybody's Protest Novel." *Partisan Review* 16 (1949): 578–585.

Beecher, Catharine. "Petty Slanders." *Hartford Daily Courant*, 18 August 1869, 1.

Beecher, Charles. *Harriet Beecher Stowe in Europe: The Journal of Charles Beecher*. Ed. Joseph S. Van Why and Earl French. Hartford, CT: The Stowe-Day Foundation, 1986.

Beecher, Charles, ed. *Autobiography, Correspondence, Etc., of Lyman Beecher*. 2 vols. New York: Harper and Brothers, 1864.

"The Birthday Garden Party to Harriet Beecher Stowe." *Atlantic Monthly Supplement* 50 (1882): A001–A016.

Blatch, Harriot Stanton, and Theodore Stanton, ed. *Elizabeth Cady Stanton, as Revealed in Her Letters, Diary and Reminiscences*. 2 vols. New York: Harper and Brothers, 1922.

Blight, David. *Race and Reunion: The Civil War in American Memory*. Cambridge: Harvard University Press, 2003.

Bowman, Christopher J. "Beecher Clan Gathers to Update Family Photo Album." *Hartford Courant*, 26 June 1983, A4.

"'Brief Sketch of the Life of Harriet Beecher Stowe' and 'Suggestions for the Holidays.'" *Hartford Courant*, 10 December 1896, 3.

Bryant, William Cullen. *The Letters of William Cullen Bryant*. Ed. William

Cullen Bryant II and Thomas G. Voss. 6 vols. New York: Fordham University Press, 1992.

"Burial of Mrs. Stowe." *Hartford Times*, 3 July 1896. Handwritten transcription. Harriet Beecher Stowe Center, Hartford, CT.

Burnett, Gene. "A Big Push from a Tiny Package." *Florida Trend*, September 1975, 81–82.

Burton, Richard. "The Author of 'Uncle Tom's Cabin.'" *Century* 52 (1896): 698–715.

"Centenary of Birth of the Author of 'Uncle Tom's Cabin.'" *New York Times*, 16 April 1900, SM14.

Charles, Eleanor. "Beecher Clan to Catch Up on 124 Years." *New York Times*, 19 June 1983, CN25.

Child, Lydia Maria. Letter to Sarah Blake (Sturgis) Shaw, 21 July 1861, bM S Am 1417 (78). The Houghton Library, Harvard University.

"City Religious Press." *New York Evangelist*, 26 August 1869, 6.

Cooke, George Willis. "Harriet Beecher Stowe." *New England Magazine* 15 (1896): 3–18.

Cooke, Rose Terry. "Harriet Beecher Stowe." In *Our Famous Women*. Hartford, CT: A. D. Worthington and Company, 1883. 581–600.

Coultrap-McQuin, Susan. *Doing Literary Business: American Women Writers in the Nineteenth Century*. Chapel Hill: University of North Carolina Press, 1990.

"The Creator of 'Uncle Tom.'" *New York Times*, 11 June 1911, LS363.

Cross, Barbara M., ed. *The Autobiography of Lyman Beecher*. 2 vols. Cambridge: Harvard University Press, 1961.

Derby, J. C. *Fifty Years Among Authors, Books and Publishers*. New York: G. W. Carleton & Co., 1884.

Dodge, H. Augusta, ed. *Gail Hamilton's Life in Letters*. 2 vols. Boston: Lee and Shepard, 1901.

Douglass, Frederick. *Life and Times of Frederick Douglass*. Hartford, CT: Park Publishing Co., 1881.

"Dramatic Readings by a Coloured Native of Philadelphia." *Illustrated London News*, 2 August 1856, 121–122.

Dunbar, Paul Laurence. "Harriet Beecher Stowe." *Century Illustrated Monthly Magazine* 57 (1898): 61.

Edel, Leon. *Henry James: The Untried Years: 1832–1870*. Philadelphia: J. B. Lippincott, 1953.

Fielding, K. J., ed. *The Speeches of Charles Dickens*. Hempstead: Harvester-Wheatsheaf and Atlantic Highlands, NJ: Humanities Press International, 1988.

Fields, Annie. *Authors and Friends*. Boston: Houghton, Mifflin, 1896.

———. "Days with Mrs. Stowe." *Atlantic Monthly* 78 (1896): 145–156.

———. *Letters of Sarah Orne Jewett*. Boston: Houghton, Mifflin, 1911.

———. *Life and Letters of Harriet Beecher Stowe*. Boston: Houghton, Mifflin, 1897.

Gardner, Eric. "Stowe Takes the Stage: Harriet Beecher Stowe's 'The Christian Slave.'" *Legacy: A Journal of American Women Writers* 15 (1998): 78–84.

Gates, Jr., Henry Louis. *The Annotated Uncle Tom's Cabin*. New York: W. W. Norton, 2007.

Gollin, Rita K. *Annie Adams Fields: Woman of Letters*. Amherst: University of Massachusetts Press, 2002.

Gossett, Thomas F. *"Uncle Tom's Cabin" and American Culture*. Dallas: Southern Methodist University Press, 1985.

Gripenberg, Alexandra. *A Half Year in the New World: Miscellaneous Sketches of Travel in the United States* (1888). Trans. Ernest J. Moyne. Newark: University of Delaware Press, 1954.

Haight, Gordon S., ed. *The George Eliot Letters*. 2 vols. New Haven: Yale University Press, 1954.

"Harriet Beecher Stowe." *American Missionary*, 50 (1896): 244–245.

"Harriet Beecher Stowe." *Hartford Courant*, 2 July 1896, 8.

"Harriet Beecher Stowe." *New York Times*, 22 December 1889, 19.

"Harriet Beecher Stowe." *New York Times*, 14 June 1911, 8.

"Harriet Beecher Stowe: Death of the Authoress of 'Uncle Tom's Cabin.'" *New York Times*, 2 July 1896, 5.

"Harriet Beecher Stowe's Centennial." *Independent*, 22 June 1911, 1384.

Hawley, Michelle. "Harriet Beecher Stowe and Lord Byron: A Case of Celebrity Justice in the Victorian Public Sphere." *Journal of Victorian Culture* 10 (2005): 229–256.

Hedrick, Joan. *Harriet Beecher Stowe: A Life*. Oxford: Oxford University Press, 1994.

Heydon, Peter N., and Philip Kelley, eds. *Elizabeth Barrett Browning's Letters to Mrs. David Ogilvy 1849–1861 with Recollections by Mrs. Ogilvy*. New York: Quadrangle, the New York Times Book Co., and the Browning Institute, 1973.

Higginson, Thomas Wentworth. *Cheerful Yesterdays*. New York: Macmillan, 1898.

Holley, Sallie. *A Life for Liberty: Anti-Slavery and Other Letters of Sallie Holley*. Ed. John White. New York: G. P. Putnam's Sons, 1899.

Homestead, Melissa J. *American Women Authors and Literary Property, 1822–1869*. Cambridge: Cambridge University Press, 2005.

Hooker, Isabella Beecher. *A Brief Sketch of the Life of Harriet Beecher Stowe, By Her Sister, Isabella Beecher Hooker.* Hartford, CT: Plimpton Mfg. Co. Press, 1896.

Howe, M. S. DeWolfe. *Memories of a Hostess: A Chronicle of Eminent Friendships, Drawn Chiefly from the Diaries of Mrs. James T. Fields.* Boston: Atlantic Monthly Press, 1922.

Howells, William Dean. "Life and Letters." *Harper's Weekly,* 27 June 1896, 630.

———. *My Literary Passions: Criticism & Fiction.* New York: Harper & Brothers, 1891.

Jacobs, Harriet. Letter to Amy Post, undated [1852?]. Department of Rare Books & Special Collections, University of Rochester Library.

———. Letter to Amy Post, 14 February [1853]. Department of Rare Books & Special Collections, University of Rochester Library.

———. Letter to Amy Post, 4 April [1853]. Department of Rare Books & Special Collections, University of Rochester Library.

James, Henry. *A Small Boy and Others.* New York: Charles Scribner's Sons, 1913.

"Jenny Lind's letter to Harriet Beecher Stowe May 23, 1852." *Hartford Times,* 6 June 1914.

Kenyon, Fredric G., ed. *The Letters of Elizabeth Barrett Browning.* New York: Macmillan, 1899.

Kirkham, E. Bruce. "Harriet Beecher Stowe's Western Tour." *The Old Northwest* 1 (1975): 35–49.

Kohn, Denise, Sarah Meer, and Emily B. Todd, eds. *Transatlantic Stowe: Harriet Beecher Stowe and European Culture.* Iowa City: University of Iowa Press, 2006.

Lathrop, George Parsons. "A Model State Capital." *Harper's New Monthly Magazine* 71 (1885): 727–734.

Lawton, Mary. *A Lifetime with Mark Twain: The Memories of Katy Leary, for Thirty Years His Faithful and Devoted Servant.* New York: Harcourt, Brace and Co., 1925.

Longfellow, Samuel, ed. *Life of Henry Wadsworth Longfellow.* 2 vols. New York: Houghton, Mifflin, and Company, 1891.

Lott, Eric. *Love and Theft: Blackface Minstrelsy and the American Working Class.* New York: Oxford University Press, 1993.

"Mark Twain's Wanderings at an End." *New York Times,* 31 March 1907, 3.

McCarthy, Justin. "Mrs. Stowe's Last Romance." *Independent,* 16 August 1869, 1.

McCray, Florine Thayer. *The Life-Work of the Author of "Uncle Tom's Cabin."* New York: Funk and Wagnalls, 1889.

"Mrs. Florine T. McCray." *Hartford Courant*, 13 March 1899, 3.

"Mrs. Stowe Wrote 'Uncle Tom's Cabin' Under Trying Circumstances." *Hartford Times*, December 1869. Typescript. Harriet Beecher Stowe Center, Hartford, CT.

"Mrs. Stowe's Birthday Party." *New York Times*, 15 June 1882, 5.

"Mrs. Stowe's Reading." *Hartford Courant*, 24 September 1871. Typescript. Harriet Beecher Stowe Center, Hartford, CT.

"The Novel That Overruled the Supreme Court." *Current Literature* 51 (1911): 209–210.

Parton, James. "International Copyright." *Atlantic Monthly* 20 (1867): 430–452.

Peterson, Beverly. "Hitherto Unpublished Letters from Oliver Wendell Holmes to Harriet Beecher Stowe." *Resources for American Literary Study* 23.1 (1997): 60–85.

Phelps, Elizabeth Stuart. *Chapters from a Life*. Boston: Houghton, Mifflin, 1896.

Pugh, Sarah. *Memorial of Sarah Pugh: A Tribute of Respect from Her Cousins*. Philadelphia: J. B. Lippincott & Co., 1888.

Railton, Stephen, director. *"Uncle Tom's Cabin" and American Culture: A Multi-Media Archive*. 1998–present. http://www.iath.virginia.edu/utc/.

Review of *The Writings of Harriet Beecher Stowe*. *Independent*, 18 February 1897, 18.

Robbins, Sarah. *The Cambridge Introduction to Harriet Beecher Stowe*. Cambridge: Cambridge University Press, 2007.

Sedgwick, Ellery. *The Atlantic Monthly: 1857–1909*. Amherst: University of Massachusetts Press, 1994.

Sklar, Kathryn Kish. *Catharine Beecher: A Study in American Domesticity*. New York: Norton, 1976.

Smith, Frances. "Mrs. Stowe's Home Life." *Drake's Magazine* 7 (1889): 440–442.

Stowe, Charles Edward. *Life of Harriet Beecher Stowe. Compiled from Her Letters and Journals*. Boston: Houghton, Mifflin, 1889.

Stowe, Charles Edward, and Lyman Beecher Stowe. "The Girlhood of Harriet Beecher Stowe." *McClure's Magazine* 37 (1911): 28–40.

———. *Harriet Beecher Stowe: The Story of Her Life*. New York: Houghton Mifflin, 1911.

———. "How Mrs. Stowe Wrote 'Uncle Tom's Cabin.'" *McClure's Magazine* 36 (1911): 605–621.

Stowe, Harriet Beecher. Letter to Eliza Follen, 16 December 1852. Estlin Papers, MS 24.123.1, Dr. Williams's Library, London.

———. Letter to Frederick Douglass, 9 July 1851. E. Bruce Kirkham Collection, Harriet Beecher Stowe Center, Hartford, CT.

———. Letter to Gamaliel Bailey, 9 March 1851. Typescript copy. Rare Books and Manuscripts Department, Boston Public Library.

———. Letter to Sarah Josepha (Buell) (Mrs. David) Hale, 10 November 1851. E. Bruce Kirkham Collection, Harriet Beecher Stowe Center, Hartford, CT.

———. *Sunny Memories of Foreign Lands*. 2 vols. Boston: Phillips, Sampson, and Co., 1854.

———. "The True Story of Lady Byron's Life." *Atlantic Monthly* 24 (1869): 295–313.

Stowe, Lyman Beecher. *Saints, Sinners, and Beechers*. Indianapolis: Bobbs-Merrill, 1934.

"The Stowe Centenary." *Washington Post*, 15 June 1911, 6.

"The Stowe Controversy." *New York Times*, 13 October 1889, 12.

"Thackeray and Mrs. Stowe, London, Friday, 3 June 1863." Undated article from unknown newspaper. Harriet Beecher Stowe Center, Hartford, CT.

Trautmann, Fredrick. "Harriet Beecher Stowe's Public Readings in New England." *The New England Quarterly* 47 (1974): 279–289.

Twichell, Joseph H. "Mrs. Harriet Beecher Stowe in Hartford." *Critic*, 18 December 1886, 301–302.

Underwood, Francis. *The Poet and the Man: Recollections and Appreciations of James Russell Lowell*. Boston: Lee and Shepard, 1893.

Van Why, Joseph S. *Nook Farm*. Ed. Earl A. French. Hartford, CT: The Stowe-Day Foundation, 1975.

Warren, Joyce. *Fanny Fern: An Independent Woman*. New Brunswick: Rutgers University Press, 1992.

Weinstein, Cindy, ed. *The Cambridge Companion to Harriet Beecher Stowe*. Cambridge: Cambridge University Press, 2004.

White, Barbara A. *The Beecher Sisters*. New Haven: Yale University Press, 2003.

Whittier, John Greenleaf, ed. *Letters of Lydia Maria Child with a Biographical Introduction*. Boston: Houghton, Mifflin, and Co., 1883.

Wilson, Forrest. *Crusader in Crinoline: The Life of Harriet Beecher Stowe*. Philadelphia: J. B. Lippincott, 1941.

Winship, Michael. "'The Greatest Book of Its Kind': A Publishing History of 'Uncle Tom's Cabin.'" *Proceedings of the American Antiquarian Society* 109 (2002): 309–322.

Yellin, Jean Fagan. *Harriet Jacobs: A Life*. New York: Basic Books, 2004.

# Index